MOUNTAIN GUIDE

The White Mountains of New Hampshire and Maine

By Ed and Roon Frost

The first **complete** four-seasons guide
for car, bike, and foot, with maps and information
on skiing (cross-country and downhill),
dining, fishing, shopping, hiking,
local lore and much more.

D1306946

Glove Compartment Books
P.O. Box 1602
Portsmouth, New Hampshire 03801

Cover artist is Don Demers, an award-winning illustrator, whose work has appeared in DOWN EAST, READERS DIGEST, SAIL MAGAZINE, and YANKEE.

Cover design is by Francesca Mastrangelo, who operates Angel Graphic Design Studio, Portsmouth, NH. Her design work has been seen in many regional magazines, such as NEW HAMPSHIRE PROFILES and SEACOAST LIFE.

Edited by Christine Davidson, who runs Wordwright Editorial Services, also in Portsmouth. The author of STAYING HOME INSTEAD, she has written both travel articles and books.

Maps are by Alex Wallach, a Maine cartographer with a masters degree in geography from the University of Vermont. Formerly with READERS DIGEST (Canada), he has produced maps for numerous guidebooks.

Typesetting and pre-press are by Ligature Typography, quality advertising and book typographers, also of Portsmouth.

MOUNTAIN GUIDE: The White Mountains of New Hampshire and Maine was printed by McNaughton & Gunn, Ann Arbor, MI.

Library of Congress Cataloging-in-Publication Data

Frost, Ed, 1940–
    Mountain guide: the White Mountains of New Hampshire and Maine /
by Ed and Roon Frost. — 1st ed.
      pp. cm.
    Includes index.
    ISBN 0-9618806-1-9
    1. White Mountains (N.H. and Me.) — Description and travel — Guide-books.
I. Frost, Roon. II. Title.
F41.52.F76 1988
917.42′ 20443 — dc19
                                      88-24475
                                      CIP

FIRST EDITION

ISBN 0-9618806-1-9

Railway illustration on p. 137 courtesy of Heritage Books, Inc.

TABLE OF CONTENTS

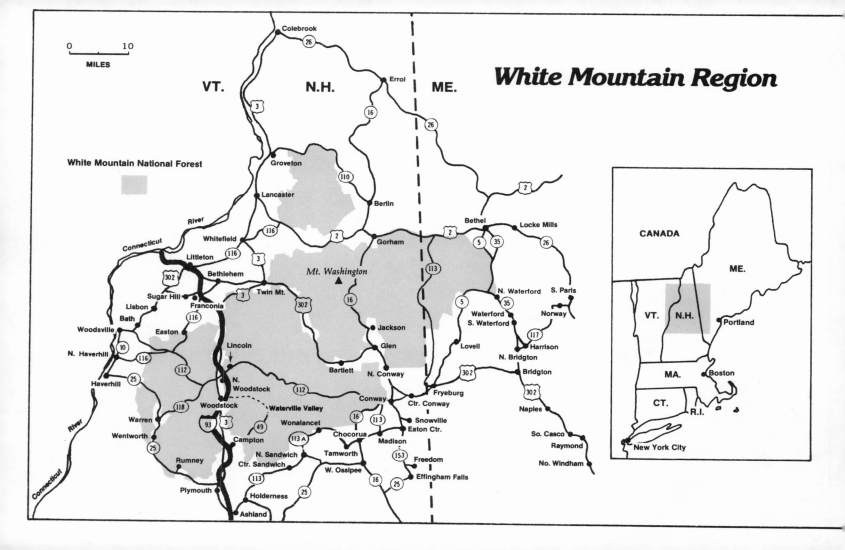

MAPS

Hiker/author Winthrop Packard: "Upon the highest mountain tops, the winds of winter make their first assaults upon the summer, driving it southward, peak by peak. . . . summer's blue and gold in the asters and goldenrod, winter's crimson and gold in the flare of maple and the glow of yellow birch."

Edward J. Blood, the first person to win a ski race down Tuckerman Ravine: "It was like watching a ribbon of white uncoil beneath me. I could hear a roar in my ears and see a blur of black as I came below the timber line. I could hear a peculiar singing sound as the skis rasped over the snow crystals, and I got the impression of a world flying up to meet me, as if I were falling from an airplane."

In LeGrand Cannon's fictional history of the White Mountains, a pioneer realizes: "This was the spring. There was in the air a sure, confident softness; there was the feel and the color of spring. There would be now no returning of winter. The trees were dusted with green, a light green but a sure one, and the sunlight was yellow and hazy and warm in his throat. The spring was now in the clearing and it lay on the hills."

Wallace Nutting, travel writer: "We cannot, in summer, escape heat except maybe on the summit of Mount Washington. . . [in] the purity of air. . . the glory of the clouds, the scent of the pine trees, and the touch of Nature."

The White Mountains of New Hampshire and Maine

Few parts of the United States are as appealing year-round as the White Mountains. Each season paints a different picture of these peaks. Every time of year brings its own special pleasures — invigorating fall air, winter sports, the subtlety of spring, or the coolness of a mountain glade on a hot summer's day.

More than seven million people visit here annually, for these peaks are within a day's drive of major population centers in the US and Canada. Close to one million acres of public land can still accommodate this crush of visitors, whether in antique-filled inns, large resorts, roadside campgrounds nestled near the National Forest, or peaceful spots several days' backpacking away from civilization.

The early settlers looked upon these mountains as barriers to cultivation and civilization. Only the hardiest pioneers dared to venture here, clearing intervale land and cutting virgin forests. By the 19th century, men realized that the mountains meant money.

Timber clogged the rivers, logs floating downstream to milltowns. Stagecoaches, then railroads and canal boats brought visitors into the mountains of New Hampshire and Maine to enjoy the marvels of nature or to while the summer away at a "grand hotel." A school of landscape painting made this area world-famous; articulate travelers decried the devastation that greed wreaked here.

Before the turn of the century, Americans came to respect the White Mountains. The Appalachian Mountain Club, which recently celebrated the centennial of its system of backcountry trails, shelters, and huts, first taught us how to actively enjoy the mountains; now they warn that overuse by hikers and skiers threatens the alpine ecosystems here. Others, like New Hampshire's Senator Weeks, who convinced Congress to create national forests, and countless youngsters, who "bought" trees in the 1920s to reforest Franconia Ridge, have helped preserve wilderness in the White Mountains. Today, the Federal government has protected more acreage in this one part of Maine and New Hampshire than exists in all of Rhode Island.

As with *COAST GUIDE: Seabrook, New Hampshire to Freeport, Maine,* our aim has been to give anyone interested in a popular area the most complete overview possible. We have organized the large, complex region of the White Mountains into scenic drives, while noting bike routes, hiking or ski trails, fishing spots, places to shop, as well as dining and lodging opportunities. Glove Compartment Books treats you, our readers, as though you were our guests. We share our favorite places but also allow you the pleasure of making your own discoveries.

How to Use *MOUNTAIN GUIDE*

Each chapter follows one complete loop through the White Mountains with sidetrips and recommendations for expanding your experiences here. Chapter I is suggested for anyone coming from the west; Interstate 93 makes this a fast, easy trip. Chapter II offers Maine's mountains and lakes just minutes from eastern highways, I-95 and the Maine Turnpike, with connections into the heart of the mountains. Chapter III describes the variety of activities along the central corridors, rte. 16 and 302, and suggests the best ways to maximize your enjoyment in a minimum of time. The highest peaks and the greatest concentration of ski areas, hiking trails, restaurants, and shops can be found in this chapter. Chapter IV details shunpikes and some of the prettiest scenery anywhere in the White Mountains along the southern routes. And for those who can't get enough wilderness, we end with the North Country, Chapter V.

As with COAST GUIDE, we've used different type faces and symbols to help you find what you want quickly. *Directions and specifics are printed in this type, so that you can quickly scan each page for the information you need.* Numerous maps will keep you properly oriented, whether you're traveling by car, bike, or foot.

> There is a wealth of history, geological and natural wonders that can enrich your appreciation of the White Mountains. We have included a good deal of this material, but present most background information in sidebars.

We have added pictographs in the margins to help you quickly find what interests you:

- **Activities for children**
- ♪ **Arts** (galleries or events, including plays or music)
- **Bike routes**
- **Boating or canoeing**
- ▲ **Camping**
- **Fishing**
- **Golf**
- ♿ **Handicapped access**
- **Hiking**
- **Historic sites and Museums**
- **Ice skating**
- ? **Information**
- **Lodging**
- **Nature**
- **Picnicking**
- **Restaurant**
- **Shopping**

⚡	Skiing (Alpine)
X	Cross-country skiing (Nordic)
≈	Snowmobiling
⚡	Swimming
⚑	Tennis

For hikers, we have included a number of trails, detailing a wide range of interesting adventures into wilderness. We also indicate the degree of difficulty of many hikes, listing approximate times and landmarks along the way. While we mention numerous hikes, like Bog Brook or Madison Gulf, as we pass trailheads en route, those we describe in detail are set off in different type, like the **Zealand Trail**.

call 536-1310
re trails off 49

But because we are not writing a book **just** for hikers, we suggest that anyone who wants to try trails that are not described in detail stop at any of the US Forest Service Ranger Stations noted in MOUNTAIN GUIDE for free maps **or** invest in one or more of the following publications: AMC MAINE MOUNTAIN GUIDE, AMC WHITE MOUNTAIN GUIDE, Daniel Doan's FIFTY HIKES IN NEW HAMPSHIRE or FIFTY MORE HIKES IN NEW HAMPSHIRE, DeLorme's MAINE GEOGRAPHIC HIKING, vol. 2.

The pressures of development make it difficult to recommend spring water in the mountains; on any hike longer than a half-hour, you should carry a water bottle or canteen. Skiers can make year-round use of a "fanny pack" (back pack #1) on hikes, carrying water, a high-energy snack, insect repellant, trail maps, camera or field guides; for easy access, turn it around into a "tummy pack." Anyone climbing above timberline needs back pack #2, adding to the items above: extra clothing (including socks and foul weather gear), food, compass, first aid kit, pocket knife, flashlight, and matches in a waterproof container. (You'll need a real day pack for all this gear.)

Fishermen, hunters, or anyone wanting to use recreational vehicles can get information at the Ranger Stations or write to Fish and Game Departments in Concord, NH 03301 or Augusta, ME 04330 for specific guidelines.

All major Alpine (downhill) and Nordic (cross-country) ski areas are listed. Maps of each area show all the trails and their degree of difficulty, as well as the number and types of lifts, snowmaking capability, and telephone numbers. Space limitations preclude identifying each trail by name; skiers are advised to carry updated trail maps.

Our information is current up to the time this book goes to the printer. To be as up-to-date as possible, Glove Compartment Books are revised, rather than simply reprinted. Nevertheless, it's always a good idea to call ahead for specific information.

We've worked hard, checking our favorite trails and routes, discovering new aspects of these mountains, and trying to select the best to share with you. We hope your experiences here will be as pleasurable and challenging as our own have been.

Ed and Roon Frost
August 1988

Chapter I THE WESTERN ROUTE

Mountains have long been a source of mystery, wonder, and inspiration to humankind. The Indians who roamed the northeastern United States were particularly awe-struck by one group of mountains. Often surrounded by clouds, these peaks must be inhabited by gods, the redskins reasoned — and therefore taboo. The earliest English settlers called the same mountains "crystal hills" because of their gleaming white appearance even in warm weather and because explorers venturing to climb them brought back crystals they believed to be diamonds.

Of all the peaks in the Northeast, the White Mountains of New Hampshire and Maine may be the most rugged — challenging explorers and scientists, road-builders as well as travelers, skiers, and hikers. For years we have tried to put our stamp on this land; in reality, it is the mountains that leave their impression on us. Wild, steep, subject to unpredictable changes in weather, they have earned the respect of rational, "scientific," technologically-sophisticated people.

While technology has made this wilderness habitable, the White Mountains remain awe inspiring. Even to the car-borne tourist, the peaks and ridges that look like velvet folds on a relief map become, in reality, a challenge to technology: the car's motor knocks and strains, climbing a steep grade; you wonder how sound your brakes are as you speed down a long hill, your

vehicle controlled as much by gravity and its own momentum as by its driver. Scaling a rocky summit can give you a sense of "owning" that mountain, as does finding the best trout stream or campsite, knowing where certain plants grow or animals live, or gliding gracefully over a snow-covered slope. But if we are wise, we will adopt a modern-day taboo, realizing that too much of a good thing can spoil it for us all.

Whether wilderness means driving along a highway with only headlights and moonlight as illumination, or whether it is snowshoeing across virgin snow with the sounds of your own movements breaking the forest's hush, nature asserts itself here in the White Mountains of New Hampshire and Maine.

There are man-made attractions as well as opportunities for shopping, luxurious accommodations, gourmet meals, dramatic and musical events, hunting, challenging ski runs, canoeing or white-water rafting, waterslides, tennis, golf, ice skating, snowmobiling, fishing, camping, watersports — literally anything you might conceivably want to do.

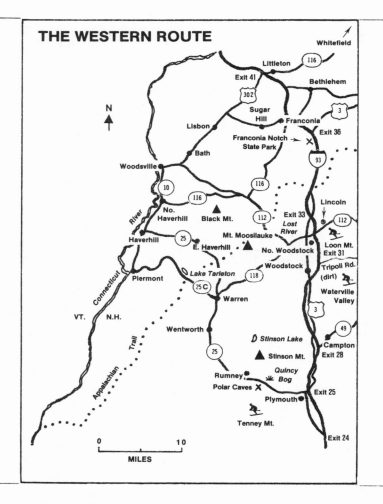

THE WESTERN ROUTE

(Map labels:) Whitefield, Littleton, 116, Exit 41, Bethlehem, 302, 3, Sugar Hill, Franconia, Exit 36, Lisbon, 93, Franconia Notch State Park, Bath, Woodsville, 116, 10, 116, Lincoln, No. Haverhill, Black Mt., 112, Exit 33 Lost River, 112, Haverhill, 25, Mt. Moosilauke, Loon Mt. Exit 31, E. Haverhill, No. Woodstock, Woodstock, Tripoli Rd. (dirt), Lake Tarleton, 118, Piermont, 25 C, Waterville Valley, Warren, 3, VT. N.H., Wentworth, Stinson Lake, 49, 25, Stinson Mt., Campton Exit 28, Rumney, Quincy Bog, Polar Caves, Plymouth, Exit 25, Tenney Mt., Exit 24, Connecticut River, Appalachian Trail, N

0 ——— 10
MILES

INTERSTATE MEETS WILDERNESS

I-93 is a model for all who propose, fund, design, or build highways. Despite the furor over this road (or perhaps because of it), I-93 offers both easy access and some of the best scenery in the White Mountains. *This divided interstate is really two highways with separate, but equally impressive vistas — depending on whether you're driving south or north. Because most visitors are coming from the south, we have detailed the route south to north. Although the north-south highway is not a mirror image of our route, perfectly reflecting our descriptions in reverse, it is well-marked with easy access to all the places we mention. Exits and mileages are similar in both directions, so readers coming down to these mountains from Canada should not be inconvenienced by our format.*

"In observing nature, as in partaking of life in general, there is always a certain degree of danger which must be accepted. . . . If we wish to understand the world in a fuller sense, we must be sometimes willing to meet it head on. While most of us may not wish to climb a tree in the midst of a windstorm [as mountaineer John Muir once did], we may have to suffer a few adversities or experience a tinge of danger. Perhaps we'll only have to get our feet wet. Or let a cold wind blow snow in our faces. Maybe even realize that there is a slight chance a tree might fall on our heads."
From NATURE'S SCHOOL, ESSAYS ON THE WHITE MOUNTAIN ENVIRONMENT AND BEYOND, 1985.

In New Hampshire, gasoline taxes are allocated for highway improvement and construction. As you "fill it up" here, think how effectively I-93, without billboards and strip development, uses your money.

The downside to a route like I-93 is that so many people can get here so easily that the fragile mountain ecology may be jeopardized, and the joy of exploration may be dampened by "Campground Full" or "No Vacancy" signs, and crowds everywhere you go.

Twice the population of New Hampshire drives through Franconia Notch every year.

But if you avoid holiday weekends (like Columbus Day, a popular time for "leaf-peepers" looking at fall foliage), I-93 is an excellent route to begin discovery of the White Mountains.

From the interstate, you pass lovely towns, rich valleys, and spectacular mountains for hiking, skiing, or simply admiring from afar. Your first glimpse of what is in store for you comes just past Exit 23, Meredith/New Hampton — towering peaks, some of which are snow-capped from fall through late spring. *Although this exit also leads to the Mt. Washington Valley, there are more scenic routes; we recommend those in Chapter III instead.*

Any exit from here on offers interesting sights and appealing ways to amble through the countryside. But if you're unfamiliar with this territory, we suggest you stay on I-93 through Franconia Notch State Park, for a maximum of mountain scenery with a minimum of driving. However, we do mention points of interest for each exit as well as suggesting different routes you might want to take there, with page numbers so that you can scan them briefly before deciding.

About 6 miles north is Exit 24, Ashland/Holderness, with several excellent restaurants (see pp. 151-2), a science center with exhibits of local fauna (page 154), and the beautiful Squam Lakes for water sports and great fishing (pp. 152-4). There is also a scenic route east to the Mt. Washington Valley and Maine's mountains, Chapters III & II. Another vista opens up along I-93 just past this exit.

> "Plymouth, beautiful for its situation on a terrace near the confluence of the Pemigewasset and Baker Rivers, is on the border of the White Mountain region and has from early times been an important town." Frederick W. Kilbourne, 1916.

"Beautiful for its Situation"

Begin your White Mountain experience at Exit 25 in **Plymouth.** *Holderness School, an independent prep school that offers a ski-racing program, is to the left at the bottom of the exit ramp.*

To explore Plymouth, turn right at the stop sign, as you exit. You'll pass Plymouth State College Stadium on the right, then take the trestle bridge over the Pemigewasset River, or the "Pemi" as it's called. Turn left at the blinking light onto Main St., also rtes. 3/25.

> It was here in Plymouth that the first baseball glove was created. Jason Draper, a local glove maker, teamed up with a Manchester businessman to manufacture gloves for the Red Sox in 1882; by the turn of the century, their plant in Plymouth was making footballs, softballs, and baseballs, as well as gloves. Boston pitcher Babe Ruth visited the Draper-Maynard factory in 1916 and even tried his hand at stitching a baseball.

This hillside city boasts a no-nonsense business district facing the brick courthouse and white Congregational Church. Skiers may want to check out gear at Guinan's Sports Center; bikers can browse at the Greasy Wheel further down Main St.

Right on Court St., just up the hill from the brick courthouse is Plymouth's Library, a small white-frame building with a tower. This is where Daniel Webster argued — and lost — his first jury trial.

> Webster's defendant here in Plymouth was so obviously guilty that the young lawyer spent most of his arguments opposing capital punishment — not exactly an idea whose time had come.

If you continue up the hill here, you will find yourself in the midst of the Plymouth State College campus. Poet Robert Frost taught psychology here when Plymouth State was a "normal school." Today the college's students and faculty almost equal the town's population.

The Plymouth State College Art Gallery, 603/536-5000, Ext. 2614, located in Hyde Hall, offers intimate viewing of an extensive collection. *Changing exhibitions of modern painting, photography, prints, sculpture, and crafts. Open Tuesday – Saturday, September to May.* In the summer, the college is also home to the New Hampshire Music Festival, 603/536-5000, Ext. 2589.

If you're ready for a bite to eat, there are several possibilities. For classic diner fare, try THE TROLLEY CAR RESTAURANT, 603/536-4433, but keep in mind that Plymouth also boasts a wonderful bakery *cum* vegetarian restaurant. SUZANNE'S, 603/536-3304, at 36 South Main St., offers beer or wine, spaghetti pie, calzone, nightly stir-fry of chicken, scallops, or shrimp with veggies, ginger, and tamari sauce. *Open daily for breakfast, lunch, or dinner.*

Our favorite restaurant in Plymouth is THE DOWNUNDER, still further south on Main St., 603/536-3983. Whether you're sitting next to the aquarium or the exotic art, you'll enjoy the generous drinks and reasonably-priced food (quiche, burgers, imaginatively-named sandwiches, like Larry's Bird).

There's a small ski area nearby at Tenney Mt., and several interesting diversions outside town. *For anyone who has time or youngsters in tow, we recommend heading up the hill on Highland St., past motels and antique shops to a left turn onto rtes. 25/3A west. After a half mile or so through a commercial area, look for the airport road on your right for the first of several sidetrips.*

Sidetrip: **Quincy Bog and Nature Center.** *The airport road takes a sharp left in front of a pretty frame house with a lovely old elm out front, then leads you through the Baker River Valley. Continue past a cemetery on the right and over a one-lane covered bridge.* There's swimming here with a parking area just past the bridge.

Turn left at the fork onto Quincy Rd. You'll see a home on a peaked mountain to your right and pass the "Plymouth Municipal Airport" on the left. Continue through farmland another mile or two, looking for QUINCY HOUSE BED AND BREAKFAST, 603/786-9277, and the Baker State Forest on the right. *Turn right at the sign for Quincy Bog just past the state forest, and left at the first fork onto a dirt road through a housing development. Continue .3 mile to a parking area.*

This 40-acre peat bog of glacial origin makes a delightful place to introduce yourself to local plants and animals. Children will have fun looking for pickerel frogs (found in large numbers here in April and May), listening to peepers, or hunting for salamanders and newts. Over 115 species of birds have been recorded here. Jointly maintained by a local ecological group and the Nature Conservancy, Quincy Bog has trails for year-round exploration and a Nature Center *which is open mid-June – mid-August.*

Quincy Bog is a good place to see the outlines of a glacial lake; peat deposits here are close to 30′ deep. In addition to the bog pond, naturalists and hikers will enjoy exploring a sedge meadow, alder and maple swamp (especially lovely in fall), sandy flood plain, granite outcropping, and typical woodland. There are several species of orchids, insect-eating plants including pitcher plants, and wildflowers.

Return to 25/3A the way you came, or if you're ready for some hiking or fishing, continue west to Rumney village.

6

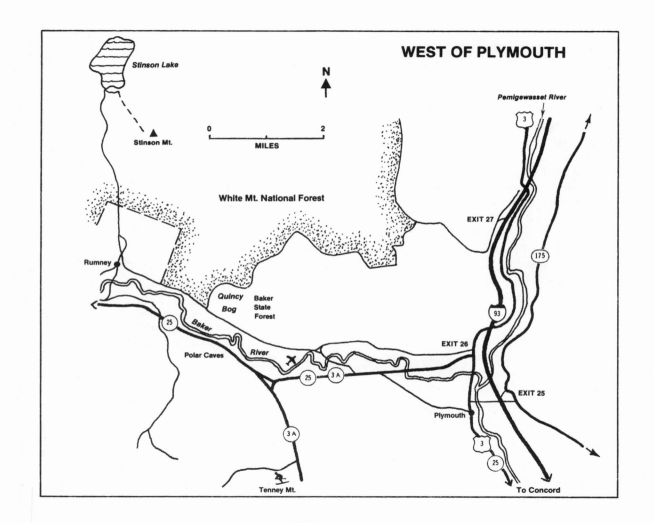

WEST OF PLYMOUTH

N

Stinson Lake

Stinson Mt.

0   MILES   2

Pemigewasset River

White Mt. National Forest

EXIT 27

175

Rumney

Quincy Bog

Baker State Forest

93

Baker

25

EXIT 26

Polar Caves

River

25   3 A

EXIT 25

Plymouth

3

3 A

25

3 A

Tenney Mt.

To Concord

Guided tours 10 am and 2 pm by a resident botanist Tuesday, Wednesday, Thursday, or by appointment, 603/786-9812. Free; no gas-powered vehicles allowed on trails. No fires, camping, picnicking, hunting, or picking of plants. Snowshoeing and cross-country skiing welcome.

Sidetrip: **Stinson Lake and Mt.** Continue west into **Rumney** village. Take the first right after crossing the bridge in town. Stinson Lake is a year-round fishing spot: ice fishing can yield trout, yellow perch, and pickerel; in warmer weather, look for small-mouth bass, cusk, fallfish, smelt, and white suckers. *Boat access to lake by a private, paved ramp; fee. Stinson Lake is one of the few lakes in the White Mountain National Forest where power boats are allowed.* Stinson Mt., an isolated, small ridge of 2870', offers a moderately easy two to two-and-a-half hour hike up to a firetower (backpack #1, see introduction.)

The road up to the lake and mountain passes the white-framed home of Christian Science's founder Mary Baker Eddy on the right. *Open May – October except Mondays and holidays.* Continue along a winding, climbing road for another three or four miles to the Hawthorne Village sign on the right. Fishermen can drive straight ahead (the road comes close to the lake there) or look for boat access near this fork. Hikers should bear right up the mountain.

The mountain road turns to dirt; in .8 mile, look for a sign to **Stinson Mt. Trail.** *To park, turn right on the trail itself, then sharp left past an old wooden frame house, and park in the field.*

Hikers should follow the dirt road a quarter mile before the trail takes a left through woods. You'll pass an old cellar with trees growing from its dirt floor, before the trail ascends to a trickling brook; here the path turns right (away from the logging road with its planked bridge). The trail becomes steep, switching back twice and passing an opening in the trees with a glimpse of the lake below and mountains in the distance. The last climb takes you through spruce and fir trees interspersed with mountain ash and striped maples; the trail curves right before opening up near the fire warden's cabin and lookout tower.

From the fire tower, you'll be rewarded with a wide view of the lake to the north and Mt. Moosilauke, its bare peak rising out of the Kinsmans in the distance; the Sandwich and Franconia Ranges to the northeast; Campton Bog to the east; forested Carr, Smarts, and Piermont Mts. to the west, especially interesting in fall.

Retrace your way, by foot and car, to rtes. 25/3A. Anyone in a hurry should turn east toward I-93, but fishermen and shunpikers will enjoy our trip along rtes. 25C & 25, (see pages 44-45). There are quiet country roads, more good fishing spots, and charming villages along the western edge of the mountains.

Sidetrip: **Polar Caves,** 603/536-1888. *Exit 26 from I-93 to rtes. 25/3A. Continue west to a rotary one and a half miles past the airport road. Take the first turn off this circle (rtes. 3/25 west) to Polar Caves, passing THE CRAB APPLE INN, a bed & breakfast, 603/536-4476, and TENNEY MOUNTAIN STEAK BARN, 603/536-9880. The caves and a large parking lot are on the left another 1.4 miles west.* Evidence of the great continental ice sheet 50,000 years ago, Polar Caves in Mt. Haycock may be of interest to all ages. *Open daily mid-May through mid-August; children under six free, if accompanied by an adult. Gift shop and snack bar; picnic facilities.*

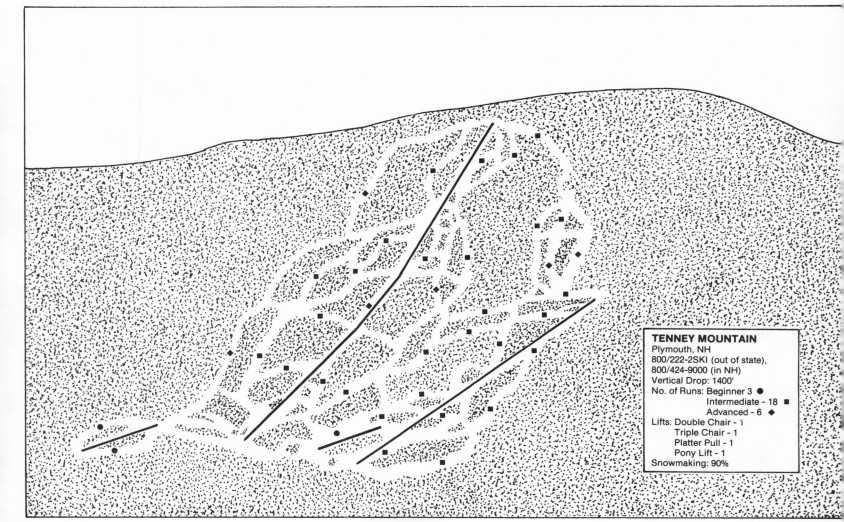

TENNEY MOUNTAIN
Plymouth, NH
800/222-2SKI (out of state),
800/424-9000 (in NH)
Vertical Drop: 1400'
No. of Runs: Beginner 3 ●
                      Intermediate - 18 ■
                      Advanced - 6 ◆
Lifts: Double Chair - 1
          Triple Chair - 1
          Platter Pull - 1
          Pony Lift - 1
Snowmaking: 90%

Sidetrip: **TENNEY MT. SKI AREA,** 603/536-1717, or 1-800/222-2SKI outside of NH. This largely intermediate mountain, south of Plymouth, may be worth discovering for any skier who hates long lift lines. A down-to-earth, family oriented area, TENNEY also offers snowboard events. *Mid-week specials Monday-Friday (except during February vacation); beginner lift tickets, group rates. Expansion for 1988 includes larger base lodge and nursery, dual course NASTAR racing, and condos. 90 percent snowmaking; ski school and shop, rentals, lounge, cafeteria. Snowboarders must demonstrate control of equipment to obtain lift tickets; snowboard lessons.*

To reach TENNEY MOUNTAIN from rtes. 25/3A west, drive to rotary and turn south on 3A. Continue about two miles south to the new (second) entrance on the right, past the Turnpike School and old burying ground. Bear left by the sign up the hill, passing condos and ski school meeting place to the lodge and rental shop.

Sidetrippers should return to the rotary and head east on rtes. 25/3A toward Plymouth and I-93.

Shortly after Exit 26 (Plymouth/Rumney), the interstate enters the White Mountains, and you'll see sweeping panoramas as you continue north. There are several state forests to your right, as well as the Squam and Sandwich Ranges. While it may be tempting to stop along these early stretches of the mountains, we recommend waiting for the Mad River/Waterville Valley area, with its network of hiking trails, choice of mountains to ski, and year-round resort facilities.

Mad River

Before you know it, you'll see signs for Exit 28 (Campton/Waterville Valley, rtes. 49/175) leading to a popular area. There's one of many White Mountain Information Centers to your right, just off this exit, as well as filling stations and ski shops. THE MAD RIVER TAVERN AND RESTAURANT on the left, 603/726-4290, is a casual stop, if you're road weary or hungry. You'll find excellent prime ribs as well as inexpensive specials, which make this restaurant popular with locals.

Also on the left, a little further along rte. 49 is CRICKET'S BAKERY AND CAFE, 603/726-3782. This sparkling clean, attractive place offers an innovative menu three times a day: St. Pauli Girl on tap, crepes, salads, club sandwiches of all sorts, burgers, and Philly steak sandwich. For breakfast, you can have Biercamulsi (oatmeal, raisins, sliced apples, nuts, and honey) topped with yogurt or served with one of Cricket's own muffins; Cuban "Old Clothes" omelette; Kentucky scramble (eggs with cream cheese, onions, and corn); or Belgian waffles.

This is pretty country with the Mad River to your right. A natural trout stream, this river is also one of several that the Forest Service keeps stocked. Bikers will appreciate the good surface and paved shoulders along 49; the road, of course, climbs steadily, though only a few grades are very steep. Part of the White Mountain National Forest, the Campton Campground

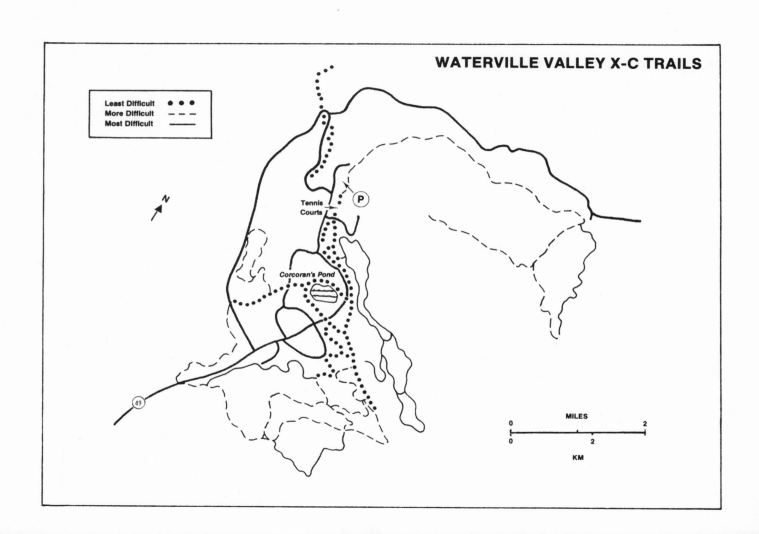

WATERVILLE VALLEY X-C TRAILS

Least Difficult ● ● ●
More Difficult - - -
Most Difficult ——

N

Tennis
Courts

P

Corcoran's Pond

49

MILES
0   2
0   2
KM

welcomes tents or trailers; this is a good base camp for fishermen or bikers.

Growing in size, as the number of visitors increases, the White Mountain National Forest encompasses close to a million acres; presently, 85 percent of the lands within forest boundaries are publicly held — the largest ratio of public to private land in any US National Forest.

A couple of miles down the road is another place to dine: CARNEVALE'S NORTHERN ITALIAN CUISINE, 603/726-3618, formerly THE WILLIAM TELL. The service is friendly, the wine list good, and there's a wide selection of pasta dishes. Almost a half mile further on the right, the Sandwich Notch Rd. comes down from a ridge above. *Open only in the summer, this mostly dirt road gives even modern auto tourists a sense of the energy and determination it took early settlers to carve out tiny settlements in these mountains; you might want to take a sidetrip to Center Sandwich from here (see pp. 155-157).*

Look for trailheads in another mile or so. **Smart's Brook Trail,** with a parking area on the right, gives experienced hikers and skiers access to trails on Sandwich Mt., but also offers a less strenuous hike over logging and dirt roads to a swimming hole among the pools of the mountain brook — it's important to remember, however, that most of the streams here in the White Mountains end up as drinking water somewhere in New England, so please treat them with respect.

Follow the trail across Smart's Brook over a highway bridge, then turn left immediately, climbing the logging road. After crossing the Tri-Town Ski Trail, this road joins a better one, leading to a swimming hole a little over a mile from rte. 49. Another three hours' tramping will bring hikers to Sandwich Mt. and other trails, but unless you have all day and an AMC WHITE MOUN-TAIN GUIDE with you, we recommend only the short hike to the swimming hole.

Continuing along rte. 49 with the Mad River now on your left, you may notice the roundness of the rocks and boulders strewn throughout the water. Unlike many rock specimens in these mountains, river rocks are well-worn from the fast-flowing water. Two and a half miles further, you'll see another spot for hikers and cross-country skiers to park on the right. *The Old Waterville Rd., which leads to the Yellow Jacket Trail, is temporarily closed to the public because of logging activity, but you may want to stop and check (a sign at the trailhead will give the latest information on its condition).*

Black flies, the bane of fishermen and hiker alike, are commonly believed to be food for trout; unfortunately fish don't eat them. The good news is that phoebes and swallows do — for good reason. While only four or five species of these troublesome flies bite humans, 25 out of the nearly 60 species in existence are pests to birds.

Fishermen need to be aware that certain black fly repellants, such as DEET, dissolve plastic. Fly fishermen should thoroughly wipe any product containing DEET from their hands, if they don't want to ruin their lines.

Hiking mountains and hills can quickly change one's sense of time. The Appalachian Mountain Club (AMC) formula for determining how long a hike will take is two mph on level ground, plus a half hour for each 1000' climbed. If you're young and in good physical shape (or both), this scale may work for you — it rarely has for us! Weather, trail conditions, and hiking experience are also important factors.

As the road grade steepens, you'll see **Mt. Tecumseh** (4004') to your left. This peak is easily recognizable because of is various ski trails. Waterfalls trickle or rush (depending on the season) down on the right, while stands of birches add interest to the river views on the left. Another mile or so on the right is yet another parking area — this time for Sandwich Mt. and Drake's Brook Trails.

Incorporated in 1829, all but 500 of Waterville's 43,000 acres are designated as national forest. For years towns-people paid no taxes; timber rights alone provided all the revenue this small community needed.

Waterville Valley, Year-Round Population 199

Next, signs appear for **Waterville Valley,** pointing you in different directions depending on what you plan to do. A complete resort with ski lodges, condos, and private vacation homes, Waterville was until recently one of New Hampshire's smallest communities. Remnants of that tiny village remain in old homes near new ones or pre-development public buildings like the Osceola Library. Developers deserve credit for blending past with present so well. New signs for "Sleigh Crossing" or "Saddle Horse Crossing" are as welcome as those prohibiting skimobiles or designating the difficulty of cross-country ski trails.

Skiing was the force behind development, and this is one resort determined that you'll enjoy the sport. *Alpine skiing on Mt. Tecumseh offers sufficient vertical drop for even expert skiers; wide fall-line trails make Waterville competitive with western US ski areas. There's usually good natural snow cover, plus 96 percent snow-making. Lift tickets are limited (so slopes aren't too crowded and lines too long) and allow mid-week access to 8 other White Mountain ski areas. Kids ski and stay free if they're 12 and under AND if one parent buys a three-day or longer lift ticket (non-holiday package). For cross-country aficionados, Waterville has 100 kms. of trails in the White Mountain National Forest, most double-tracked, patrolled and groomed daily. Lessons, rentals, nursery; race programs for both Alpine and Nordic Skiers.* The brainchild of former Olympic racer Tom Corcoran, Waterville has a reputation as a ski mountain that works, especially for families. In addition, the resort hosts more World Cup competitions than any other ski area in North America. *Recreational NASTAR racing, coin-operated practice course, even a challenging 6 km. cross-country race training track are available here.*

But you don't have to ski to enjoy a visit to the Valley. Waterville also offers ice skating, sleigh rides, and

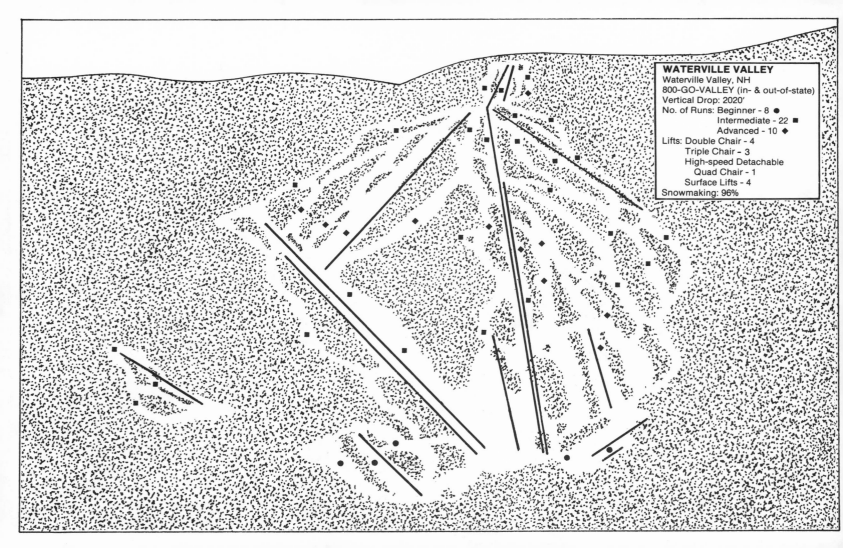

WATERVILLE VALLEY
Waterville Valley, NH
800-GO-VALLEY (in- & out-of-state)
Vertical Drop: 2020'
No. of Runs: Beginner - 8 ●
Intermediate - 22 ■
Advanced - 10 ◆
Lifts: Double Chair - 4
Triple Chair - 3
High-speed Detachable
Quad Chair - 1
Surface Lifts - 4
Snowmaking: 96%

a $2 million indoor fitness center. *Swimming pool, racquetball, tennis, squash courts, jogging track, Nautilus, free weights, aerobics. Also saunas and steam rooms, whirlpool, tanning, and massage available.* There are plenty of places to eat here, as well — from warming huts with hot chocolate or lobster bisque to O'KEEFE'S, 603/236-8331 with fireplace fare like Boston schrod or roast duck. And most of the Valley's rooms have their own kitchens.

Despite all its new buildings, Waterville Valley is actually an old resort. Sport fishermen came here in the 1850s, and a small hotel was built in 1860. These early visitors hiked, played croquet or tennis, and even bowled in an alley built here in the valley. By the 1900s golfers had developed a rough course.

Like many resorts that cater to skiers, Waterville's inns and condos can be a real bargain when the snow has melted. Spring rates may be a third of winter ones, as golfers replace skiers. *For reservations, call 1-800-468-2553 or 603/236-8371.* In summer the resort hosts its annual Festival of the Arts: American pop and classical programs on weekends under a tent and on the lawns at Mt. Tecumseh. *July — August, admission (some tickets include dinner); 603/236-4161.*

From Mt. Tecumseh in the west to the picturesque, triple-peaked Tripyramid in the east, Waterville also has mountains for climbing — many four-thousand footers. Once the snow melts and the dirt section of Tripoli Rd. reopens, the Valley becomes popular again — with young and old clad in thick socks and heavy boots for hiking.

As backpacking and tenting grew popular in the 1960s, it also became fashionable to distinguish the expert hiker from "goofers," those novices who hike without adequate preparation. The "Four Thousand Footer Club," composed of hardy folk who have climbed mountains of substantial height, was a way some hikers could test their mettle. Yet one outdoorsman who attended a meeting at the Appalachian Mountain Club in Boston was chagrined to find "two dogs in the auditorium," who'd done as well as he. "What's more, there's a whole bunch of people who are doing 4,000 footers in the winter."

Camp sites, below treeline, are available in the Sandwich Range Wilderness. Mt. Tecumseh Trail, Snow's Mt. Trail (sometimes difficult to follow because of Water-

ville's continuing development), and Mt. Osceola Trail take hikers up from the valley, but there are interesting short walks here as well. Trail information and maps are available at Waterville's "Jugtown" store; trails are also described briefly in AMC WHITE MOUNTAIN GUIDE.

An easy hike any age can enjoy is **Cascades Path,** beginning at the base of the Snow's Mt. Ski Area. A mile-and-a-half walk along the brook to the falls makes a relaxing, rewarding adventure; backpack #1 (see page ix). *From the base of the ski area, climb the ski slope a short way, then descend gradually through old-growth hardwoods to the brook and continue up to the Cascades.*

Sidetrip: **Tripoli Road.** In summer, this is nice shortcut to I-93 north and an important starting point for many trails. *From the SNOWY OWL INN or BLACK BEAR LODGE, turn right on Snow's Brook Road, looping around toward rte. 49 north, between the tennis courts and golf course. Turn left on 49, then left again before the Osceola Library onto West Branch Rd. Cross over a one-lane bridge, slowing down for the horse crossing, then turn right and continue into the National Forest.*

The road alternates between pavement and dirt. A little over three miles from where you turned onto West Branch Rd., you want to look for the **Mt. Osceola Trail** and parking on the left. Climbing the highest peak in this area, the trail is, at times, pretty easy, at others very rough and steep; allow two and a half to three hours to reach this 4430′ summit (one-way, so double this time adding lunch and snack breaks in planning this hike). This is a trail where backpack #2 can come in handy (see Introduction).

Climb an old tractor road to gravel switchbacks. Head east across the southern slope of Breadtray Ridge for a moderate 1.3 mile climb toward the ridge top, and in another mile, this trail crosses a brook via a log bridge.

The trails, bridges, steps, camp sites and shelters here in the White Mountain National Forest are all created by dedicated people — mostly volunteers who love these mountains. Donations and memberships in hiking and mountaineering groups help assure continuation of their valuable work.

After another series of switchbacks, you reach the summit ledge (3.2 miles from Tripoli Rd.) for excellent views of Mt. Tripyramid and the Franconia Range.

For experienced hikers prepared for a much longer trek, this trail connects with one to Osceola's East Peak and the Greeley Ponds Trail, ending on the Kancamagus Highway, (page 149).

Tripoli Rd. meanders up and down, passing through Thornton Gap, across countless streams, with access to several trails (Mt. Tecumseh and East Pond, the latter a two-and-a-half to three-hour round-trip). On a holiday weekend, this road becomes a wooded version of

Hampton Beach, with huge signs inviting guests to join in the party — and tents everywhere and anywhere, as long as they're close to the road. After leaving the National Forest, Tripoli Rd. descends, then passes under I-93 at Exit 31 (look for Russell Crag on your right).

> "The Woodstocks with their river and their various drives. . . are an admirable rest region, since they are within the capacity of persons of modest means." Wallace Nutting, 1923.

North Woodstock

Those who skip Waterville (or return on 49 the way they came) and continue north on I-93 have a marvelous view of Franconia Notch. Just past the exit for Woodstock and before the access to Tripoli Rd. Exit 32, North Woodstock/Lincoln, is a popular stop. One of our favorite country inns is in **North Woodstock.** You'll find mountain roads to explore, Lost River (one of the least offensive commercial attractions anywhere), and some excellent hiking nearby.

Begin at THE WOODSTOCK INN on Main St. in North Woodstock, 603/745-3951. *Open for breakfast and dinner. WOODSTOCK STATION, a converted railroad depot behind the inn, serves lunch and a more* *casual dinner; the same kitchen but lower prices at the STATION.* Even though the Victorian dining room at the inn is fairly expensive, it offers first-rate service, and you certainly get your money's worth gastronomically.

We split a generous crock of garlicky snails before our salads; the complimentary house appetizer made a first course unnecessary. A homemade fruit sorbet cleared our palates, so we could choose freely from the expansive menu. Venison was well-prepared, as were tournedos with pepper and boursin. Veal with shrimps and artichokes, fresh charbroiled swordfish, and coquilles Saint Jacques are other choices. A complimentary liqueur in a tiny chocolate cup accompanied coffee.

North Woodstock has remained a delightful country town, despite its proximity to an interstate highway. You can buy aged cheese for a snack at Fadden's General Store, where old floorboards ripple underfoot and antique implements dangle from the ceiling. The Moosilauke Public Library shares its home with the Woodstock Fire Department. A mile north on rte. 3 is **Clark's Trading Post,** with its collection of commercial clutter, and amusements: a steam locomotive, trained bears, 1890s fire station, bumper boats, and the Mystical Mansion. *Open mid-May – late-June, weekends; late-June – Labor Day, daily. Admission with reduced rates for elementary-school aged children; those under six are free.*

Florence Clark, whose son runs Clark's Trading Post, made history by climbing Mt. Washington in winter via dog sled — becoming the first woman to do so, but at great physical cost. After three grueling attempts, she somehow managed to climb to the summit without the crampons that supposedly had been left for her, the dogs often flat on their stomachs clawing the ice. Speaking about her animal team, she later said: "No matter how tough the going, they never lay down and quit. But sometimes I wonder why I did it." Clark's red sled, built by a Berlin high school shop class, is part of the display at the Trading Post.

You can continue north on rte. 3 through the commercial stretch ahead, page 23, but we recommend a drive west to Lost River with at least a view of Mt. Moosilauke, pronounced "Moos-i-lock" or "Moos-i-locky," the choice is yours.

In the Shadow of Moosilauke

If you're ready to explore a bit, this is a fine place to do so. Take rte. 112 west of North Woodstock past Lost River Valley Campground on the right *(showers, store; swimming and fishing)* to **Lost River** itself, another three miles ahead. *Open mid-May–mid-October; fee (children under six free). Parking, picnic area, gift shop and snack bar. Although boardwalks lead you through the jumble of rocks here, sturdy footwear is recommended.* A "geological wonderland," Lost River offers a series of basins and caves modeled by swift water action into all sorts of shapes: Guillotine Rock, Hall of Ships, the Lemon Squeezer, and the small but spectacular Paradise Falls.

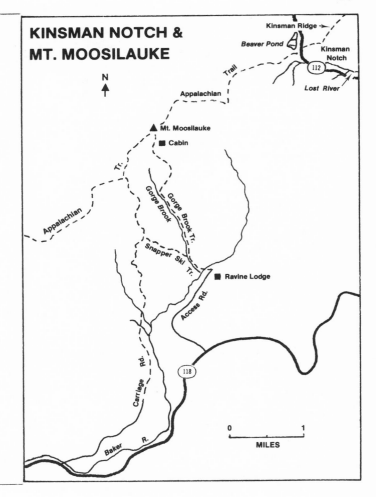

KINSMAN NOTCH & MT. MOOSILAUKE

Tradition says that two boys were fishing here in Kinsman Notch, when one "disappeared as though the earth had opened up and swallowed him." Actually, he had dropped down into a pothole and needed to be fished out. Later his brother returned with a group of friends and discovered the Cave of Shadows and the "lost river," so named because it disappears periodically under huge glacially-deposited boulders.

Lost River makes a nice excursion for kids, especially if one adult wants some time off to fish or hike, while the other babysits. The Appalachian Trail, which runs from Georgia to Maine, crosses rte. 112 about a half mile past the entrance to Lost River. Known to hikers simply as the "AT," this is a well-maintained trail, blazed in white. *From the right side of the road, the trail leads along the Kinsman Ridge, a very challenging hike that is rougher than it appears, but one that rewards the experienced hiker with beautiful mountain ponds and views of Mts. Lafayette and Lincoln.*

From the left side of rte. 112, you can hike to Mt. Moosilauke's summit, 4810', and down to the lodge off rte. 118, where the rest of your party can meet you. *No overnight camping or fires permitted on the mountain. Trail guide is available from Environmental Studies Division, Dartmouth Outing Club, Dartmouth College, Hanover, NH 03755.*

Just a little west of Lost River, rte. 112 leads to **Beaver Pond,** where the kids can look for evidence of these sharp-toothed animal engineers and adults can fish for trout. This road leads west past excellent fishing along the Wild Ammonoosuc, connecting with rte. 302, pp. 38-43. Or if you have a little time to spare, you might consider a drive down rte. 118.

Whenever hiking above treeline, it's important to be aware of the danger of hypothermia, even when the weather is warm in valleys below. Most cases occur above freezing, with rain, wind, and temperatures below 50 degrees. The symptoms include uncontrollable shivering and drowsiness, as well as impaired speech, motor and mental functions. In mild cases the victim can be revived by drinking warm (NEVER hot) liquids, getting into dry clothes, and wrapping up in a sleeping bag — preferably with another warm body. As amusing as this last part may sound, hypothermia can be extremely serious and is sometimes fatal.

From Lost River return the way you came, back toward North Woodstock, just past the campground. Make a sharp right onto 118 near the confluence of Jackson and Moosilauke Brooks.

The rocks in the stream make a good place to picnic in warm weather. If the trees are leafless when you drive southwest on 118, fantastic views of the Presidentials appear to the left. Beginning at the far left are Lafayette, then Lincoln and Flume, the Pemigewasset River and the Kancamagus Highway (the eastern section of rte. 112), then the hulks of Mts. Hancock and Hitchcock, and finally Mt. Washington, often snow-capped but with its observatory outlined at the summit in clear weather. In summer you'll have to hike to see any real views. Because 118 is steep, it is not recommended for biking.

> "Moosehillock, of Moosilauke, is one of four or five summits from which the best idea of the whole area of the White Mountains may be obtained. It is not so remarkable for its form as for its mass. It is an immense mountain." Samuel Adams Drake, 1882.

Just after crossing the line into **Warren** township, the road descends sharply and **Mt. Moosilauke** looms to the right. The Indians called this mountain "a bald place" and the name still fits. There used to be quite an elegant summit house, or hotel on the top.

> Prospect House atop Mt. Moosilauke opened July 4th, 1860 with a grand celebration: patriotic speeches, a brass band, demonstrations by Indians, rides up and down the carriage road on the large two-horse pleasure wagon. The first meteorological station on a summit in the White Mountains was on Moosilauke. J.H. Huntington, a geologic surveyor with a degree from Amherst, and A.F. Clough, a Warren photographer, recorded an unusual phenomenon: a terrible storm with wind velocity of 97 mph. When their wood supply ran out in February, the two were forced to descend the mountain in 70 mph winds and subzero temperatures. They were almost blown off Moosilauke, but their experience led eventually to similar winter observations on Mt. Washington.

Dartmouth College took over the summit hotel in 1920, putting in bunks for 80 hikers. Today the mountain remains Dartmouth's. Although the original building burned in 1942, there is now an emergency shelter 400' south of the summit.

Look for the access road on the right, shortly past the Warren town line. This road leads to the Dartmouth Outing Club's Ravine Lodge, a good place to park, meet hikers, or begin your own four-and-a-half to five-hour loop of the mountain. The lodge is open May — October to hikers within the Dartmouth family.

Start your climb of Mt. Moosilauke on the west side of the Baker River across a footbridge in front of the Lodge. After a short distance, turn left along a path on the west bank then right onto Gorge Brook Trail. In a quarter mile the Snapper Ski Trail branches left, offering

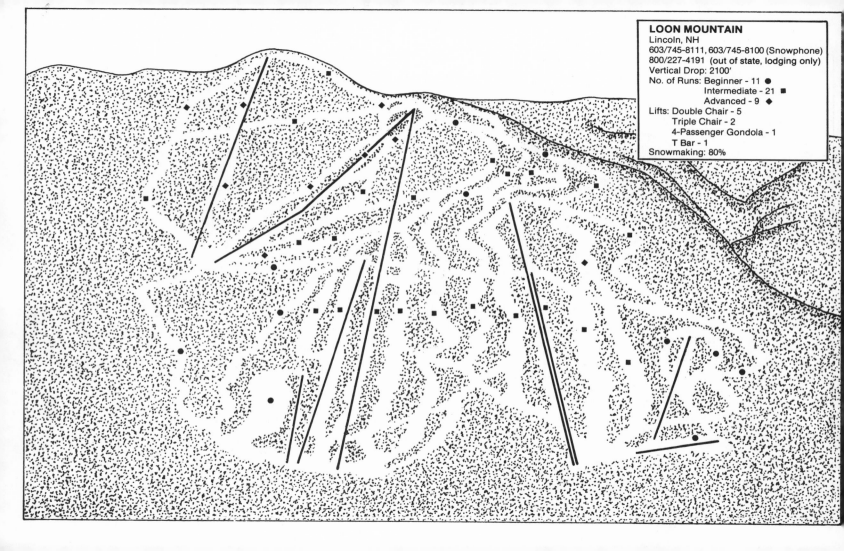

LOON MOUNTAIN
Lincoln, NH
603/745-8111, 603/745-8100 (Snowphone)
800/227-4191 (out of state, lodging only)
Vertical Drop: 2100'
No. of Runs: Beginner - 11 ●
Intermediate - 21 ■
Advanced - 9 ◆
Lifts: Double Chair - 5
Triple Chair - 2
4-Passenger Gondola - 1
T Bar - 1
Snowmaking: 80%

an alternate and/or return route. **Gorge Brook** *is more direct and safer in bad weather, rising steadily toward the summit along an old logging road and offering views of the brook's falls and pools. You'll cross the brook twice before the trail gets steep, one mile up. Continue up the main trail through spruce and firs, listening for blackpoll warblers, who inhabit 3000' heights.*

Roger Tory Peterson describes the blackpoll warbler's song as, ". . .a thin, deliberate, mechanical zi-zi-zi-zi-zi-zi on one pitch, becoming slightly louder and more emphatic in the middle and diminishing toward the end."

As you approach treeline, the climb becomes more gradual and you're rewarded with wonderful views. You pass the emergency cabin. Then the trail is marked by cairns (piles of rocks often painted with bright colors to mark trails) and leads north to the summit ledges and the stone foundation of the hotel. From Moosilauke, you have a 360-degree view of the White Mountains and the gentler Green Mountains in Vermont.

Back on rte. 118, you have several choices. First, you can continue west toward Warren and the Morse Museum with its unique collection of curios from around the world. Second, you can head back to North Woodstock, and drive straight north through the com-

merce at Lincoln *to ski at LOON MT. or view Indian Head on the way to Franconia Notch. The third choice is to get back on I-93 from North Woodstock.*

Loon Mt.

If you've never been north to Franconia and its notch, we recommend continuing in that direction. One of the reasons for roads like I-93 is to avoid commercial clutter in places like **Lincoln,** yet for many people, this is half the fun of traveling. If you're one of these or have youngsters in tow who are ready for a swim in a heated pool, rather than a mountain stream, continue north on rte. 3.

Amidst the maze of waterslides and motels, you might want to look for LOON MT. on the right, just off the Kancamagus Highway, rte. 112. The state's longest aerial ride with wonderful mountain views leaves from here and takes only eleven minutes to reach the summit; self-guided nature trail, cave walk among glacial boulders, and four-story sky tower. *Fee. Summit cafeteria; at base: gift shop, pottery shop, crafts barn, and another cafeteria. THE MOUNTAIN CLUB at LOON offers tennis and racquet ball, in addition to its indoor pool; both condos and rooms available year-round, 1-800/433-3413. For information on lodging in the Lincoln area, call 1-800/227-4191. RACHEL'S, 603/745-8111, serves new American cuisine three meals a day.*

Perhaps the most accessible of New Hampshire's

major ski areas, LOON MT., keeps getting bigger, 603/745-8111 (24-hour snow phone: 603/745-8100). "The first mountain" for thousands of skiers, LOON has almost as many intermediate slopes as it does beginner and expert ones combined. *Beginner's and mid-week specials, also lower rates before Christmas and after March 20. Juniors ski free on ski-weeks (except over Christmas vacation); children under six ski free anytime. Ski school, rentals, children's program and day-care.*

Recently, LOON has added snowboarding to its repertoire. *Rentals and instruction at Snowboard Center.* And its Ski Touring Center, near the Octagon Lodge, offers over 14 miles of groomed and tracked trails for no fee. *Cross-country rentals and lessons.*

Lift ticket sales in the Northeast have almost doubled in the past eight years, putting considerable pressure on national forests. LOON MT. hopes to double its terrain and skier capacity in the next five years as part of a $15 million expansion — employing workers from a defunct paper mill, but using parts of the White Mountain National Forest. Stephen Blackmer, policy specialist with the Society for the Preservation of New Hampshire Forests, the state's oldest and biggest conservation group, says, "Environmentally, Loon is a huge improvement for the area."

Michael Kellett of the Wilderness Society disagrees: "Not long ago there seemed to be lots of mountains, and ski areas could go their own way. What's happened is that we're running out of mountains." Unfortunately, infrastructure (roads and sewage treatment plants) doesn't always keep apace with development of more ski slopes and condos, as winter traffic jams here in the White Mountains will attest.

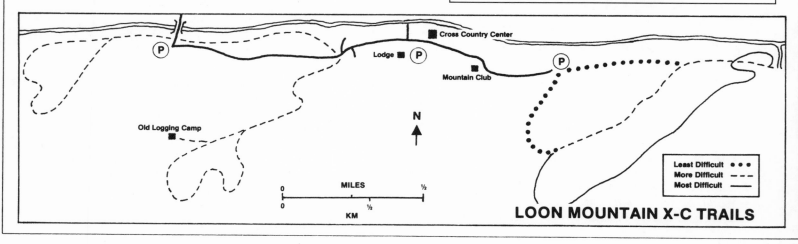

P

P

Cross Country Center

Lodge

P

Mountain Club

P

Old Logging Camp

N

MILES
0 ½
0 ½
KM

Least Difficult ● ● ●
More Difficult ─ ─ ─
Most Difficult ───

LOON MOUNTAIN X-C TRAILS

Faces in the Mountains

Use exit 33 off I-93 or continue north on rte. 3 — either way, you'll get a look at one of this area's most famous landmarks, a face that seems carved out of stone. For those who would rather avoid the commercialism of this stretch, just stay on I-93 which turns into Franconia Notch Parkway with its own selection of sights, including the most famous profile.

The Indian Head Motel on the right has the best view of a rock formation at the top of Mt. Pemigewasset that looks just like — you guessed it — an **Indian Head.**

Legend has it that an Abenaki chief, wounded in a battle with the Algonquin Indians of New York, took a chief's daughter as his booty and bride. Although he grew to love the Algonquin squaw as much as life itself, she left him after hearing that her father was dying, but promised her husband to return before the harvest moon. Pemigewasset waited for her near the mountain that bears his name, and the following spring, Abenaki braves found their leader's bones next to Lonesome Lake. Looking back at the mountain, they saw his profile carved in stone, in everlasting vigil for his bride.

Believe it or not, rte. 3 is an official New Hampshire bike route, and in fact, the passage through Franconia Notch State Park is eased by bike trails. *Speed limit is 45 mph on the parkway; two lanes northbound, one lane southbound.* There's a trailhead on the west side of rte. 3, about 200 yards south of the Indian Head Motel. You can hike two and a half hours round-trip up *Mt.*

Pemigewasset or wait for a second trail that's a little less steep (and more clearly marked) in the park ahead.

FRANCONIA NOTCH

In another half mile, you'll find yourself in **Franconia Notch State Park** with trailheads for hiking, bike paths throughout, as well as uncommercial but fascinating sights that have attracted tourists for centuries. Begin at the **Flume Visitors Center.** *Open May 30–October 15. Maps of attractions within park, film, free bus transportation, restroom facilities; admission. Information on trail conditions, facilities, and weather is available at Lafayette Place parking area on the west side of the parkway.*

There's a wonderful view of the southern mountains as you drive into the Trailhead Parking Area at the Flume, and from here backpackers can hike the Whitehouse Trail to the Appalachian Trail, which links Mt. Lafayette, 5249′; Mt Lincoln, 5108′; Little Haystack Mt., 4840′; Mt. Liberty, 4460′; and Mt. Flume, 4327′, the highest peaks in the Franconia Range.

Second only to the Presidentials in height, these mountains were originally called the Haystacks because of their shapes, then later renamed the Franconia Range. The Appalachian Trail follows the crest of mountain peaks for over 20 miles here. The AMC maintains 8 mountain huts plus a base lodge at Pinkham Notch, making it possible to cross the White Mountains with little more than a checkbook, water, and a bag of gorp in your pack. *The portion of the*

Franconia Range above treeline can be extremely dangerous in bad weather because of its narrowness and unusual exposure to lightning; nevertheless, the high, serrated ridge is strikingly beautiful, suggesting the ruins of a huge cathedral with its interesting rock formations. AMC Huts, the Pemigewasset Wilderness, and Lafayette Place Campground offer a variety of outdoor experiences to suit any taste. For information on huts, which provide hikers with bunks, toilets, and meals, contact Reservation Secretary, Pinkham Notch Camp, Box 298, Gorham, NH 03581, 603/466-2727.

A round-trip loop from the parking lot north of the Flume to Mts. Liberty and Flume takes 6 1/2–7 hours; 3327' vertical rise. Mt. Liberty alone takes five hours or more; 3060' vertical.

The Flume itself is well worth a visit. Originally, a huge boulder hung suspended above this narrow, 800-foot gorge in the flank of Mt. Liberty. A series of waterfalls cut through the granite to create this flume, and it took an avalanche in 1883 to loosen the rock. Scouring marks on the Flume represent the work of that slide, while the mountain stream was responsible for smoothing the sides of the gorge.

> 93 year-old Aunt Jess Gurnsey is said to have first discovered the Flume, when she was out fishing. Considering her age, she must have been both agile and tough, even "a little out of her head" as legend suggests.

The Pool, a 40-foot pothole formation with a covered bridge nearby, and **Avalanche Falls** are within walking distance. *Paths are gravel and occasionally steep. Free bus; admission for Flume and Pool.*

In 1853 "Professor" John Merrill came to the Notch, where he built a crude boat to accommodate sightseers who wanted a closer look at the falls that bring the river into the Pool. Known as "The Hermit," Merrill spent 30 years here as tour guide and off-the-cuff philosopher.

Ahead and across the Parkway via the underpass is **The Basin,** a 60' wide glacial pothole formed by the Pemigewasset and the sand and stones the river carried with it. Made of Conway granite, a combination of pink feldspar, gray quartz, and black mica, the walls of the Basin have been scoured by erosion over the years. *Free; handicapped access. Picnic and toilet facilities nearby.*

One of the easiest huts to reach (and surprisingly, one of the least crowded) is **Lonesome Lake,** with its eight-sided, eight-pitched skylighted roof. Three quarters of a mile around, the lake itself is a tarn, or dark-colored mountain pond, with Cannon Mt. rising steeply to the north and Franconia Ridge to the east. AMC operates this hut as a family shelter with small bunkrooms instead of the usual men's and women's dorms; this is an excellent place to introduce young children to hiking and the outdoors. *Open mid-June to mid-September and reached from Lonesome Lake Trail,*

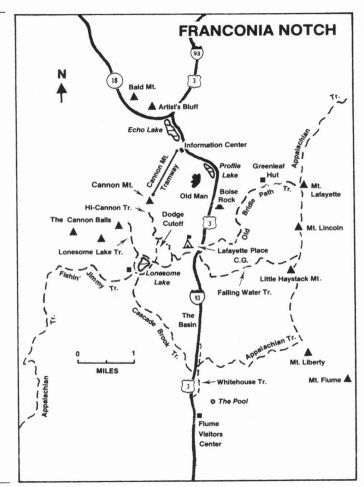

FRANCONIA NOTCH

Cascade Brook Trail, Fishin' Jimmy Trail from Kinsman Junction, or Dodge Cutoff from Hi-Cannon Trail. Small fee includes lemonade and lodging; meals extra. No camping permitted near hut or lake.

> Thomas Boise of Woodstock drove a team of horses over the first road through the Notch, but on one trip was caught by a fierce snowstorm. Seeing this large boulder with its sheltering ledge, he killed his horse, wrapped himself in its hide, and survived under the rock, although the search party that found him had to cut the frozen horsehide off him.

Further north into the Notch is more trailhead parking (for the Old Bridle Path Trail, leading up to the Greenleaf Hut and Mt. Lafayette, and Falling Water Trail, leading to Little Haystack), as well as roadside picnic facilities. Lafayette Place Campground is across the parkway. *To reach this camping area from northbound I-93, follow signs to the Tramway Exit and head south from there. Park at Lafayette Place Campground if you plan to hike to Lonesome Lake and its hut.*
Another mile on the right is **Boise Rock.** *Parking, toilet and picnic facilities, as well as a mountain-fed spring, although you can see the rock as well from the parkway.*

> On Lafayette the fall color is richest near the top, paling into green down toward the valley. "Once or twice on the way [up Lafayette] the gray brow of Mt. Cannon looks in through gaps in the foliage, from its great height, seeming to lean across the Notch and peer solemnly down from directly overhead, so narrow is this deep defile between two mighty mountains." Winthrop Packard, author/hiker, 1917.

New Hampshire's Profile

Within the next mile and a half are places where you can pull over to observe a rock formation that has fascinated visitors to Franconia Notch since the first white man saw a face there almost two hundred years ago. Even before there was lodging here in the Notch, stage-wagons brought travelers here to see the **Old Man** and the magnificent scenery.

> Opinions vary concerning this profile in rock. One of its first viewers, a tax collector, claimed it resembled Thomas Jefferson, then President; author Nathaniel Hawthorne saw the face of a loving father there in 1832. American poet Lucy Larcom thought the profile resembled a "relentless tyrant," while Swedish novelist Fredrika Bremer saw "a very old man in a bad humor. . . with a nightcap on his head, who is looking out from the mountain half inquisitive." Characteristically, P.T. Barnum offered to buy the Old Man. Whatever you may see there, you need only move a few hundred yards in either direction to turn the face into just another mass of rugged rocks. Today the same profile can be seen on the state's road signs and a US stamp.

Each year Plymouth's Niels Nielsen, the official caretaker of the Old Man, climbs atop Cannon Mt. to check the tie rods and bolts that keep this famous profile from slipping into the valley below.

> "Some of us may indeed . . . experience wildness when viewing the Flume from a crowded trail or the great cliffs of Cannon Mountain from Route 3. But to drink deeper of this special tonic of wildness, we need to remove ourselves from the more crowded areas where humans prevail. A short distance from even the most popular trail is a nature that 'pastures freely.' There you will find age-old processes still at work: the remains of giant trees being quietly decomposed into the forest floor; the springs that seep from the ground to form brooks and then rivers; the scattered feathers that tell the story of a life and death struggle. A small hemlock ravine can tell the same story as its bigger cousin, the Flume. And on a small unnamed hill, you can still experience the essence of wilderness." Gene Twaronite, teacher and columnist, 1985.

Profile Lake on the left side of the parkway is a popular picnic spot. *Visitors' center has parking, restrooms, telephones, and first-aid facilities.* Sorry, no boating or swimming allowed here, but you can enjoy both another half mile further at **Echo Lake.** *Beach, visitors center; swimming, fishing, and boating.*

We recommend that you pull off at the Tramway parking lot first — for trailheads, skiing, or just playing tourist. *The Information Center has a gift shop, snack bar, clean restrooms; bus and auto parking.* Even if there's no snow, Cannon is worth a stop for the year-round views from the tramway: Mt. Lafayette and the Franconia Range to the east, the Connecticut River Valley and Canada to the north, the mountains of Vermont to the west, and the Pemigewasset Valley to the south. And the tramway summit connects with numerous trails, both hiking and skiing. Cannon itself is the largest "talus" mountain in the area, made up of piles of broken rocks of all sizes. Rocks on its ledges form the "Cannon" and "Cannon Balls" from which this mountain takes its name; the formations can be seen from Profile Lake.

The New England Ski Museum next to the Tramway is a good way to learn something about this sport without the expense or effort of actually trying it. *Museum is open daily 10 am–4 pm; admission reduced in ski season. 25-minute multi-image slide show; changing exhibits.* One of several state-run ski areas, CANNON is also an exciting mountain in winter. Primarily a day-trippers' mountain, this is the one to ski during the crowded February vacation, since there are no condos in the park. *Limited lift tickets; surcharge for five-minute tram trip. Multi-day tickets interchangeable with other area resorts. Expert slopes above Echo Lake; 8 in all for advanced skiers, 14 intermediate and beginner trails on gentler northern face. Ski school; planned activities for non-skiing youngsters.*

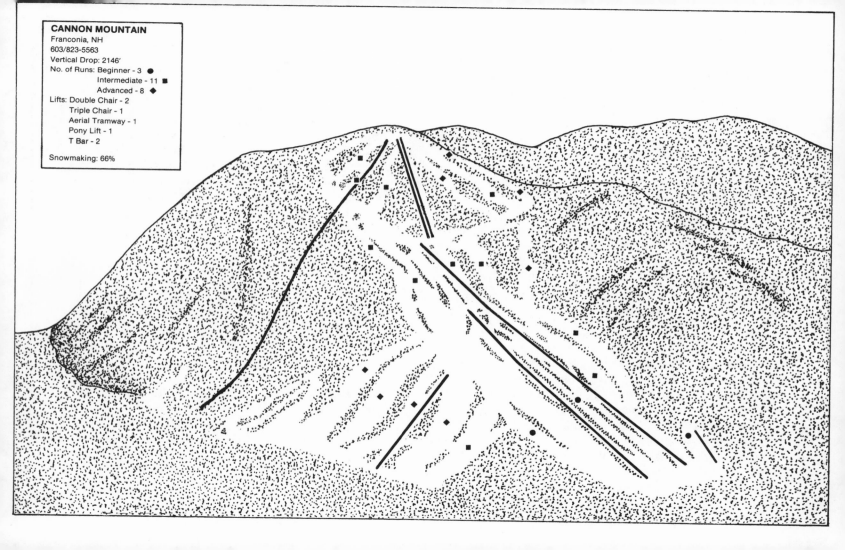

CANNON MOUNTAIN
Franconia, NH
603/823-5563
Vertical Drop: 2146'
No. of Runs: Beginner - 3 ●
　　　　　　Intermediate - 11 ■
　　　　　　Advanced - 8 ◆
Lifts: Double Chair - 2
　　　Triple Chair - 1
　　　Aerial Tramway - 1
　　　Pony Lift - 1
　　　T Bar - 2

Snowmaking: 66%

Site of America's first ski race and first ski school as well as New England's first winter resort, Cannon boasts yet another "first" — the original aerial tramway. Called Murphy's Folly when it was built during the Depression, this aerial funicular was the far-sighted vision of New Hampshire's governor; it now subsidizes much of the park system at Franconia Notch.

From here, return to the parkway, after deciding where you want to go next. Exit 3 from the parkway leads along rte. 18 to Echo Lake for boating, picnicking or hiking; this is also a nice route to the town of Franconia, with its inns and country roads to sample. Or you can continue north toward Littleton as the parkway becomes I-93 once more.

Franconia

We recommend a stop in Franconia, whether you turn off toward this charming community from the parkway or the interstate. *From parkway exit 3, turn left on rte. 18 passing Echo Lake/Old Man Viewing Area.* Look for **Artist's Bluff,** a favorite hiking overlook preserved during interstate construction, and **Bald Mt.,** both on the right; Echo Lake and its parking lot are on the left.

Rte. 18 essentially parallels I-93 to Franconia, a mile or two after leaving the park, but does offer a shorter route to lodging and dining south of town. Not long after leaving the park, you'll see signs for the FRANCONIA INN. *If you're ready for a bite to eat or want to spend the night, turn left, heading west on Wells Rd.*

Genteel lodgers of the old summer hotels in the Notch favored Bald Mt. for hiking.

The architectural design of Profile House, once located where today's Tramway is based, can perhaps best be described as 19th-century monumental — its twelve cottages, each three stories tall, were lost in the hotel's shadow. The hotel's lobby was 250 feet long; the octagonal dining room seated 600. There was a water-powered elevator and sparkling water was piped in from a mountain brook.

While the Boston Symphony Orchestra performed at Profile House twice a week in the summer, the most famous event here was the arrival of then President U.S. Grant on August 27, 1869. Wearing a high silk hat, black suit, and linen duster, he was covered with dust from a fast coach ride to the hotel.

Ferns will keep you company along this pretty paved road through the woods. You'll see the HORSE AND HOUND INN, 603/823-5501, recommended by BON APPETIT, on the left. Popular with skiers, the pine-paneled dining room offers an extensive menu, including three kinds of roast duck.

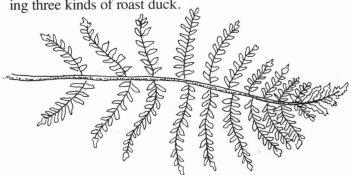

A pond and nice views appear on your left, and in another mile the road brings you to rte. 116. *Turn right toward the airport and Franconia.* FRANCONIA INN, 603/823-5542, maintains close to 30 miles of cross-country trails (some of which link up to trails in nearby Sugar Hill, if you're up to the steep "Inn Connector" Trail). *Rentals; lessons in barn.* The lovely peach-colored dining room serves meals daily to guests as well as the public. From French toast with sauteed apples to salade Nicoise, stuffed mushrooms, veal, and fresh seafood, the food is carefully prepared here and the service is friendly.

Sidetrip: **Hiking Without Roughing It.** For those who like to hike but prefer the luxury of a hot bath, a firm mattress, thick towels, and good food to roughing it in a tent or AMC hut, NEW ENGLAND HIKING HOLIDAYS, 802/253-8017, has the answer. Organized and managed by Clare Harrison, who has four years' experience guiding hikers and organizing outdoor vacations, this Vermont-based group offers numerous weekends and week-long trips with stays in delightful New Hampshire or Maine inns. In the White Mountains, you can hike from Franconia over to Crawford Notch and Conway, or combine hiking with tennis and big band sounds at THE MOUNT WASHINGTON HOTEL. *Rates include pickup at area airports, van shuttle from hiking areas to inns. For information, contact NEW ENGLAND HIKING HOLIDAYS, RR 2, Box 542, Stowe, VT 05672.*

Ham Branch, west of rte. 116, is a first-rate trout stream. A half mile past the inn, Lafayette Rd. goes off to the left (turn here if you want to go to Sugar Hill; see sidetrip, page 33). Then 116 becomes a bit more commercial, before you see signs for the ***Robert Frost Museum.***

Sidetrip: **Frost Place.** *Turn left at the sign and cross over bridge. After .1 mile turn left again onto a dirt road, up a hill; look for parking .2 mile on right.* Still a wonderfully quiet place where you can hear the wind in the trees and birds singing, this simple farmhouse seems little changed since the poet lived here. The name on the mailbox looks as though it might have been painted by "R. Frost" himself.

"The mountain held the town as in a shadow
I saw so much before I slept there once:
I noticed that I missed stars in the west,
Where its black body cuts into the sky.
Near me it seemed: I felt it like a wall
Behind which I was sheltered from a wind.
And yet between the town and it I found,
When I walked forth at dawn to see new things,
Were fields, a river, and beyond, more fields. . ."
Robert Frost
From NORTH OF BOSTON, 1914.

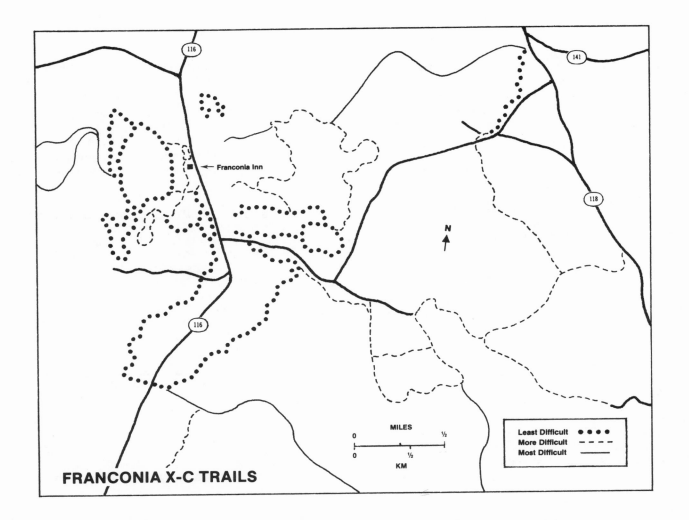

FRANCONIA X-C TRAILS

Mountains were a unifying force in Frost's work, and anyone (literary or not) will thrill to the views from his home. *Open weekends spring through fall (summer, Tuesday – Sunday); donation. Two rooms contain memorabilia, including signed first editions; narrated slide show, guided tour, half-mile nature trail, summer readings by resident poet.*

"Not a poem, I believe, in all my six books," Robert Frost wrote in his sixties, "but has something in it of New Hampshire. . . . I lived, somewhat brokenly to be sure, in Salem, Derry, Plymouth, and Franconia, New Hampshire, from my tenth to my forty-fifth year. Most of my time out of it I lived. . . on the edge of New Hampshire, where my walks and vacations could be. . . . So you see it has been New Hampshire, New Hampshire with me all the way." Later in life, Frost said he found it "restful just to think about New Hampshire. At present I am living in Vermont."

This road is part of our Sugar Hill Sidetrip, see page 33 for a pretty loop, or continue back the way you came to rte. 116.

If you return to 116, you'll see Ham Branch again on the left, as the road leads into the village of **Franconia.** There are some nice old homes along here, then a mile past the sign to the Frost place, you cross a bridge over the Ham, before coming into the busy part of town. If you go straight ahead, South Rd. leads to Bethlehem, page 140. We recommend turning left onto rte. 18, instead, to explore a little of Franconia first.

18th Century Village Meets 1960s Craftsfolk

In sharp contrast to the development spawned by most ski areas, this village in the shadow of Cannon remains a sleepy, low-key community with some of the flavor of its 1772 beginnings. The Gale River and various feeder streams are still fresh enough for brook trout, and the town remains as charming as it was when Hawthorne, John Greenleaf Whittier, Washington Irving, and William Cullen Bryant visited here.

Sidetrip: ***Rt. 141.*** *If you opted for I-93 rather than 18, Exit 36 puts you onto rte. 141, a faster route into Franconia. Turn right where this road "T's" into 18 for restaurants and inns along this stretch.*
If you head left instead of right, you'll come to LOVETT'S INN, 603/823-7761. Herbs from the garden and local produce are the basics for meals here: lamb with chutney, chicken in brandy, herbs, and cream. Breakfasts include blueberry, apple, or butternut pancakes; shirred eggs with tomatoes and mushrooms; fried cornmeal mush with local maple syrup.

Recently bought by a Boston-based group, LOVETT'S INN was a farmhouse in the 18th century and is today on the National Register of Historic Places.

Heading north toward Franconia on 18, you'll pass a motor lodge and family campground on the left before the bridge; then rte. 142 comes in from the right. The stream on the left here is actually a river — the Gale — and will become considerably wider ahead. Look for the VILLAGE

HOUSE RESTAURANT, 603/823-5912, on the right. Serving three meals a day, this is a popular place to eat. Ahead are antiques for sale, pretty houses, and barns.

Less than half a mile past the VILLAGE HOUSE and also on the right is the Abbie Greenleaf Library. Next door is the Franconia Town office with a museum in between. *Open year-round with research materials, photos, information on the iron works. Tuesday 9–2:30, Wednesday 9–noon; 603/823-7752.* Across the road, you'll notice Dow Academy, an interesting frame schoolhouse that was the gift of Moses Arnold Dow, a successful Littleton magazine publisher who was reputed to print "everything sent in" to him.

Continue north on 18/116. You'll see the Franconia Village Store on the left with the local craft guild nearby. Then on the right is a collection of enterprises that includes a bakery, wool shop, Gale River Outlet (discount women's wear created for the Garnet Hill mail-order catalog), and Anne McKnight Gallery. Chuck Theodore sells nature photography (signed and numbered, limited editions) as well as calendars, postcards, posters, sweatshirts, and T-shirts at the Rivendell Gallery of Fine Art on Streeter Pond Rd., off rte. 18 north. Franconia College, a product of the 1960s that exists no longer, spawned a number of first-rate craftspeople in this area.

A little further ahead on the left is a picnic area and the ruins of an old stone furnace used in smelting iron ore. The sole example of the post-Revolutionary iron industry in the state, this furnace produced iron for farm tools, cookware, and the famous Franconia Stoves.

Continuing north on 18/116, you'll find access back to I-93. Or if you have time and are interested in antiques, old inns, biking, or cross-country skiing, take the sidetrip below.

Sidetrip: ***Sugar Hill.*** *From 18/116, .1 mile north of the picnic area/iron furnace, turn left onto 117. There are no paved shoulders and some steep grades along this road, but it is usually not heavily traveled. Experienced bikers will find this a challenging, but rewarding route.*

The road climbs up from Franconia past the SUGAR HILL INN AND COTTAGES, 603/823-5621, on the right — look to the left here for incredible views of Cannon Mt. There are even more fantastic views ahead by the iris farm.

Sugaring in this part of New Hampshire is reminiscent of the old Indian method: on the first thaw, squaws cut down elms and stripped them of bark — making wooden bowls and bark troughs. Then, the Indians cut two-inch deep gashes in maple trees, inserting the troughs. When sap began to flow, the women brought huge wooden vessels to catch the sap — storing as much as 100 gallons at a time, before boiling it in brass kettles stolen, according to an Englishman held captive, from the white settlers.

Ahead on the right is one of the area's oldest and most popular eateries. POLLY'S PANCAKE PARLOUR, 603/823-5575, offers genuine pine-paneled country flavor — no frills here, but plenty of attention to honest value. Out front, there's an illustration of the various mountains (from Washington through the Kinsmans), so you can distinguish those you've hiked from those you've skied.

The restaurant itself is as eclectic as they come, with reminders of the past, like old sheet music covering the ceiling. The ham and bacon are cob-smoked; soups are delicious. You'll find the pancake choices both varied and filling. And there are maple products for sale in the gift shop. About the only thing you can't get here is any kind of alcoholic beverage, but your waitress will automatically bring you coffee — no matter what the time of day.

Sap is said to flow on a warm day that follows a cold night, probably a chemical reaction (gas in cell walls expands and contracts, driving the sap up then down). Sugaring season — when today's visitor is most likely to find buckets or plastic milk jugs hanging from maple trees — lasts about a month. It takes 25 gallons of sap to produce a gallon of syrup. For the best grade, look for pale amber color, rather than dark molasses brown.

At the top of the hill, almost a mile past POLLY's, you'll see a fine old inn, THE HOMESTEAD, 603/823-5564, on the left, with The Sugar Hill Sampler behind it. The Sampler sells antiques and crafts as well as displaying memorabilia of the area's early settlers. *Open daily 9:30–5:30; from late June to late October or by appointment.* A comfortable inn that's been in the same family for generations, THE HOMESTEAD offers bed and breakfast only,

but you will find a place to dine further down this road. *Or you might want to continue straight on rte. 117 for another loop that connects with Lisbon, see Ammonoosuc Valley Sidetrip, page 38.*

Turn left before the inn. The views to the left, as you head down the hill are spectacular, and there are pretty houses on the right. In close to half a mile, you'll see the SUNSET HILL INN AND SKI TOURING CENTER, 603/823-5522, on the left. An old-fashioned place with a 9-hole golf course and tennis courts, this inn serves a changing menu to the public as well as its own guests. Salmon steak, chicken Marsala, veal blanquette are among the choices here.

From the inn, the paved road jogs left, then dead ends just past the intersection with Lafayette Rd. Turn left by the huge frame house and barn onto Lafayette, passing an apple orchard and stone house with a picket fence on the left. The road gives you stunning views between the stands of birches and hemlocks (no hunting). Continue down past another pretty old place on the left; the grades are steep, but at least you're heading down all the way.

Toad Hill Rd. comes in on the right by a boulder. There are more views and an old 1779 house on the left, before Ridge Rd. *Turn left if you haven't been to the* **Frost Place,** *see sidetrip page 30, or if you have, continue straight on Lafayette to 116.*

I-93 North

Even though you're getting further and further away from one of the main ranges of the White Mountains, there are interesting places to visit from the interstate north of Franconia. For hay-fever sufferers, *Bethlehem* has long been a resort community, though a refresh-

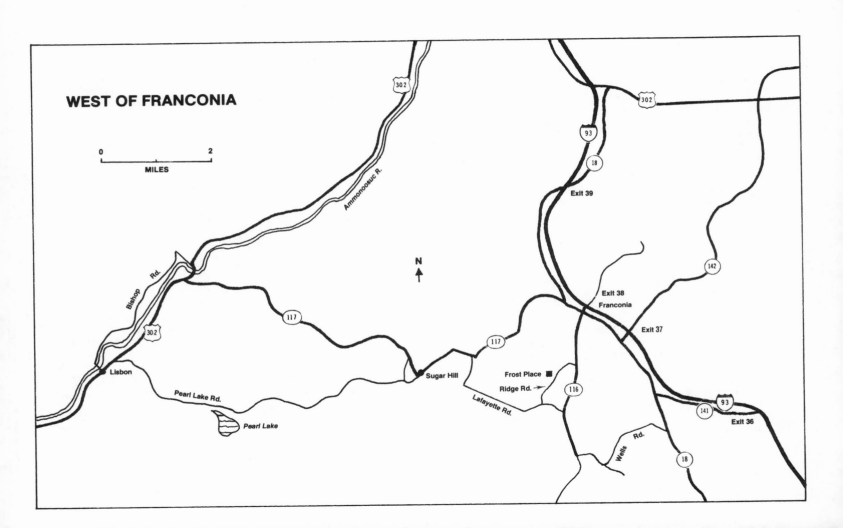

WEST OF FRANCONIA

ingly undeveloped spot. *Take Exit 40, turning right onto rte. 302 east (see page 140 for descriptions of Bethlehem and other stops along rte. 302).*

Another mile and a half along the interstate brings you to the first of two exits for Littleton, historically an industrial center, but also an interesting city in the beautiful Ammonoosuc River Valley. If you're ready for a stop, there are inns and restaurants here; certainly, Littleton has long been a way station for travelers going in any direction. *From here you have several choices: continue north on I-93 into Vermont toward I-91 and Canada; connect with rte. 116 north toward rte. 3 and the loop around the northernmost section of the White Mountains (see Chapter V), or head south on rte. 302 through charming colonial villages toward rte. 10, which will take you to Hanover (home of Dartmouth College) and eventually the Berkshires, in Massachusetts.*

> Littleton's first permanent settlers arrived in 1769 and created population growth immediately with the birth of their fifth son. The Caswells' original house was destroyed by a flood the following spring, but they persisted, building another home near the mouth of Parker Brook, where a boulder commemorates their determination.

Whatever route you decide on, we recommend a stop in **Littleton** first. *Take rtes. 116 and 18 north from Exit 41, across the river and into town, turning left on rtes. 10 and 302.* Built on several of the many natural "shelves" that line the Ammonoosuc, this city has

been an important trading center for northern New England. It was the river that brought development here, beginning in 1799 with a dam. From distillation of potato whiskey to manufacture of carriages and sleighs, from the Kilburn Brothers Stereoscopic View Factory in the late 19th century to Moore Station, a hydroelectric plant on the Connecticut River, Littleton has contributed substantially to the region's economy.

> The anti-slavery movement was also strong in Littleton, which became an important stop on the "Underground Railroad" running slaves to freedom in Canada.

Coming in from Exit 41, you'll pass BISHOP'S ICE CREAM SHOPPE, 603/444-6039, on your right. *Open daily mid-April to mid-October.* Cross over the Amoonoosuc before turning left for downtown. Look for Tilton's Opera Block, an unaltered collection of commercial buildings on the left. Granite keystones and sills draw attention to the bricks along the arched windows.

> When Henry L. Tilton designed this block in 1881, the double doors on the first and second floors were to be entrances to the concert halls on the third floor.

The Kilburn Block, a little ahead on the right, is less impressive, but does show the Georgian revival style so popular at the turn of the century. In the next block, the Littleton Public Library is another example of this, with its Palladian windows, arched openings, and heavily toothed cornices.

> Like those in many American towns, Littleton's library was a gift from philanthropist Andrew Carnegie.

If you have time, you might like to take the walking tour of Main St. *The Chamber of Commerce, located in the Queen Anne-style Community House ahead on Main St., has a free brochure on twelve historic sites downtown. Open Monday – Friday, 9–5; 603/444-6561.*

> An imposing three-storied exterior with Doric portico and fluted columns has changed little since Harry Thayer's red coach brought visitors to what was once the White Mountain House in Littleton. In its glory day, Thayers Inn boasted gracious hospitality and modern conveniences as well as elegant architecture.

You'll see THAYERS INN, 603/444-6469, on the left, before Community House on the right. As you head out of the downtown area, BEAL HOUSE INN, 603/444-2661, with lodging and antiques is on the right. *Bear left down the hill, just past Beal House Inn for rte. 302 west or access to I-93 north.* Further along rte. 302 are numerous fast-food franchises and THE CLAM SHELL, 603/444-6445/6501. Serving lunch (or Sunday Brunch) and dinner daily, this seafood and steak restaurant is popular with locals and tourists alike. *If you're interested in continuing north from Littleton on the New Hampshire side of the Connecticut River, I-93 connects to rte. 135 for some excellent trout fishing and views of the Green Mountains en route to Lancaster. Or the interstate will lead you into Vermont itself to I-91 with a fast route north or south.*

We recommend your taking route 302 west from Littleton. (You'll actually be going south here.) If your time is limited, head south along the Ammonoosuc River Valley through some lovely towns and villages toward rte. 25, page 38, for the loop east, or rte. 10 toward Hanover and the Berkshires.

Or if I-93 has only whetted your appetite for these rugged White Mountains, head east on 302 toward the quiet resort of Bethlehem, with wonderful views of the Presidentials and Mahoosucs en route to the central corridor (Chapter III) and Maine (Chapter II). For those interested in the North Country, continue northeast on rte. 116 to Whitefield, page 165.

SOUTHBOUND ON 302

South of Littleton, 302 takes you down the Ammonoosuc River Valley with a kind of geology more like Littleton's than that found in most of the White Mountains. There are interesting towns, colonial architecture, and connections south or east.

Outside town, this road merges with rte. 10 and goes through a variety of scenery: old farms, lumberyards, car dealerships, colonial burying grounds, trailer parks. On the left, the often snow-capped summit of Mt. Washington rises above the surrounding hills and peaks. Closer to the highway, suburban sprawl melds into rural poverty, horse farms, and antique shops. If you can ignore the lack of zoning and concentrate instead on the river next to you, you'll make worthwhile discoveries ahead in *Lisbon.*

About five miles south of Littleton, you'll pass an old kiln, then see signs for AMMONOOSUC INN in an open meadow on the right. The sign should alert bikers, as well as anyone ready to eat or play a little golf, of a pleasant sidetrip.

A colonial settlement, Lisbon has attractive buildings from every period thereafter. It is also near Sugar Hill's inns and views, if you're in need of lodging or didn't explore this lovely area earlier.

Although this part of 302 is listed as an official New Hampshire bike route, we don't recommend it either immediately south of Littleton or through Lisbon, because of traffic. Bikers who've developed a little moun-tain muscle and aren't put off by hills might want to try a loop off 302 to the AMMONOOSUC INN and the old part of Lisbon, then on to Sugar Hill for the night. This loop makes a nice sidetrip for drivers as well; see map (page 35).

Sidetrip: **Ammonoosuc Valley.** When you see the sign for the AMMONOOSUC INN, look for a bridge over the river, and turn right over that bridge. In about a half mile, turn left onto Bishop Rd. This road climbs up a gentle grade with the river on the left. You'll see a golf course in the valley below you, and in about .7 mile, THE AMMONOOSUC INN, 603/838-6118, appears on your right above the road. You don't need to be a golfer to enjoy the fare at COBBLERS' RESTAURANT: crab-stuffed mushrooms, fried calamari, or steamed mussels for starters; among the entree choices are veal Marsala, beef tenderloin in puff pastry topped with boursin, Cajun-style chicken, swordfish with dill butter, barbequed ribs with stuffed shrimp. *Open for dinner Sunday – Thursday from 5–9 pm, Friday and Saturday until 9:30, Sunday Brunch 10–2. Children's menu; closed Mondays in winter.*

The broad meadows that line the Ammonoosuc River in Lisbon were once considered by Eleazar Wheelock as one possible site for Dartmouth College; instead, Wheelock encouraged his brother-in-law to settle here. In 1778 Lisbon was one of 35 New Hampshire towns that talked of joining the independent republic of Vermont.

Continue on Bishop Rd. for another mile or so, past an old house with a picket fence, to a stop sign. *Turn left by New Hampshire Electric Cooperative, still keeping the river on your left.* The road winds closer to the Ammonoosuc, with houses uphill on the right. Just past Witherton's Cog Railroad, you'll see the Lisbon Police and Fire Department in the red building on the right.

Turn left here onto School St. to return to 302/10 and the center of town. For further explorations of Lisbon, turn right. You'll pass a wood-shingled Episcopal Church with a lovely white-frame house behind, as well as many well-tended homes. Nearby, the Lisbon Regional High School has taken over an impressive, towered building of some age. Brooks meander through this part of town, and construction dates distinguish homes on both sides of the river. The Lions Club Community Field exudes the kind of civic pride we wish every small town had.

Heading back over the river toward the center of Lisbon, you'll see a large wrought-iron, Victorian-era lamppost where School St. meets 302. *Turn right for one block (bikers may want to walk through this busy section of town) on 302, crossing the street onto Landaff Rd. across from Indian Head Bank. Here's where your hills really start, but hopefully, bikers are in shape for them.*

Cross the railroad tracks and take the first left, passing a small store and residential area. At the yield sign, con-

tinue up the hill, then turn left again onto Savage Hill Rd.

This paved road crosses a bridge; given a choice of routes, you want to stay on the paved one, keeping the brook to the right. Continue up this winding country road, turning left at (but not going over) the bridge at the next fork. Pearl Lake is on your right. Pearl Lake Rd. climbs next to an apple orchard. You pass through woods to a lovely brick house on the left. Continue through a fine stand of evergreens that opens up with mountain views, bearing right past a tiny pond.

"The trees are large but not huge. Certainly they are second or third growth, perhaps even younger. But here and there are some good sized hemlocks and spruce which are well on their way to becoming forest giants. A large gnarled red maple looks like it has been growing here a very long time. There is a strong sense of the primeval here. Slowly but surely this place is becoming wilderness again." From NATURE'S SCHOOL, 1985.

Ferns, pines, and occasionally birches will be your companions for a while. Then houses begin to appear, letting you know you've arrived in ***Sugar Hill***. A little over 6 miles from Lisbon, Pearl Lake Rd. runs into rte. 117; continue east through the village if you're in need of lodging or something to eat. You'll see the pretty Sugar Hill Meeting House (1830) and Harmon's Country Store before reaching HILLTOP INN, a bed and breakfast on the left, 603/823-5695. *Children and pets welcome.*

In another half mile, you'll find THE HOMESTEAD INN, a more old-fashioned bed and breakfast on your right. (See Sugar Hill Sidetrip, pages 34.) Or turn left on 117 to 302, for the largely downhill ride back toward Lisbon.

Rte. 302/10 passes a campground, then the New England Electric Wire factory, one of several major employers (and a reason so many of Lisbons's homes are well-maintained or being restored).

> Mining was a leading industry here in the 19th century — one Lisbon vein of iron ore was the richest in the nation, and for a time more than $50,000 worth of Lisbon gold was in circulation.

Yankee Original Antiques sets the atmosphere for this old town, hugging the Ammonoosuc. *If you didn't take the Ammonoosuc Valley sidetrip, turn right at the wrought-iron, antique lamp post in the center of town, and follow School St. a little way to get a real feel for this town; sidetrip, page 38.* On the southern end of Lisbon, 302 passes one of the prettiest Methodist churches in New Hampshire.

A mill marks the end of town. ***Landaff,*** with twelve identical millworkers' houses, overlooks the river. And .3 mile further a single picnic table awaits under a solitary pine.

The Baths

After a rusting trestle bridge and a tall stand of sumac, rte. 302 passes through farmland. The half dozen homes nestled up against an evergreen forest on the left and overlooking the Ammonoosuc on the right comprise ***Upper Bath*** village, dating back to 1840 or earlier. From the four-chimney frame farm house north of town through the "Rounded House," a brick building that was once a law office, this community seems frozen in time. Only cars parked in driveways or an occasional TV antenna remind you that this is indeed the 20th century. The old elms that once lined the highway have mostly died, but today there are huge firs, wonderful willows, and hydrangeas in well-cared for yards. *The traffic moves fast here and there's no place to park except on narrow shoulders, so a quick look may be all you can expect.*

> The four terraces in Upper Bath are typical of geological formations in the Ammonoosuc and Connecticut River Valleys. As glacial ice melted, soil and rock readjusted to meet the changing levels of meltdown, leaving the land permanently terraced.

Rte. 302 climbs through a dense wood of pointed firs that obliterates river views, then descends into the town of ***Bath.*** An old burying ground and an 1895 house reflect historic flavor in a village that has seen better times. While an 1836 stone home and others remain as reminders of Bath's proud past, asbestos siding and TV dishes accurately describe the present.

> The numerous covered bridges that New Hampshire preserves so proudly today were once frowned upon by clergy as spooning and kissing places.

Look for an old covered bridge here, off to the right. An 1848 Opera Hall now sells gifts and handicrafts. Next door is one of the most delightful country stores anywhere — the Brick General Store. A vintage Coke cooler, classic green rocking chairs, weathered doors, and interesting architectural features will charm you as much as the daily specials: the day we visited, a sign proclaimed, "Today it's warm, so the soup is chili."

If it's warm when you drive through Bath, be sure to roll down your windows to hear the river rushing south. 302 passes lovely bottom land before the valley narrows. *Woodsville,* another four or five miles south, has another covered bridge, about a mile west on 302 after this road diverges from rte. 10, the Dartmouth Highway. The river is best for fishing in June; canoeists from Littleton use the covered bridge as a place to leave a second car. *It is important to pull your boat out here, before encountering a dam ahead.*

Unless you're heading to Vermont on 302, we recommend continuing south a bit on rte. 10, to the lovely old community of Haverhill, with some wonderful fishing en route east to Plymouth and I-93. Or turn east on rte. 112 toward Kinsman Notch and the Kancamagus Highway, Chapter IV.

The Ammonoosuc joins the Connecticut River, a blue-ribbon trout stream, here in Woodsville, with fine views into Vermont. Early settlers in this part of New Hampshire used the river as their highway; the first bridge across the Connecticut at this point was built in 1804, but it was railroads that put Woodsville on the map. As you continue south on rte. 10, you'll pass a historic marker commemorating the Rogers' Rangers, who drove the St. Francis Indians from New England, making this valley safe for settlement.

The Ox-Bow of the Connecticut

Four or five miles south of Woodsville, the road passes through **North Haverhill.** Founded in the 18th century, this town boasts a Civil War statue and the only place to eat for miles around, THE VILLAGE PANCAKE HOUSE AND BAKERY, 603/787-6588. Fall travelers can enjoy fresh cider or apples from the Indian Corn Mill or sample wares at the fairground on the right.

"Moosehillock resembles a crouching lion, magnificent in repose. . . . This immense strength, paralyzed and helpless though it seems, is nevertheless capable of arousing in us a sentiment of respectful fear. . . . This mountain received a name before Mount Washington, and is in some respects. . . the most interesting of the whole group." Samuel Adams Drake, 1881.

"You ought to have seen what I saw on my way
To the village, through Mortenson's pasture today:
Blueberries as big as the end of your thumb,
Real sky-blue, and heavy, and ready to drum
In the cavernous pail of the first one to come!"
Robert Frost, 1914.

There are views of Black Mt. (2836′) outside Benton, and massive Mt. Moosilauke to the east of rte. 10, as you continue south. Black has a long quartz ledge with wide views for day hikers; but old house buffs will want to continue south to one of New England's prettiest villages.

Sidetrip: **Black Mt.** Allow four to five hours from rte. 10. *Continue south on 10 for another three to four miles, just past Oliverian Brook, a trout stream. Turn left at the junction of rte. 25 and drive another four or five miles to **East Haverhill.*** Turn left in the center of town onto Lime Kiln Rd., bear left a mile-and-a-half at the fork, continue about the same distance on dirt to the parking area on the right. **Chippewa Trail** can be found to the left. Slip through an opening in the fence, descend a small slope, cross a road and turn right onto a logging road which forks ahead (hikers should bear left, climbing up to a pasture). Cross the pasture toward the left into the woods, where the climb steepens. Arrows, blazes, and cairns point you up the mountain through spruces. If you hike in late spring, you'll see masses of the purple shrub rhodora; in summer, you may find blueberries ripe for picking.

About an hour and a half from the time you parked, you'll come out onto the open shoulder. Walk 100′ to the right for a view to the south, or continue climbing to the bright quartz knob (using toeholds and handholds, mountaineer-style). Go down a short col (a low point between two peaks), then up a cliff to the uppermost ledge, keeping left around the cliff's base. From the bare summit, you'll see Moosilauke surrounded by forests, with bulky Mt. Kinsman to the northeast, obscuring some of the Franconia Range.

Birders may see swallows from the summits, and possibly hawks or ravens. Warblers and white-throated sparrows often inhabit the spruces here. *Although you'll see Black Mt. Trail at the top, you should descend the way you came, back to your car.*

Each species of organism seems to find its separate niche. For instance, warblers all inhabit the same type of forest, with different species occupying different altitudes and subtly different environments. Similarly, woodpeckers move straight up the trunks of trees in their search for food; brown creepers move upward in a spiral, catching different insects; while nuthatches move down, finding bugs the others missed.

If you continue south on 10, you'll soon find yourself in *Haverhill,* a charming collection of colonial and Federal homes overlooking the Great Ox-Bow of the Connecticut River. Northeast of the common are two historic old homes: the 1812 Governor John Page House, and next door with a plaque in a boulder out front, the home built for Colonel Charles Johnston, hero of the battle of Bennington and one of the town's founders. Constructed in 1769, the Johnston house is the first frame home in Haverhill (note the architectural details, like "dentil work," here).

> At Bennington, Johnston had to carry important orders from General Stark through the woods to another division but, instead, came upon British and Hessian soldiers in ambush. An officer, sword in hand, claimed Johnston prisoner, but the American, with only a stout staff as a weapon, knocked the sword out of the Hessian's hand and, grabbing it, declared the officer his prisoner and a "dead man" if the other soldiers didn't throw down their weapons. Turning to his men, the officer admitted, "We are prisoners of war," and Johnston marched them back to the American encampment.

The Old Coos Pike

The large common in Haverhill, divided by Court St. (formerly the Coos Turnpike leading 18th- and 19th-century travelers to Plymouth), is unusual. In most New England towns such an expanse in the middle of a settlement would be "commonly" owned, hence the name, but here only the abutters own the common. A brick Congregational Church and Haverhill Academy (born again as a junior high school) own part of the northernmost common, which explains the playing field and jungle gym.

The second common boasts an array of attractive old homes, from Wintra's Homestead (1805) facing the highway to Williams Tavern next to Court St. Those interested in antiques or lodging would be advised to continue south on rte. 10 to 1812 Antiques and the HAVERHILL INN, a bed and breakfast establishment, 603/989-5961. But there is a dirt road at the east end of Court St. that connects, eventually, with rte. 25C, passing some wonderful fishing spots on the way to the town of Warren.

Sidetrip: *Lake road to Warren. Turn left onto Court St., past the Haverhill Library and an unusual brick Greek Revival home.*

New Hampshire's last public hanging took place in Haverhill in the 1860s. At one such event, the sermon preceding the hanging lasted two hours and was circulated far and wide: three pages exhorting the criminal, 13 pages haranguing the audience. No wonder this custom died!

The paved part of Court St. ends east of town; take the right-hand fork, heading straight. The road climbs past giant ferns and what looks like the newest innovation in chicken houses, then several old farms. The road narrows and will slow you down in places; there are good mountain views, however.

Three miles outside of town, past farm buildings on both sides of the road, turn right on a paved road that climbs up a hill before it runs into rte. 25C, where you turn left. Eastman Brook, a nice trout stream, is to the right of this road, which roller-coasters its way to Lake Katherine, also on the right. Fishermen should keep going a bit further to **Lake Tarleton** on the left, barely visible from the road. *Look for a pullover, then a road down to the lake about 1.2 miles past East Armington Estates. Tarleton offers lake as well as brook trout, salmon, bass, pickerel, and hornpout;* **Lake Armington,** *a little further along 25C on the right, is good for warm-water fishing.*

Shortly after crossing the Warren town line, the road passes the Wachipauka Pond Trail, leading up Webster Slide Mountain, and a four-hour hike to rte. 25, see AMC WHITE MOUNTAIN GUIDE. Rte. 25C makes a steep descent, through logging activity, into a broad valley. Then, past a lumberyard, the road brings you into the village of Warren, with the Morse Museum, 603/764-9407, and its collection of African animal trophies and curios from around the globe. Open end of June – Labor Day, 10 am–5 pm, 7 days a week; free.

From here you can bear right onto rte. 25, below, to Wentworth, Rumney, page 7, and Plymouth, page 4. Or return via our trip along rte. 118 to Moosilauke and on to North Woodstock, page 16.

Rte. 10 continues south, with the Connecticut River and Vermont providing most of the scenery, through Piermont and Orford, where the road straightens out and becomes a New Hampshire bike route around Lyme and down to Hanover. Unless you're Dartmouth-bound or interested in the Berkshires, we recommend heading back to just north of Haverhill for more hiking and fishing on rte. 25 east en route to Warren, Wentworth, and finally Plymouth. *Less than a mile north of the Haverhill common, look for rte. 25 and turn right.*

EAST ON RTE. 25

Oliverian Brook — you guessed it, another trout stream — is on the left as 25 passes through the small settlement of **Pike.** In another mile or so, you'll pass the Pike School and **East Haverhill,** before crossing a wide valley. With the industrial revolution, a number of farms were abandoned in New Hampshire and other New England states; others have been deserted in this century, as farming becomes more expensive and less productive here in the mountains.

Just past the Benton town line, hikers will see AT signs on either side of rte. 25 (to the right, the Wachipauka Pond Trail; and a number of the others as well on the left). The Appalachian Trail leads to Mt.

Moosilauke on the left side of 25. The road continues through a fairly desolate area with only mountains and an occasional trailer on the way to the Baker River Dam on the left, and **Warren** village, just ahead.

Rte. 25C comes in from the right just before the Warren Honor Roll and Civil War statue. South of Warren, rte. 25 narrows, crosses a bridge, then enters **Wentworth** township. *Anyone who's hungry or looking for a place to stay should be alert to the junction with 25A, just past a couple of antique shops.* On the right, WENTWORTH INN, 603/764-9923, invites diners (who should call for a reservation) to share what the chef prepares nightly for guests or to come by for breakfast.

To the left side of rte. 25 is the triangular town common, several interesting old buildings, and HOBSON HOUSE, 603/764-9460, another bed and breakfast inn that's happy to serve meals to the public. *Open year-round with full breakfast and a five-course dinner included in special winter rates.* Both inns are very reasonable places to stay, a short drive to a number of ski areas, and a good base for antiquers.

Named for Governor Benning Wentworth, the town was settled before the Revolution, but a flood in 1856 wiped out much of the community. Nevertheless, there's a beautiful old church with mountain ranges behind it; Wentworth boasts not one but two post offices, although the older one no longer sells stamps.

The Baker River Valley

Continuing southeast on rte. 25 from Wentworth, you'll soon have the White Mountain National Forest on your left. There's a campground three miles outside town. Look for a recently-built information booth and rest area on your left in another two or three miles. *Handicapped access.*

As early as 1712, the English were interested in this area. Captain Thomas Baker, an adventurer from Northampton, Massachusetts, led 32 men to explore what is now Coos County. From the Pemigewasset to the Ox Bow of the Connecticut River, the company encountered Indians, peacefully acquiring trinkets from some but killing others.

Baker's treatment of the Pemigewassets is perhaps the hardest to reconcile. These friendly Indians, who grew corn in the valley and hunted otters and beavers along the sandy banks of the river, were attacked for no apparent reason — other than the wealth of furs the tribe had acquired. Baker's men killed the Pemigewassets' chief, raided their village, and drove the formerly peaceful Indians into Canada.

Rte. 25 continues toward Plymouth, with the Baker River on the left. If you have time, you might want to fish or hike outside Rumney, or picnic and cool off at Polar Caves, page 7, another three miles ahead. For those who would like to explore the White Mountains further, we recommend heading south on 25 past Plymouth to Holderness, continuing east on 113 for a shunpikers' tour of the Sandwich Range on page 151, then continuing to the heart of the White Mountains (Chapter III) or Maine's peaks (Chapter II).

Chapter II   THE EASTERN ROUTE – THE WHITE MOUNTAINS OF MAINE

Until recently, the mountains of Maine have played second fiddle to New Hampshire's peaks. For one thing, only a small section of the White Mountain National Forest goes into Maine; for another, the road system is more primitive than the high-speed corridors of New Hampshire. But for many people, the relatively "undiscovered" quality of southwestern Maine offers exactly the kind of get-away-from-it-all experience they need.

There are small villages to explore — places where progress is measured by the number of push-button telephones, rather than the number of condos and outlets. You will pass lakes and brooks, often traveling on dirt roads that look as though no one has driven them for years. There are plenty of restaurants (including some excellent places that feel like a time-warp from the fifties), as well as quaint 18th-century inns. There's first-rate skiing and even one 4000 footer to "bag," yet the feeling is distinctly laid-back here in Maine's White Mountains.

To reach these peaks, you have several choices. Most routes from the south converge in Naples, a busy lakeside summer resort framed by the moutains. The fastest combines some freeway driving with a good surfaced, two-lane road, route 302. *Take the Maine Turnpike to Exit 8, Westbrook/Portland. Turn right at the light just past the toll booth (and roll up your windows — Westbrook is known for its paper mills and rotten egg odors). After one and a half miles through an industrial area, you want to turn left at the stop light onto rte. 302, Forest Ave. This stretch of road is often busy, particularly through the shopping malls and fast-food outlets 10 miles ahead in* **North Windham.** *Drivers are advised to look out for turning traffic.*

Indians Called It "Stretch of Water"

The first scenic attraction en route is **Lake Sebago,** 15 miles north of the Westbrook Exit, on the left. There's a boat landing in **Raymond.** Lake Sebago is the site of many summer camps, as well as the source of Portland's drinking water supply.

Originally the home of landlocked salmon (Salmo Salar Sebago), this lake is 15 miles long, 11 miles wide, and 400 feet deep in places, which makes it a favorite fishing spot even today. Fly fishermen will find salmon hard hitters; Sebago is a great place for ice fishing as well. Lake trout (toque) and brookies, bass, white and yellow perch, rainbow smelt, chain pickerel, whitefish, black crappie, and brown bullhead (hornpout) can also be caught here. *For further information on fishing in Maine, call 207/657-2345.*

Hugging a narrow strip of land between Thomas Pond and the lake, **South Casco** has an attractive, newly-restored inn and 100-seat playhouse. The recently remodeled THOMAS INN AND PLAYHOUSE, 207/655-3292, serves sandwiches, soups, steaks, chicken Parmigiana, angel hair primavera. *Open for lunch and dinner every day. Look for their sign and turn right as you enter South Casco. If you miss the first right turn, you can still get there by turning right at the second street; look to your right for the large yellow-frame inn and barn.*

Sebago Lake State Park, a couple of miles north and off to the left of 302, offers opportunities to fish, canoe, or picnic. Although there will be other lakes ahead with mountain views as well, this park is a nice place to stop and stretch your legs. If you've never experienced the incredible softness of mountain lake water, Sebago Lake is also the place for a swim. *Sand beaches, boat rentals, restrooms, bathhouses, picnic tables and grills, play equipment, and snack bar. Open May through mid-October; 207/693-6613 (camping information), -6611 (picnicking).*

Nathaniel Hawthorne's family moved to Raymond after his father's death. Young Nathaniel spent some of his happier days in the woods along the lake, reading or playing with a black friend, William Symmes. Later, while living in Salem, Massachusetts, the author wrote fondly of his childhood experiences here: "I have visited many places called beautiful in Europe and the United States but have never seen the place that enchanted me like the flat rock from which I used to fish," on Lake Sebago.

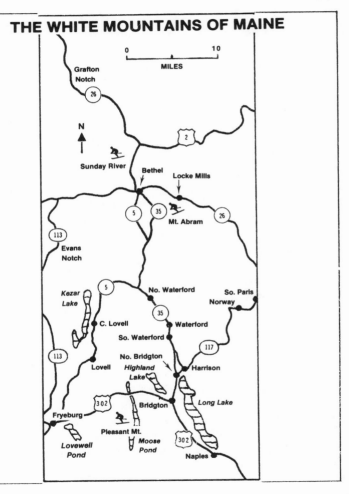

THE WHITE MOUNTAINS OF MAINE

Presidentials Mirrored in Long Lake

Before you know it, you'll be in **Naples,** sited in a picture book setting with a large, clear lake framed by the mountains. The focus here is water: water-skiing, sailing, seaplane rides, and the Songo River Queen for lake touring.

Gourmets may want to stop at THE EPICUREAN INN, 207/693-3839, a white-frame, mansard-roofed house south of town *just past the boat rentals on the left, across from where rte. 302 and 35 diverge.* You may think you're in someone's home as you enter through the Victorian living room. The decor is ersatz at best (from oil paintings in gilt frames to cocktail glasses that look as though they came from a yard sale), but the staff knows its food — and drink.

You may choose from European (grilled pork tenderloin en brochette with aioli or veal with port and pears) or Eastern dishes (shrimp Tandoori or oriental scallops with pan-fried noodles), even if you're the only guests in the dining room. The menu changes every two weeks. Pate has sturdy flavor that can be heightened with mustard or softened with jelly. The wine list is extensive and select. *Open Wednesday through Sunday, September – June, seven days a week in July & August 11:30–2 and 5–9. Because there are only nine tables, and diners tend to linger, dinner reservations are strongly requested; lodging available.*

If it's summer, Naples also offers several more casual places to eat. From May through October,

RICK'S CAFE on rte. 302, 207/693-3759, serves up blackened fish, Tex/Mex and Creole cooking overlooking Long Lake, or try the more informal SANDY'S AT THE FLIGHT DECK, 207/693-3508, right on the lake itself.

In the 19th century, Mainers took advantage of water to get around — even here in the western mountains. Water locks, like those on the Songo River, allowed boats to move from one level of water to another without shooting the rapids. The Songo River Lock, about five feet in height, was just one of 27 locks that linked Long Lake with Portland. ". . . the Songo [is] the crookedest river in the world. . . only a mile and a half, as the crow flies, from its mouth to its source, but you have to travel 6 miles and make 27 turns to sail through it." Cliff Stevens, purser on the Songo River line in the early 1900s.

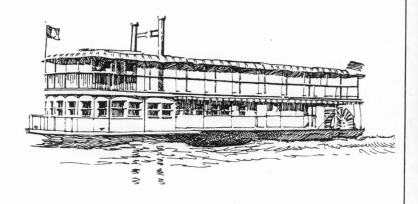

Sidetrip: **Songo River and Long Lake.** From the boat landing on 302 in Naples, board a replica stern-paddle wheeler that offers daily trips along the Songo River and Long Lake; mailboat rides are on Long and Sebago Lakes. Cruises and charters are available in season (weekends, June and September; daily, July 1 – Labor Day). Dinner cruises Wednesday evenings July & August 7–9:30; cruise to locks takes two and a half hours, also one- or two-hour cruises on Long Lake. Fee; snack bar on board. 207/693-6861.

> In addition to water sports, Naples has a history of taking politics seriously. Through the early part of this century, all town buildings had two entrances: one for Republicans and another for Democrats. Each party also insisted on having its own flagpole.

Past the busy lakefront, you'll find the **Naples Historical Society Museum,** on the left up the hill just past the Methodist Church. *Open daily July and August, 10–4 or by appointment; free. Slide show on canals and steamboats; local history exhibits.* Children will enjoy seeing the two-cell jail; history buffs can look into archives from the original town office.

Rte. 302 continues for seven miles along the west side of Long Lake, passing a few motels and campgrounds, as well as craft shops and lovely old homes. High up on the left, a mile past the center of town, you may notice a 1796 brick-end house. Built by one of Naples' first settlers, "the Manor" still had hollow logs for pipes when it was restored in the 1930s.

> Sited for its views of Long Lake, "the Manor" originally backed up against primeval forest that stretched all the way to Bridgton. As late as the 1930s, the King's "broad arrow," a mark made in the 18th century to reserve mast pines for the Royal Navy, could still be seen on trees here.

Almost a mile further on the right, you'll see signs for Mast Cove Artisans, a gift and craft shop worth a stop — if only to enjoy tea and lake views. *Afternoon tea from 1–4 pm in season.* As rte. 302 continues north, there are other casual restaurants with more complete menus. THE COLONIAL, 207/647-2547, welcomes buses as well as small parties. *Open year-round daily 11–9.* On the left just ahead, J.T.'S PARTNERS, 207/647-3669, has everything from steak and seafood to quiche and cocktails. *Open year-round Sunday – Wednesday 7am–9pm, Thursday – Saturday until 10pm.* In another couple of miles, you'll find yourself in **Bridgton.**

Antiques, Antiques, and more Antiques

Lovers of vintage furniture, jewelry, or collectibles will enjoy Bridgton's many shops. *Current listing of area antique shops is available from Bridgton Chamber of Commerce, Bridgton, ME 04009; 207/647-3472.* The Wales & Hamblen Antique Center on Main St. has everything from old quilts to turn-of-the-century greeting cards. Ricker House Antiques on North High St. displays lovely old pieces in a restored 18th-century cape with original Rufus Porter murals. Craftsworks,

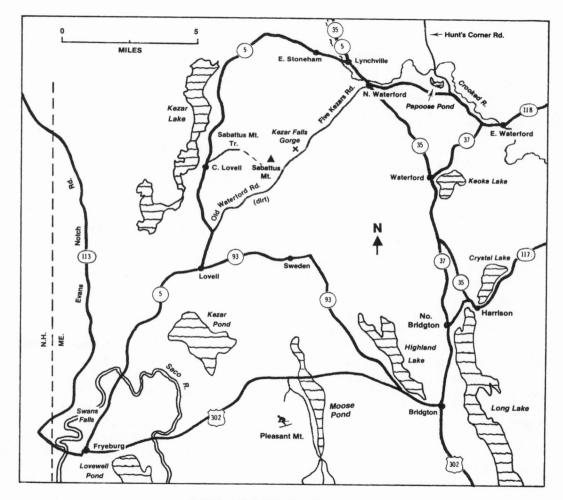

BRIDGTON-LYNCHVILLE

in a restored old church en route, stylishly mixes sportswear, baskets, books, and toys with rugs and pottery.

> Water has always been important to Bridgton. The first settlers sailed up Sebago Lake, the Songo River, and Long Pond, as Indians had done earlier; canal boats carried goods to and from town later when the locks were built; and mills along Stevens Brook brought industry to the community — from sawmills to gristmills and dowel mills.

There are several attractive dining choices here as well. On the right across from the small mall on rte. 302 as you enter town, THE BLACK HORSE TAVERN, 207/647-5300, serves Cajun and American food. TARRY-A-WHILE, 207/647-2522, offers Swiss cooking and a pretty drive to Bridgton's Highlands. *After passing Craftworks on your left, you'll see Highland Lake, with its sandy beach and spectacular mountain views to your right. Turn right here, and continue along the lake.* You'll notice Joyce Kilmer's poem, "Trees," has been memorialized in a stone wall here.

Past the NOBLE HOUSE BED AND BREAKFAST, 207/647-3733, you'll come to a fork in the road; bear left toward TARRY-A-WHILE. A stone wall climbs along the ridge with you. At the top you'll see the Highlands sign on your right with spectacular sights to your left. Past well-tended, turn-of-the-century homes, TARRY-A-WHILE is on your left across from the golf course. THE SWITZER STUBLI (mean-

ing: small, friendly room) DINING ROOM, 207/647-2522, offers Swiss cuisine — wiener schnitzel, cordon bleu, or raclette, that wonderful cheese and onion pancake — created by a chef flown in every summer from the owners' native Alps. *Open mid-June through Labor Day: breakfast 8–9 am; dinner 6–8:30 pm.*

As you return, the views along the two and a half miles back to town are different, though certainly no less impressive. There are more antique shops and lodging in the comfortable Victorians that continue along rte. 302 west. For those heading north on 117, please skip to page 57.

Pleasant Mt.

302 west is scenic — with hiking, skiing, and sight-seeing en route. For those who want the flavor of the White Mountains without turnpikes, strip development, or outlet shopping, this route from east to west gives a genuine sense of the area. But even the trip west to Pleasant Mt. is a nice excuse to explore Maine a little more. *A mile from the center of Bridgton, rte. 93 splits off from 302; bear left or west on 302. Those who are heading north to Lovell or Kezar Lake should bear right on 93.*

As rte. 302 heads west, you'll begin to see mountain vistas. The road passes Beaver Pond on the left, then Moose Pond extending as far as the eye can see to either side of the road, with **Pleasant Mt.** reflected on the water's still surface.

Sidetrip: *PLEASANT MT. SKI AREA,* 207/647-8444. *This popular "family" mountain is almost a mile from the sign on 302, where you turn left. The ski area has a reputation for reasonable rates and weekday specials, if not the most challenging skiing in the White Mountains. Beginner as well as regular lift tickets; rentals, nursery and day care, group rates.*

Sidetrip: **Ledges Trail.** *Continue along the road past the ski area and condos. Hikers should drive another two miles through beautiful woods on this hilly, bumpy road to reach the trailhead.*

*For the three-to-four hour round-trip hike up this 2000′ mountain, look for a red "M" painted on an old pine on the right side of the road, just past Moose Cottages. There is parking here for a couple of cars only; otherwise, you need to pull **fully** off the road, so as not to block the fire route.*

*Begin the **Ledges Trail** on the gravel fire road, following red blazes, through raspberries growing wild to a fork where the road widens. Bear left, crossing two small brooks, before the climb steepens. In about a mile, you begin climbing over a rock outcropping (the Ledges themselves). As you move out of the trees onto these rocks, you'll have fine views to the south over Moose Pond. Continue climbing toward the northwest, passing over a second open ledge area with excellent views west. The climb steepens over low-bush blueberries and more ledge, but you can continue moving northwest over another rock outcropping, before heading north to the summit and fire tower.*

On a clear day, you'll be rewarded with spectacular views of the Presidentials running north-south on the horizon; Carter Dome is visible over the west tongue of Pleasant Mt. To the northwest is Kezar Lake, with Lovewell Pond to the southwest outside Fryeburg. *Return the way you came. Sidetrippers may continue on the Pleasant Mt. Rd. to the tiny village of **Denmark,** where 117 leads back to 302 and Bridgton, or retrace your route to 302 west; we recommend the latter.*

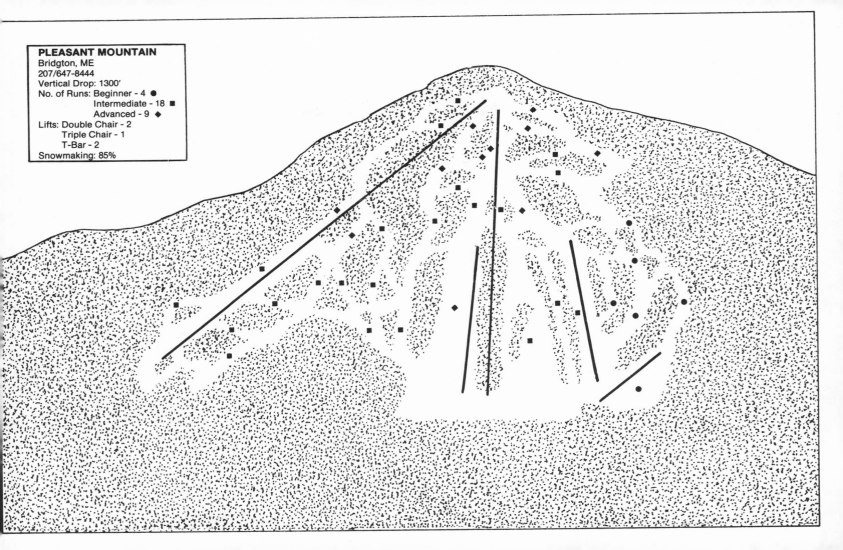

PLEASANT MOUNTAIN
Bridgton, ME
207/647-8444
Vertical Drop: 1300'
No. of Runs: Beginner - 4 ●
　　　　　Intermediate - 18 ■
　　　　　Advanced - 9 ◆
Lifts: Double Chair - 2
　　　Triple Chair - 1
　　　T-Bar - 2
Snowmaking: 85%

Land of the Pequawkets

Three to four miles further west of the Pleasant Mt. Rd., 302 crosses the road to Denmark on the left and Hemlock Bridge Rd. on the right.

Covered Bridge Sidetrip. Approximately three miles north on Hemlock Bridge Rd. is the last remaining covered bridge in the Fryeburg area. Built in 1857, Hemlock Bridge used Paddleford truss construction with wooden arches crossing the Saco River. This is a canoe launch site.

Rte. 302 continues through a boggy area with Pleasant Pond to either side, then the Saco River winds under the road. Between here and Fryeburg, one of the most famous Indian battles took place at Lovewell Pond, which may be hard to see from the road when the leaves are out.

A little west of here, on the right side of 302, is the *Jockey Cap Trail,* which leads to a huge 200-foot boulder, near the motel that bears its name. *Trail begins between motel and store/gas station. A three-minute walk brings you to the face of the gigantic rock.* If you look carefully, you may be able to find a cave where the Indian woman, Molly Ockett prepared herbal cures from plants found here.

Jockey Cap boasted Maine's first ropetow in 1936 when skiing began to flourish in the White Mountains, but it was discontinued a year later as the more substantial Mt. Cranmore in New Hampshire began operations.

Rte. 302 turns left in *Fryeburg,* a pretty town in the Saco River Valley with wonderful mountain vistas. Heading toward New Hampshire, you'll pass Fryeburg Academy where Daniel Webster once worked, a quaint Congregational Church, and the tiny Fryeburg Museum. *Open Thursdays 2–4 pm, year-round.*

In 1725 Captain John Lovewell and the Massachusetts Rangers attacked the Indian town of Pequawket in "one of the bloodiest and most obstinately contested battles" ever. While both Lovewell and the Indian leader Paugus, "whose name was terror throughout the length and breadth of the English frontiers," were killed, the battle effectively ended the Indians' power in this area.

Although only a young woman at the time, the legendary Indian Molly Ockett claimed to have survived this raid by hiding in the bushes near the pond. She later befriended the English settlers, and as she roamed the mountains from Fryeburg to Bethel, Molly shared her knowledge of herbs and roots with her white friends.

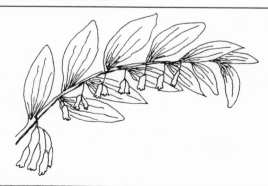

Before he began his law career, Webster served as preceptor of the Academy. "Nothing here is unpleasant," he wrote of this community. "There is a pretty little society; people treat me with kindness and I have the fortune to find myself in a very good family."

On the right you'll see THE OXFORD HOUSE INN, 207/935-3442, which serves delicious dinners nightly, as well as Sunday brunch. Flowered wallpaper, gorgeous cypress paneling, original fixtures keep this restaurant as impressive looking as it must have been when a rich lumberman built it. The menu, printed inside old sheet music, is just as splendid: dine on salmon Pommery, thick lamb chops with a mint sauce, or tender veal Oxford carefully-prepared and presented with fresh flowers.

Across the street is the stone Fryeburg Library, 207/935-2731, with a room devoted to Hollywood cowboy Hopalong Cassidy, better-known locally as Clarence Mulford. Bradley Memorial Park in the center of town is a good place to stretch your legs; boaters and fisherfolk might want to make Fryeburg their base of operations for a while. Trout, landlocked salmon, bass, pickerel, and pan fish are abundant in local lakes and ponds. If you're planning a fall trip to the White Mountains, try to schedule this town for the first week in October, when fairgoers more than double the town's population.

The Fryeburg Fair, the Granddaddy of Them All

For a visit to the fair, canoeing, or a loop up to Kezar Lake and Lovell, *turn right onto 5, where 302 enters Fryeburg.* Rte. 5 passes lovely old homes with still more mountain views. Canoeists should look to the left for signs for boat access from Swans Falls. *Turn left at the first main road on the north end of town. RIVER RUN, 207/452-2500, shuttles boaters from parking lots in Brownfield and Hiram to start canoe trips here. AMC maintains a campground at Swans Falls; 207/935-2765 for reservations information. SACO RIVER CANOE AND KAYAK, 207/935-2369, is located on the right side of rte. 5.*

Just outside of town is the Fryeburg Fairground, where every fall you can watch an ox-pull, teenagers roping calves, children trying to catch baby pigs in a sack (an event known as a pig scramble), and women throwing cast-iron skillets. If you have time for just one New England fair, this is the one! Concessions, contests, harness racing, and bake-offs attract visitors from far and wide. *Admission; camping nearby.*

We recommend continuing north on rte. 5 to Maine's mountains, Kezar Lake (where novelist Stephen King has a home), the National Forest, Bethel, and SUNDAY RIVER SKI RESORT.

The road narrows north of the fairground, though it continues to be well-maintained for most of our route. There's more canoe access three miles outside of town. Then rte. 5 crosses the Saco. After the 1847 Fryeburg

Town Hall, the road has little scenic to offer; only its roller coaster hills add interest until you cross the river again (look to your left for a fantastic view).

The Voice of the Loon

In no time, rte. 5 brings you into **Lovell** village, a sleepy community of old brick and granite homes and antique shops. A distinctly New England establishment, the One Stop Store/Mobil Station has everything from fishing creels to T-shirts, including take-out and lunch-counter fare. Rte. 5 climbs a steep hill, and you'll see the Old Waterford Rd. on your right. *Hikers or anyone with a sturdy vehicle might want to take this road, if the weather's good and dry — see page 60.*

"How naked a wild lake in the northeast would seem without the *whaaahoooooooooooaaah* plaintive wail, or the bizarre preening antics of an energetic, self-engrossed, uninhibited loon." Scott Sutcliffe, wildlife biologist, 1979.

Shortly after the well-maintained Lake Kezar Country Club on the left, the road surface deteriorates. But in only a couple of miles, you'll be in **Center Lovell** with more spectacular views, pretty old homes, and a first-rate inn. The CENTER LOVELL INN, 207/925-1575, serves Northern Italian cuisine either fireside or overlooking the lake and White Mountains (even providing a diagram to help diners and guests pick out mountains). *Open Friday, Saturday, Sunday for dinner, 5 pm on; lunch, Sundays only, 11–2.*

Former owner Eckley T. Stearns was appointed governor of Florida; returning to Maine, he renovated the house, adding a mansard-roofed third floor to remind him of his ante-bellum Southern days.

Look for Sabattus Rd. just north of the inn, if you're in a climbing mood. This pretty country road takes you past farmhouses on the left, with fiddleheads and trilliums in spring. *After a little over a mile, follow the gravel fork on the right up past another attractive house, also on the right. Parking for the trailhead is one-third mile up the gravel road on the left; the trail begins across the road from the parking area (look for the weathered sign next to a big, old pine).*

Sabattus Mt. Trail *parallels a stone wall, then crosses another as it gently climbs the ridge. For only a 500-foot vertical climb and an hour's round-trip hike, you are rewarded with one of the finest panoramas anywhere: Pleasant Mt. and Kezar Lake to the south, with North*

Conway and the drumlin-shaped mass of White Horse Ledge to the right; to the west the Presidentials from Kearsarge to the Carter-Moriah range; to the northwest, the mountains around Evans Notch. Easiest descent is by retracing your steps.

Rte. 5 continues north with Kezar to the left; look for the WESTWAYS sign, 207/928-2663, also on the left 7 miles north of Lovell village. This low-key resort was, in the past, a corporate retreat. *Water sports, nature trails, tennis, bowling, raquetball, riding stables, access to two challenging golf courses; cross-country and downhill skiing nearby.*

> Called one of the world's most beautiful lakes by NATIONAL GEOGRAPHIC, Kezar Lake has long attracted the rich and famous, yet it remains delightfully uncommercial today. Rudy Vallee, vintage radio and screen star, had a home here in the 1930s and used to paddle across the lake to parties. Even earlier, William A. Fairburn, a prominent naval architect from Bath, Maine, built his own Xanadu, called Westways, on the lake; servants were sworn to secrecy, protecting not only personal foibles of family and corporate executives vacationing here, but also business decisions.

The shimmering lake is beautifully set off against a backdrop of jagged peaks. Surprisingly, for all its loveliness, Kezar is still relatively affordable — a summer cottage can still be rented here for only $250 a week.

> "This is a unique spot. It has good vibes. People will come down here with a frump on the face, very uptight, especially if they are from one of the big cities. . . . They sit down here in the boathouse and listen to the loons, go for a swim, go for a canoe ride, and they get quite happy," WESTWAYS' Nancy Tripp, 1987.

Rte. 5 continues northeast through North Lovell and East Stoneham to the junction with rte. 35 in Lynchville — and a fascinating signpost. Turn sharp left for Bethel, page 61, with more fishing en route. This is the point where both routes from Bridgton meet.

From Bridgton North

For those heading north from Bridgton, simply return to the stoplight at the junction of rte. 117 and 302, turning onto 117, which connects with rte. 37 in a few miles.

Sidetrip: *Harrison. For a visit to another pleasant mountain lake town, continue east on 117, skirting the north end of Long Lake. Harrison hugs the shorelines of Long and Crystal Lakes. In Harrison, continue north on 117 to* Crystal Lake Park with picnic facilities and a swimming beach. Down on Main St. is Great Expectations Antiques, next door to the ice cream parlor. Nearby, you'll see THE CASWELL HOUSE RESTAURANT, 207/583-6606, overlooking Long Lake. Lobsters and steamers, spinach and pasta salad, light fare on the deck make this a popular place in summer. *When you're finished exploring, just head north on rte. 35 to Waterford, page 58.*

Rte. 117 north passes Long Lake on the right, although it may be hard to catch more than a glimpse of water through the trees in summer. *Three miles north of Bridgton, turn left on rte. 37* for the village of **North Bridgton,** with its charming colonial houses and the campus of Bridgton Academy. Past the settlement, rte. 37 is narrow and winding, an archtypical country lane with stone walls, clumps of birches, and the obligatory old burying ground.

The Glines Neighborhood Cemetery is where Captain John Haywood, hero of Concord, lies. Whether you're interested in grave rubbings or the wisdom of our ancestors, you're sure to notice the epitaph on Haywood's slate stone:
"Pause stranger, ere you pass by —
As you are now, so once was I.
As I am now, soon you'll be
Prepare for death, to follow me."

Along this stretch of road, you begin to feel truly part of the mountains, as rocky-faced hills come into view. *Because of its narrowness, this road is not recommended for cyclists. Four miles or so out of North Bridgton, rte. 37 merges with 35.* BEAR MOUNTAIN INNE, 207/583-4404, is a bed and breakfast place on the left, overlooking Bear Pond. Fishermen will be pleased to know that salmon, trout, hornpout, bass, and perch can be caught here. The inn has its own private beach, and there is a public boat landing on the pond.

The Bear Mountain Grange and an old church are part of **South Waterford,** but the more substantial village of Waterford lies ahead, beautifully sited on Keoka Lake. This is yet another fine mountain lake for boating, fishing, or picnics; there is a small sand beach next to the Selectmen's office.

Past Is Present in the Waterfords

There are four inns here in the Waterfords: gourmet enough to attract Portlanders out for a Sunday drive and downright elegant for those dropping children off at any of the nearby summer camps (and after spending all that money for your youngsters, don't you deserve a treat as well?). The LAKE HOUSE, 207/583-4182, in the center of *Waterford* village was an 18th-century stage coach stop; today it is filled with antiques and good will. Featuring regional and fresh foods, the menu includes seafood, duck, veal, and lamb. Desserts and breads are baked on the premises; the wine list offers 125 different vintages. *Open daily from 5 pm in summer; closed Tuesday – Wednesday, the rest of the year.*

From the front porch, you can look out at Artemus Ward's former home, an 1805 frame house. Ward, whose real name was Charles F. Browne, appealed to 19th-century newspaper readers with his dry wit and apparent lack of learning. (In reality, he was a clever enough writer and printer to work for publications like THE CLEVELAND PLAIN DEALER and VANITY FAIR). Next door to his home, L.R. Rounds & Co. is an old-fashioned country store and post office, the kind of place Ward/Browne might have patronized himself.

In a series of letters, "Artemus Ward" introduced himself to his fans and described the world as he saw it:

"I was born in the State of Maine of parents. As an infant I abstracted a great deal of attention. The nabers would stand over my cradle for hours and say, 'How bright that little face looks! How much it nose!'"

In describing his home, Ward wrote: "The village from which I write to you is small. It does not contain over forty houses all told; but they are. . . shaded with beautiful elms and willows. To the right of us is a mountain — to the left a lake. The village nestles between. Of course it does. I never read a novel in my life in which the village didn't nestle. Villages invariably nestle. It's a kind of way they have."

Rte. 35 bears left through town, passing the KEDAR-BURN INN, 207/583-6182, on the left. This period home is carefully maintained by two bachelors. *Open year-round for breakfast and dinner; closed Mondays. Reservations advised.* There are three or four nightly specials in addition to the regular menu of sausage-stuffed mushrooms, fresh chowder, crab-stuffed shrimp, veal picatta, or individual beef Wellingtons.

Sidetrip: **East Waterford.** For the third inn, take rte. 37 toward East Waterford, and look for the sign to THE WATERFORD INNE & ANTIQUES, 207/583-4037, about two and a half miles out of town. Turn left onto Chadbourne Rd. to an attractive yellow-frame house with a red barn attached. This homey, country-style place offers just one selection at each meal; bring your own bottle, if you want wine. *Reservations only. Because Chadbourne Rd. ends shortly past the inn, return to rte. 37, then turn left until you reach rte. 118 and turn left again, passing Papoose Pond and the Crooked River on the right, before coming to North Waterford.*

Rte 35 climbs up several hills, after crossing Kedar Brook, but the road deteriorates a bit, while it becomes more scenic. There's a Christmas Shop, *open year-round, every day but Monday,* on your right as 35 heads down to **North Waterford.** Besides Tut's General Store and the post office, the OLDE ROWLEY INN, 207/583-4143, is the only act in town. *Catering; New England fare served nightly Wednesday – Saturday, 5–9 pm.* You might want to use this cozy, attractive home-away-from-home as a base of operations, exploring the numerous ponds and lakes in the Waterford area.

Sidetrip: **Kezar Falls Gorge and Lovell.** If you want to spend some time hiking, or if your car has sturdy shocks, you might want to head west at the sign for "Five Kezars," past the church onto Lovell Rd. *You'll cross Warren Brook and see Jewett Pond on your right before this road turns to dirt. Look to the right for pullovers and Kezar Falls Gorge. This deep, winding gorge falls 10 yards with smaller falls as well. Look for an esker, which will point you to the gorge, approximately three miles from the village.*

> An esker is a gravel ridge, most frequently found in New England; once a stream bed in or under glacial ice, eskers are especially long here in Maine. They may run scores of miles without a break and can be up to 100 feet in height. Often the only dry, open route through heavily forested, swampy areas, eskers were used by Indians and early settlers as paths; today, many have disappeared, their gravel dug away for construction uses.

At the second fork in this road, bear right, passing stone walls, bracken, lichen and ferns. The road is paved again in places, usually near someone's private "camp." *Continue straight ahead.* There are very rural homes ahead, and you might even pass a resident on horseback as the Old Waterford Rd., now completely paved, heads down toward Kezar Lake, page 57.

Outside North Waterford, rte. 35 merges with rte. 5 for a good road north to Bethel. Signs at the junction in Lynchville may boast names of exotic-sounding places,

but all are found in Maine. The next twelve miles are pretty, with more mountain and lake views as the White Mountain National Forest appears on your left. *Rtes. 5 and 35 diverge again ahead; we recommend you take 5 on the left for a faster route, with a very nice sidetrip on the way.*

Sidetrip: *Moses Patte's Brook.* Seven or eight miles north of Lynchville on rte. 5, look for a road on the left (there's a camping sign on the right and an old barn covered with license plates on the left.) The Forest Service has a four-mile self-guided tour here that's wonderful for naturalists and fishermen. *Brochure is available at the Ranger Station; 207/824-2134. Numerous turnouts and stops, keyed with numbers to coincide with information in the brochure. Since trails in this area have recently been relocated, hikers should ask for updated information on Albany Mountain Trail, with fine views in all directions from the open summit ledges. This area is also popular for small game and deer hunting in the fall.*

Starting with the brook itself which flows into the Crooked River and eventually Sebago Lake, you'll see openings in the forest that early settlers made (a good place to find ruffed grouse, woodcock, deer, or hares). In some places, white pine woods have replaced cleared fields. Nearby, the dam supports a 22-acre marsh for ducks and other waterfowl.

Moses Patte operated a mill on the brook here for many years; look for its foundation about a mile downstream from the dam, which the Forest Service maintains. Settlers planted over 300 apple trees in this area, which you will

see blooming in springtime.

> Multiple use is a major challenge the White Mountain National Forest faces today. At Patte Brook, timbering, hiking, fishing, hunting, wildlife, and water management co-exist peacefully.

Further south after bearing left at the second fork you'll see a glacial bog, an old homesite, and a place for a short hike with views of the upper end of the marsh, a nesting area. You may continue south to the 18-acre Broken Bridge Pond for trout fishing and canoeing. A second pond, Crocker, offers campsites as well as fishing; this is a good place to look for moose. *7 sites on a first-come, first-served basis; fee mid-May – mid-October.*

Return the way you came, unless you're heading to Evans Notch, page 81; or the heart of the White Mountains (Chapter III). In the latter case, head straight north from Crocker Pond to **West Bethel** *and rte. 2. If this is your first trip to Maine's mountains, we recommend rte. 5 north past Songo Pond on the right to* **Bethel,** *and SUNDAY RIVER SKI RESORT.*

Historic Bethel

Founded in 1774, this community of 2,500 may seem like a bustling place after the tiny villages you've just passed in the Waterfords. But travelers will find still more old-fashioned relaxation, as well as a real working town.

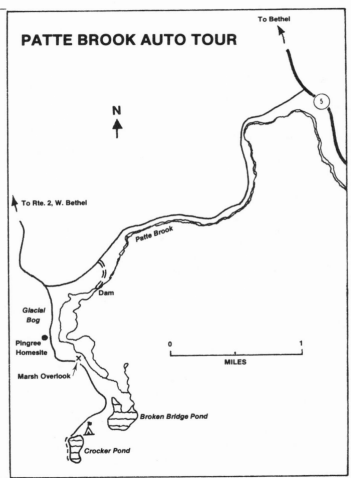

PATTE BROOK AUTO TOUR

Bethel was originally named Sudbury Canada because the first settlers came from Sudbury, Massachusetts and had fought together in Canada against the French and Indians. In 1781 Indians carried off three of the settlement's ten citizens, but the Indian Molly Ockett was able to save a trapper from captivity. The town grew quickly once the Revolution ended, changing its name to Bethel, a Biblical name meaning house of God.

Farming and sawmills brought prosperity to Bethel in the early 19th century, but the arrival of the Atlantic and St. Lawrence Railway in 1851 made the town popular as a summer resort with Bostonians and New Yorkers alike. Around the turn of the century, physician John Gehring came to Bethel to recover from a nervous breakdown, and the town's image as a health spa began. Gehring recovered so completely that he set up a clinic here, combining outdoor physical activity with contemplation of the area's natural beauty. He and one of his patients, William Bingham II, founded the BETHEL INN in 1913, where today's guests enjoy skiing and golf instead of cutting wood or planting trees, as Gehring and Bingham's patients did.

There's comfortable lodging at THE BETHEL INN AND COUNTRY CLUB, 207/824-2175, as well as at numerous bed and breakfast inns in the area. Pleasant, tree-lined streets, the attractive campus of Gould Academy, a fair share of shops and restaurants — and best of all, no fast-food franchises — make this a nice place to stay a while. The wide Androscoggin River courses along the north end of town. Beyond the valley are more mountains — the White Mountain National Forest to the west, the Mahoosucs and Longfellow Ranges to the north — offering year-round recreational opportunities, including two ski areas.

At present, tourism is an important part of the local economy but hardly Bethel's only commerce. A number of wood-based industries, as well as farming, education, and crafts, keep the population here diverse and friendly. Let's hope the town fathers realize that Bethel's appeal comes from the town's authenticity — it doesn't look or feel like a place that caters exclusively to visitors — and that they'll do what they can to preserve its diversity.

Walk Around Town

This is the kind of place that practically begs you to stop and walk around. Using THE BETHEL INN as a starting point, there are several areas you can explore on foot. *From the third green of the golf course, down Mill Hill Rd.,* are the ruins of early stone dams, part of Bethel's first industry.

Back up Mill Hill Rd. toward the Common, you'll see a Greek Revival house, "The Willows," once a retirement home and now a guest cottage at THE BETHEL INN. Across the street, but facing the Common, is THE MILLER INN AND OPERA HOUSE CONDOMINIUMS, 207/824-2312. This 1880s building was formerly a store, auditorium, oil distributorship, and restaurant; on this same site Bethel's first inn was built in the 19th century.

In 1774 Eleazer Twitchell of Dublin, NH cleared land that his father owned and built a sawmill, then a gristmill in Bethel. Today foundations of the two mills remain, and Gould Academy has an archaeological dig at the site.

A raging fire in 1865 leveled both the original inn, Bethel House, and a huge home next to it, known as the "Castle" and owned by Eleazer Twitchell, who ran Bethel's mills.

If you continue beyond the Opera House and walk down Church St. past THE CHAPMAN INN, 207/824-2657, another bed and breakfast place, you'll find shops as well as historic buildings.

Formerly the home of William Rogers Chapman, an outstanding musician and long-time conductor of the Maine Music Festival, THE CHAPMAN INN was once the site of important musical events.

On the left side of Church Street, you'll see a lovely old Congregational Church.

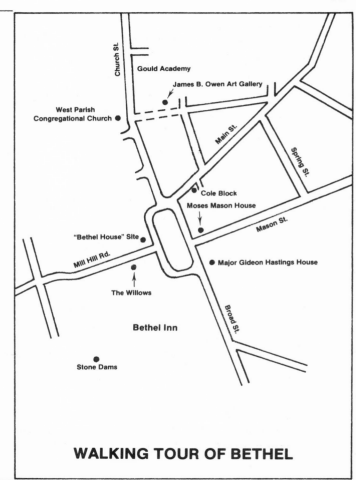

WALKING TOUR OF BETHEL

> The Reverend Daniel Gould, Revolutionary war veteran and Harvard graduate, was the town's first pastor in 1799 and later founded a school for boys here.

Gould Academy has interesting art exhibits at the James B. Owen Gallery, *behind* the Administration Building. *This wooden-frame Greek Revival structure, once a private home, is open 9-3 weekdays and on weekend afternoons; changing exhibits.*

Walk back up Church St., browsing in the shops, then turn left after Groan & McGurn and head down Main St. You'll pass the Cole Block, on the right, completed in 1891 before its owners went bankrupt.

The FOUR SEASONS INN, 207/824-2755, is on the left as you continue down Main, as is Bonnema Pottery. This family-run ceramics outlet has goblets, bowls, and casseroles that reflect the natural beauty surrounding Bethel.

Across the street, past the Cole Block, you'll see Bethel Craftworks with a variety of hand-made collectibles, including the owners' hand-dyed baskets. MOTHER'S, 207/824-2589, is a comfortable restaurant nearby, in a renovated gingerbread home. Delicious homemade breads, hot drinks in winter, veal Michel in gingered lime sauce, Cajun chicken, rainbow trout are specialities at this reasonably-priced eatery.

On your way back up Main, look for the Chamber of Commerce on Philbrook St., then take a left on Spring St. and a right up Mason back toward the common. On the right, facing the common is The Bethel Historical Society, 207/824-2908, with its period house museum. Formerly the home of the Masons (he was a prominent doctor, businessman, and state representative; she was the temperance leader in Oxford County), the building contains 8 rooms decorated with Rufus Porter murals and Federal-style furnishings. In addition to a handsome fan-light door with sidelights, there are 6 fireplaces. *Open Tuesday – Sunday, July 1 to Labor Day; by appointment the rest of the year. Research facilities weekdays by special arrangements. Fine collections of luster and Chelsea ware, pewter and Portland glass.*

> When Dr. Moses Mason decided to build his home on granite, folks were afraid the walls would cave in; only the blessing of Rev. Daniel Gould was believed to have brought construction to a safe completion in 1813. Among the many collections here is a series of moose horns, said to have been given Mason by Metallak, the last of the St. Francis Indians in Maine.

Also facing the BETHEL INN on the common is the Major Gideon Hastings House (private). This clapboard Greek Revival home is typical of the "castles" Maine's timber barons built in the 19th century.

> Returning to his hometown after the Civil War, Hastings began lumbering in what is now the White Mountain National Forest. Although no one lives in "Hastings Plantation" in the Wild River Valley any more, this turn-of-the-century boom town still bears the Major's name.

The nearby HAMMONS HOUSE, 207/824-3170, is an elegant 1859 home on the National Registry of Historic Places that doubles as a bed and breakfast inn.

Sidetrips for Exploring

Sidetrip: *To Waterford or Norway.* For a venture into Maine at its most rural, take Broad St. south past THE BETHEL INN and HAMMONS HOUSE. *The road bends sharply to the left, passing THE POINTED FIR B & B, 207/824-2251, on the left. As you leave town, this road climbs a hill.*

The views from the ridge are spectacular. To the right are the White Mountains and to the left is **Mt. Abram,** easily identified by its ski trails. *In another two miles, the road ends at rte. 35. Turn left to head back into the center of Bethel.*

Or turn right for several miles of isolation as the road winds through a small valley in the township of **Albany.** This part of the country is so desolate there aren't even any telephone poles. *Rte. 35 eventually hooks up with rte. 5, but we suggest bearing left onto an unmarked road, just before you reach rte. 5. After passing the Albany town hall and a few trailers, the road passes through pretty woods*

before climbing a ridge. Off to the right are fantastic views. You'll pass the Round Mt. Grange and the Albany Congregational Church before the road turns to dirt for about a half mile.

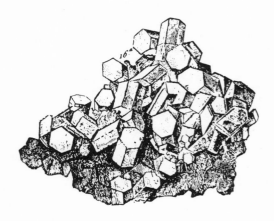

> The Albany area is rich in minerals: particularly feldspar, from which amazonite and moonstones are cut; pink and green beryl, whose cut stones are valued for their intense color.

This dirt road connects with Hunts Corner Rd. that leads to rte. 118. After another five miles of solitude, you will pass a camping area at Papoose Pond on the right before coming to a stop sign at rte. 118. Turn left, and in about two miles, you will come to the rather nondescript settle-

ment of **East Waterford.** *A half mile further you'll see LOU'S FAMILY RESTAURANT, 207/743-6997, with good, plain cooking in clean surroundings (the kind of place kids tired of camp cooking will love). Rte. 37 comes in on the right; you should take this road if you haven't visited the charming village of* **Waterford**. *After turning onto rte. 37, look to the right for the sign to the WATERFORD INNE, page 59. Three miles down the road are Keoka Lake and the pristine colonial buildings of Waterford, page 58.*

If you don't turn onto rte. 37, you will continue on rte. 118. Canoeists may be interested in the ***Crooked River*** that meanders through forest and town to some steep rapids (portage here, please, *unless* you're an expert in white water). The road continues east past Little Pennes-seewassee Pond and Pennessewassee Lake (we dare

you to say these Indian names fast ten times). There are opportunities for boating or picnicking here.

If you head straight east at the lake, you'll come to **Norway,** *page 70, and the riverside town of* **South Paris**, *page 183.*

Sidetrip to Norway and South Paris.

If you're partial to mountain lakes, biking, or mineral collecting, the old road to Norway is meant for you. *Take rte. 26 south from Bethel for five miles toward* **Locke Mills** *and the MT. ABRAM SKI AREA. This is a busy main road, but it is wide enough to be handled by cyclists.*

Look for the sign to MT. ABRAM on the right when you reach Locke Mills. After turning right, take a sharp left onto Greenwood Rd., just after crossing the railroad tracks and the bridge over the Alder River.

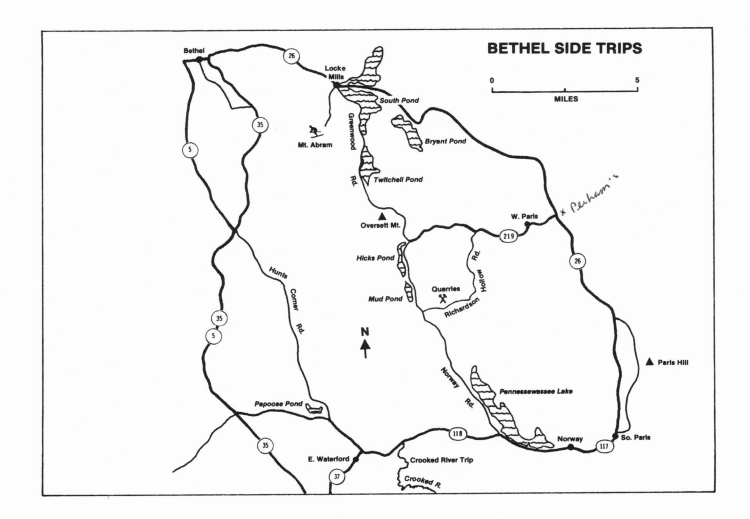

BETHEL SIDE TRIPS

0 — MILES — 5

Bethel

26

Locke Mills

South Pond

Bryant Pond

Greenwood Rd.

Mt. Abram

Twitchell Pond

Oversett Mt.

W. Paris

219

x Pecham's

26

Hicks Pond

Hunts Corner Rd.

Richardson Hollow Rd.

Quarries

Mud Pond

Paris Hill

N

Norway Rd.

Pennessewassee Lake

Papoose Pond

118

Norway

So. Paris

117

35

5

35

5

35

E. Waterford

Crooked River Trip

37

Crooked R.

For the next 15 miles, you will experience an unforgettable trip through some of Maine's prettiest inland scenery. Almost as soon as you make the turn onto Greenwood Rd., you will travel right next to the shoreline of South Pond on the left, with rocky hills coming down to the water's edge. In the distant north are low mountains of varying shades of blue. The road passes through stands of evergreens, birches, and beeches; the landscape is strewn with boulders.

> There are only two deciduous trees that don't shed their leaves in the fall: beech and oak.

After traveling along the edge of South Pond for about two miles, you will come to Twitchell Pond. Both ponds are edged by comfortable summer places that seem as though they belong here. After skirting Twitchell Pond for about a mile the road leaves all signs of civilization and heads into the woods again, with views of Oversett Mt. ahead. A small brook winds along beside the road.

Two miles south, the road climbs a gradual hill before reaching the crossroads town of Greenwood. *Rte. 219 goes off to the left here to West Paris and rte. 26. Continue through the intersection, bearing right onto Norway Rd.* This route passes through pretty, open farmland before skirting mile-long Hicks Pond on the right. A few camps are nestled along the shoreline; the hills come down dramatically to the edge of the water. Next is Mud Pond, smaller and with even fewer houses than Hicks Pond.

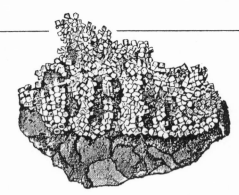

Sidetrip for mineral collectors. If you turn left onto Richardson Hollow Rd., just past Mud Pond, you will come across four quarries, where you are welcome to prospect for specimens at no charge. The three sites owned by Perham's of West Paris can be explored without prior permission, while the Tamminen Quarry is privately owned, but can be visited after securing permission. *Owner Nestor Tamminen lives in the white house on the left as you turn onto Richardson Hollow Rd. The following directions and descriptions are presented in the order they can be found on Richardson Hollow Rd.:*

• **Harvard Quarry.** *Drive .4 mile east on Richardson Hollow Rd. to a parking area on the right. The road to the quarry is on the left across the road from where you park. Walk along this road, marked by red blaze marks, for about 20 minutes to the foot of the dump area. The easiest way to reach the working face of the quarry is to follow a trail through the woods to the right of the dump; the upper part of the dump is very steep with loose materials underfoot.* Look for purple apatite, beryl, cookeite, garnet, quartz, green and black tourmaline. Amethyst, cassiterite, columbite, green gahnite, lepidolite, petalite, scheelite, spodumene, vesuvianite, and vivianite xls. specimens have also been found here.

• **Tamminen Quarry.** Before exploring this quarry secure permission from Nestor Tamminen. *Sometimes he conducts explorations for visitors; small fee. Park in the same area as you would for the Harvard Quarry, and walk down the hill to the rear of the parking area. You will see mine dumps on both sides of the road. Pass to the right of the water-filled Waisanen Quarry to a crossroad. The Tamminen Quarry is just ahead.* Species to look for: amblygonite, montmorillonite, pollucite, pseudocubic quartz crystals, and altered spodumene.

• **Waisanen Quarry.** *Follow directions above to the Harvard Quarry. Walk through the back of the parking area and down the hill to this quarry on the right.* While the quarry is usually filled with water, you can explore the dumps on both sides. Look here for purple apatite, bertrandite, columbite, herderite, spodumene, gem tourmaline, triphylite; also crystals of white quartz covered with parallel growths of smoky quartz have been found here.

In the early 1940s, some of the finest quality mica specimens in New England were found at Nubble Quarry.

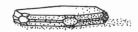

• **Nubble Quarry.** *Drive .7 miles from the beginning of Richardson Hollow Rd. Park on the left. Follow the red blaze-marked trail on the right for about 10 minutes to the quarry.* Besides mica, look for green apatite, beryllonite, chrysoberyl, garnet, gem quality smoky and rose quartz.

Just beyond Richardson Hollow Rd., bear left on Greenwood Rd. toward Norway. For the next five miles or so the road passes through a mixture of farmland and woods (some showing signs of recent logging), pretty farmhouses and trailers. As you approach Norway, the houses become more numerous and suburban-looking. *Eventually you will come to a stop sign at rte. 118. Turn left, skirting the south-*

ern end of Pennesseewassee Lake to the center of **Norway,** three miles ahead.

In town, look on the left for a magnificent white colonial house with three chimneys and a fan over the door. This is the home of the Norway Historical Society. Across the street is the ADVERTISER-DEMOCRAT building, where writer Artemus Ward learned the printing profession.

After driving through the work-a-day business district of town, you will pass attractive large houses, including a few brick colonials, before you reach the busy commercial strip of rte 26. *For area restaurants, see descriptions on page 183. Turn left onto 26 to head toward South Paris and Bethel, or turn right toward Gray and Portland.*

A Year-Round Resort

It seems whenever you visit Bethel, there are plenty of outdoor activities. In warm weather, you can choose between boating, fishing, or hiking. See hiking trails for Evans Notch, page 75; Hastings Plantation, page 76; and Grafton Notch State Park, page 177. Or stop by the Ranger Station on rte. 2 just north of town for further information on the White Mountain National Forest. Birders will find ruffed grouse common along dirt roads and trails, spruce grouse on mountain summits.

In winter the quiet is often broken by skimobiles, which speed through the Wild River Valley into Conway, New Hampshire. There's also cold-weather hiking in the WMNF. But in recent years, the Bethel area has gained a reputation among skiers. Altogether, there are 50 miles of cross-country trails here: THE BETHEL INN has 16 miles to groom; SUNDAY RIVER INN,

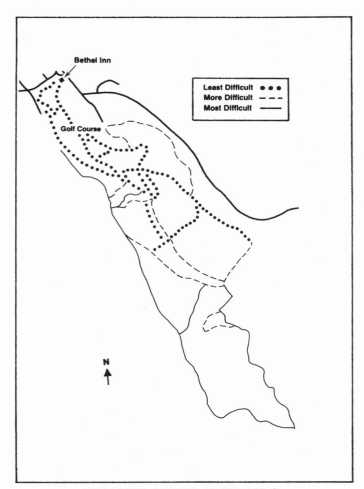

BETHEL INN X-C TRAILS

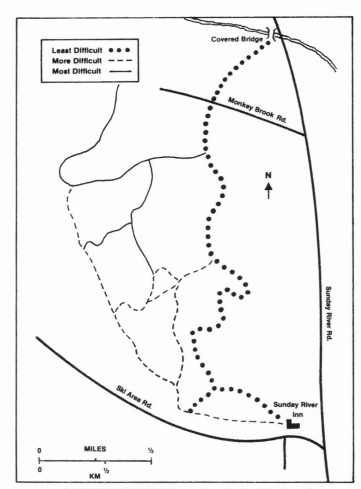

SUNDAY RIVER INN X-C TRAILS

207/824-2410, takes care of another 25 miles.

For downhill skiing, MT. ABRAM, 6 miles east of town in Locke Mills, page 179, 207/875-2601, continues to be a local favorite. To the north, SUNDAY RIVER, 207/824-2187 (or for reservations 1-800/367-3314; in Maine 1-800/443-1007), keeps on growing — with new, challenging trails down yet another mountain in 1988/89.

Drive 8 miles north of Bethel, off rtes. 5/26/2, to a left on the Sunday River Rd. You'll see the SUNDAY RIVER INN first, then "New England's fastest growing resort." Numerous chairlifts boost skier capacity here to 2400 an hour, with lift lines averaging under 10 minutes. As of this writing, there are 56 interconnecting trails, including the new "White Heat" (the East's longest, widest, and steepest lift-serviced trail) on five peaks with 88 percent snowmaking capacity.

Three ski shops, several restaurants, cafeterias, and lounges; day-care and nursery facilities as well as ski
programs for young children. There are over 600 condo units, including several hotels with swimming pools. An hour's free skiing every morning to test conditions also helps justify lift-ticket prices.

North of Sunday River

The Mahoosucs as well as New Hampshire's North Country beckon the serious lover of mountains. The Umbagog Lake region between Maine and New Hampshire is still largely undeveloped. There are fewer amenities in this area, but those that do exist, like THE BALSAMS RESORT in Dixville Notch, will seem very special. Reverse the rte. 26 description, Chapter V, if you want to sample the White Mountains of New Hampshire.

Hikers don't have far to go for a day's climb to Mahoosuc Notch, which, in turn, connects to the Appalachian Trail and Old Speck Mt., one of Maine's highest peaks.

We recommend AMC MAINE MOUNTAIN GUIDE (although parts of this area are mentioned in the AMC WHITE MOUNTAIN GUIDE as well), or MAINE GEOGRAPHIC HIKING, vol. 2 for anyone who has the time to explore this region for a few days. From the Appalachian Trail in Evans Notch, the two hours to Mahoosuc Notch is considered "the most difficult mile" *anywhere* along the entire trail — Georgia through Maine — but is much less strenuous from the Sunday River area, since much of the climb here can

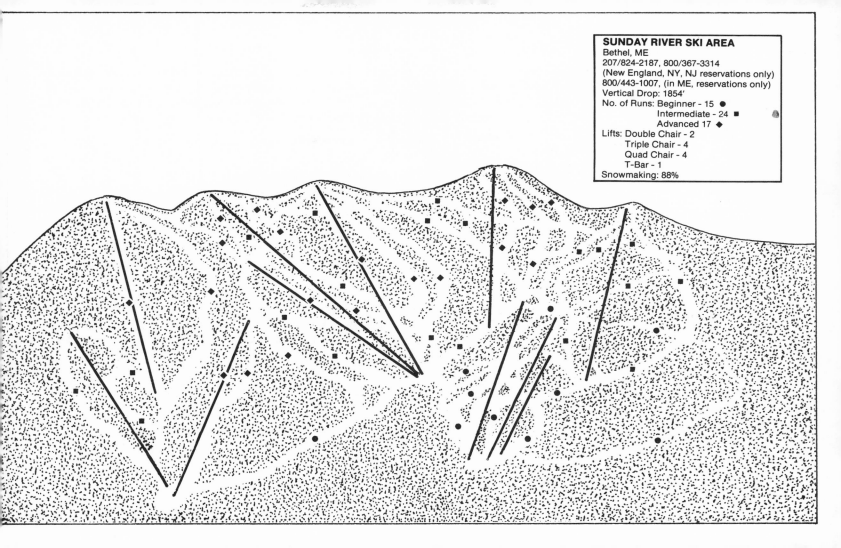

SUNDAY RIVER SKI AREA
Bethel, ME
207/824-2187, 800/367-3314
(New England, NY, NJ reservations only)
800/443-1007, (in ME, reservations only)
Vertical Drop: 1854'
No. of Runs: Beginner - 15 ●
　　　　　　　Intermediate - 24 ■
　　　　　　　Advanced 17 ◆
Lifts: Double Chair - 2
　　　Triple Chair - 4
　　　Quad Chair - 4
　　　T-Bar - 1
Snowmaking: 88%

be made by car. *Take the road on the west bank of the river, past the entrance to the ski area for about four and a half miles; the road crosses to the opposite bank near the Sunday River Covered Bridge.*

> Popularly-known as Artist's Bridge, this 1872 structure looks over a swimming hole with flat ledges.

Follow the road another 4.2 miles, then turn left onto a bridge over the headwaters of the river in Ketchum. (If you miss this turn, you'll quickly come to a dead end ahead by some cabins, and you can retrace your steps back to the bridge.) One-tenth of a mile past this bridge, you want to turn right and head north for another mile and a half, just beyond Goose Eye Brook. Here you turn right again; the road then deteriorates for the next two miles, finally becoming impassable.

Leave your car and hike the rest of the way to a logging yard, with a faint trail at the far side. (This trail follows the southern bank of a brook draining Mahoosuc Notch.) You have about a mile and a half to reach Mahoosuc Notch, where you can connect with Mahoosuc

Trail (the AT) and Speck Pond Trails. *There is a popular, though unofficial tenting area before the Notch for backpackers who intend to spend some time hiking here. The Mahoosuc Trail is another 100' up the north slope of the brook; see map, page 176.*

Mahoosuc Notch is one of the premier sights of Maine: a long, open gash between Mahoosuc and Fulling Mill Mts. The notch is filled with a huge jumble of house-sized boulders, covered with moss and twisted roots of trees. The trail provides for ample exploration, as it winds between the boulders here.

About 20 miles west of Bethel is one of our favorite roads — with plenty of opportunities to hike, fish, camp, or simply enjoy the scenery from your car. *Take rte. 2 west of town along the Androscoggin River.* There are few signs of civilization, beyond Groan and McGurn Tourist Trap & Factory Outlet in West Bethel.

Further along rte. 2, just past an old house on the right, you'll see a trail sign on the left for Wheeler Brook Trail, which climbs Peabody Mt. and leads over to the campgrounds in Hastings Plantation. In winter, this makes a challenging ungroomed cross-country trail. *If you make a loop and walk north on the Evans Notch Rd., back to your car in the field here on rte. 2, it will take four and a half to five hours (see AMC MAINE MOUNTAIN GUIDE for trails in this area). Look for the Evans Notch Rd., rte. 113, shortly ahead on the left in the town of Gilead.*

In the summer of 1975, recent high-school graduate Jay Johnson walked down the dirt road from his family's cottage in Maine and began hiking alone across the White Mountains: "My longest day of the trek came as I left the ridge near South Peak in the Mahoosucs, descended into Mahoosuc Notch, climbed Old Speck Mountain and walked along highway Route 26 to the Grafton-Upton town line. The next day I continued along old Route 26 past Umbagog Lake to the quaint town of Errol, where I made my last food pickup. On the lawn across from the post office I unpacked and repacked all the food. It was a bizarre scene, as I had newspapers, food packages, and boxes scattered all over the place. It's a wonder someone didn't have a car accident driving along the road as he took a second glance at the nut on the lawn."

A Warm-Weather Route

If you can't decide whether you'd rather be in New Hampshire or Maine, take a drive down the scenic **Evans Notch Rd.,** and you'll be able to see both. Bikers accustomed to steep grades and long-distance cycling will enjoy the coolness of this route — not to mention its views and campgrounds. It is important to realize, however, that this road is not maintained in winter, so unless you have cross-country skis or a snowmobile, plan to take this trip when you're *sure* the road is clear of ice and snow.

While the Evans Notch Ranger District does not maintain any ski touring trails, snowmobiles use this road, packing down the snow for skiers and hikers. As always, when different uses are made of the same land, caution

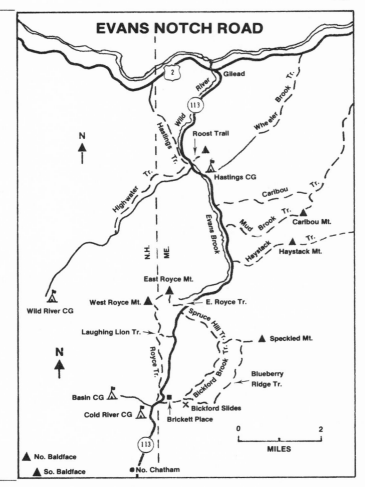

and cooperation are important! From May to November, when you don't need to worry about snow, the Forest Service allows only restricted-use camping (no fires or tents except at designed sites).

For the first three miles the road follows the Wild River, passing through dense woods. Fishermen will appreciate the numerous places to pull off on the right. *Look for brook or rainbow trout; motor boats or canoes are unlawful here. There is also a suspension foot bridge nearby that leads to the Hastings and Highwater Trails. The bridge makes a good place to swim or fish in the Wild River. For further information on fishing regulations in the Evans Notch area, contact NH Fish and Game Dept., 34 Bridge St., Concord 03301 and/or Dept. of Inland Fisheries and Wildlife, 284 State St., Station 1, Augusta, ME 04333.*

Just before the bridge, we leave the Wild River and follow Evans Brook — a lovely mountain stream. *Hikers will find numerous trails here and 6 backcountry shelters within walking distance of rte. 113.* On the left is the **Roost Trail,** an easy, short climb up to a bald outcrop. This is an excellent trail for people who have had little experience hiking, because the reward is great and effort small. Vertical is 400′; distance, round-trip, one mile.

*Trail starts north of the bridge, but parking is south, off to the right by signs to **Hastings Plantation.** Climb the log stairs up a steep bank for 100 feet, then bear*

Novice hikers may not realize that log steps, bridges over marshy spots, and terracing on trails are not just for their personal safety, but often to prevent hikers ruining a trail by overuse.

right (east) and ascend gradually along a wooded ridge, over a brook at .3 miles, climb a bit more steeply to emerge on a small rock ledge, "The Roost." This 1300' point gives you a wonderful view through the Notch, and a side trail brings you down to more spacious ledges: to the southwest are East and West Royce Mts.; Howe Peak, with the Moriahs behind, is directly opposite you; to the southeast, Caribou Mt.; and northwest, Bald Cap leading to Mahoosuc Notch.

Five and a half miles down the dirt road past the parking lot for the Roost is Wild River Campground, and a little further south on the left side of 113 is Hastings Campground. Either makes an excellent base camp for day trips here. *Open during summer to tents and trailers; two handicapped sites at Hastings. Fee includes well water, garbage collection, toilets.*

> Like much of the north woods, Hastings Plantation was over-logged. In the 1930s, 67 acres were replanted in white and red spruce, creating much of the forest you enjoy here today.

Wheeler Brook Trail, which loops north to rte. 2, see page 74, connects to Hastings Campground. Another .4 mile south, on the left, is the head of the Caribou Trail. If you're here in late spring or early summer, you'll pass rushing water and a 25' waterfall. Two tent pads and a shelter are available near the summit.

Less than a mile further south, look for Mud Brook Trail, another way up Caribou Mt., that begins near a small waterfall. Another mile ahead is the Haystack Trail, a fairly long but easy hike through Miles Notch and back to rte. 2 across from the West Bethel Post Office. Allow yourself five to six hours, and leave a car in West Bethel.

> To tell the difference between a spruce and a fir, feel the needles: spruce has prickly needles; those of various fir trees will feel soft.

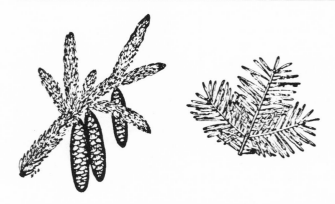

For these last few miles, the road winds through fern-covered dells and mixed woods, occasionally crossing a mountain stream — sometimes the same one, more than once. If your favorite color is green, visit here in spring or early summer to get enough of this shade to last you a while. But if the leaves are sparse, you can see where the mountains wall in the road from both sides and will know you have arrived at the notch itself.

After several more miles on the right is parking for the head of the East Royce Trail, which follows an old logging road next to a brook for 1.5 miles to the summit of East Royce Mt., the northernmost peak of the Baldface Range. The views of the Presidential Range from the summit are spectacular. On the other side of the road is Spruce Hill Trail, which will take you to the top of Speckled Mt. The latter loop is somewhat difficult and takes about 6 hours.

A bit further on the right is the Laughing Lion Trail, a pleasant hike through mixed woods that connects with Royce Trail and up East Royce Mt. (It's slightly longer than the East Royce Trail.)

> Evans Notch gets its name from Captain John Evans who was placed in command of troops fighting the Indians along the Androscoggin, after Stephen Farrington and others from Fryeburg marched up the Cold River Valley through this notch to aid the settlers at Bethel.

For those who don't feel like hiking but are ready for a view, there's a scenic stop before the Laughing Lion trailhead, then later on the left is the **Cold River Overlook** with *parking on the right.*

> From this watershed, brooks running south flow into the Saco River; those running north feed into the Androscoggin.

Almost two miles further south, you'll see an old brick house on your left. Built in 1812, the Brickett Place is maintained under an agreement with the Lexington, Massachusetts Boy Scouts; it is an important trailhead.

> John Brickett built his Cold River Valley home from bricks he made himself (the closest source of lumber then was a planing mill in Fryeburg).

*Look for Bickford Brook Trail and Blueberry Ridge Trail, which eventually connect with each other. While the round-trip up Speckled Mountain is 6 1/2 hours minimum, many people enjoy making a mile loop up to the **Bickford Slides** (a series of flumes and falls in the brook), then descending along the steep Blueberry Ridge Trail, eating tiny Maine berries in late July. The Slides are two dramatic waterfalls — the upper one cascades into a clear pool, but swimming in the frigid alpine water is only for the hardiest of souls. Several picnic spots can be found along the way.*

> The National Forest campgrounds in this area are open mid-June through September, except for Cold River, which stays open year-round.

Ahead on the right is the entrance to Cold River and Basin Campgrounds; both are popular places to fish. *Handicapped sites; picnic areas. Basin also has a boat ramp. Usual Forest Service amenities.* In close to another mile, rte. 113 leaves the National Forest, entering a wide valley. *The road surface deteriorates somewhat here.*

Farmhouses, some quite large, dot the open meadows. In about two miles, you'll find yourself in the tiny settlement of **North Chatham.** *Hikers should look for a brick and granite house, then a bridge. Leaving from the right side of 113, Baldface Circle Trail, a 10-mile loop of both North and South Baldface, offers close to four miles of views. Since fire swept the tops of these mountains, the vegetation is stunted — making this one of the finest hikes in the area. There is a shelter on the trail, just below the ledges of South Baldface; see AMC WHITE MOUNTAIN GUIDE.*

Signs of rural enterprise abound along 113. Our favorite: "Laying Hens, 75 cents ea., Blueberries."

In New Hampshire or Maine?

Continuing south, you'll see more and more signs of civilization, including brick farmhouses with ornate wooden trim. Five miles after entering New Hampshire, rte. 113 crosses into Maine again.

Ahead is the crossroads hamlet of **Stow,** with its town hall the only building to identify where you are. And in another four miles, you'll come into **North Fryeburg,** with its lovely old Universalist chapel dating back to 1838. *From here you can turn left, passing Horseshoe Pond and Fryeburg Harbor toward rte. 5 and Lovell. Or continue south toward Fryeburg.*

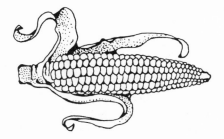

After crossing 6 miles of flat corn fields in the rich Saco River valley, rte. 113 enters New Hampshire for a second time. In another mile, it turns left, bringing you into an exotic landscape of isolated round mountains, rising out of bottomland. You're back in Maine for the third time here. *Before you cross the Saco River, you'll see a sand beach to your left.* Look for River Handicrafts on your right as you enter Fryeburg.

Chapter III   THE HEART OF THE WHITE MOUNTAINS

For those who want to maximize their mountain experience in a minimum period of time, we recommend the central corridors through the Presidential Range, rtes. 16 or 302. Both take you past some of the most famous peaks in the White Mountains, including the highest in the Northeast. Both routes offer numerous hiking, fishing, and skiing opportunities — not to mention shopping (much of it at discount prices in strips of outlet malls), first class dining, and lodging.

The bad news is that both routes are two lane for most of their lengths. In general, rte. 16 is the more heavily traveled, but both routes share the same busy stretch through North Conway. (Travelers coming through Conway on rte. 16 can avoid stop-and-go shoppers and tourists in North Conway by taking the West Side Rd., see page 87.)

Rte. 16 gives you a westerly view of the Presidentials, passing near the cross-country trails of Jackson and WILDCAT's expert slopes en route north. There's wilderness within hiking distance of Pinkham Notch and even closer to the road in "Thirteen Mile Woods." From Errol, you can head east on rte. 26 to Maine or west through Dixville Notch toward Vermont (see Chapter V). Or if you have only enough time for the Conways, you may return south along rte. 153 to 25 (Chapter IV) and back to 16, missing the worse of

weekend or holiday traffic.

Rte. 302 wanders into New Hampshire from Fryeburg, Maine (Chapter II) and past Conway Lake with its excellent fishing to link up with 16 by the outlet malls in North Conway. From Glen, the road leaves 16 and heads west through perhaps the most spectacular of the White Mountain notches, with skiing at ATTITASH and BRETTON WOODS (for a comparison of Mt. Washington Valley ski areas, see pp. 92-3). From Twin Mountain, you have choices to make: heading south to Franconia, if you skipped Chapter I; west to Bethlehem and then south along the Connecticut River, pp. 41-3; or north for real wilderness. From either Littleton or Twin Mountain, you will find routes that lead toward the North Country, Chapter V.

ROUTE 16

From I-95, bear left just south of Portsmouth, toward the Spaulding Turnpike, a toll road which speeds you through southeastern New Hampshire. En route you'll pass boggy woods, a favorite haunt of moose, those shy, clumsy creatures that look as though nature made a mistake.

Despite its huge size, the moose has a heart little bigger than that of a horse. Chasing one of these animals, who are rarely aggressive except in mating season, seems crueler even than shooting one — following a frightened moose in a four-wheel vehicle will probably only give it a heart attack.

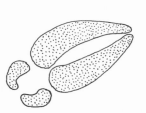

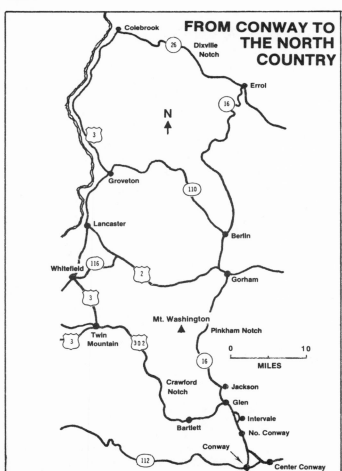

FROM CONWAY TO THE NORTH COUNTRY

The first good view of the mountains comes around *Ossipee;* you'll also see lakes if you're traveling when the leaves are off the trees. The peaks off to the right of SUNNY VILLA, 603/539-2252, are only a taste of what is to come. This cluster of shops and restaurants, some of which have handicapped access, make a popular place to stop for a bite to eat.

If you're ready for a country road or tired of traffic, *look for rte. 25 ahead in* **Center Ossipee,** *then turn right at the junction.* Known as "Ossipee Trail," this road leads through a collection of colonial buildings in Effingham Falls, four or five miles east, page 159 — a shunpiker's delight, or simply another way to get to Conway if there's too much traffic for your taste along this stretch of 16.

> Between 1849 and 1881, Whittier visited the White Mountains periodically, most often staying at Bearcamp River House in West Ossipee, which he described as a "quiet, old-fashioned inn, beautifully located, neat as possible" near the banks of the river. "Franconia from the Pemigewasset", "Sunset on the Bearcamp", "Among the Hills ", "The Wife: an Idyl of Bearcamp Water" are only a few of his works inspired by his stays in these mountains.

John Greenleaf Whittier especially liked this area, admiring the mountains (mostly at a distance) and writing about them, so it's not surprising that the locals named a mountain for him. Mt. Whittier, further north on rte. 16 in **West Ossipee,** is probably far more commercial than the poet would have liked, with a water slide, a restaurant, one of the area's largest flea markets, and a defunct ski area. But **White Lake State Park,** 603/323-7350, one mile west in Tamworth, is the kind of idyllic setting Whittier might have enjoyed. *A mile or two north of rte. 25 west, look for the sign and turn left.*

White Lake has a lovely sand beach and incredibly soft water. Two separate camping areas with a total of 173 tent sites; trout fishing (brook, rainbow, or brown) and hiking are popular here. Picnicking, playground, parking, and other facilities; entrance and camping fees in season. Open mid-May to Columbus Day, 8–8 daily.

Chocorua, the Most Photogenic Mountain

Just a couple of miles north on rte. 16 is the charming village of **Chocorua.** Chocorua View Farm, on the left specializes in antique furniture, clothing and tools. Next door, Country Primrose sells dried flowers, dolls and country crafts. This is another place to begin serious wanderings, if you have the time. The Tamworth/Sandwich area is well-worth exploring and offers delightful inns and shops as well as quiet country roads for biking (see Chapter IV).

Turn left past these shops, onto rte. 113, a minor connector in these mountains; THE FARMHOUSE BED AND BREAKFAST, 603/323-8707, at 113 and Page Hill Rd., serves its own fresh eggs for breakfast.

> "Chocorua in [one] of those mountains that stand so much by themselves as to focus our attention. Its sharply serrated and peculiarly individual outline make it perhaps the most marked feature in the state for getting one's bearings. . . The environs of Chocorua comprise various exquisitely beautiful drives." Wallace Nutting, 1923.

A classic view of Mt. Chocorua, one of the first landmarks of the White Mountains, appears after you pass through town on rte. 16. Tall pines and Chocorua Lake make a stunning foreground for the mountain's 3475' height. No buildings can be seen along the water from the road. *Look to your left as you approach the lake for Fowler's Mill Rd., almost two miles from the intersection of 113. Boat access and fishing on the lake.*

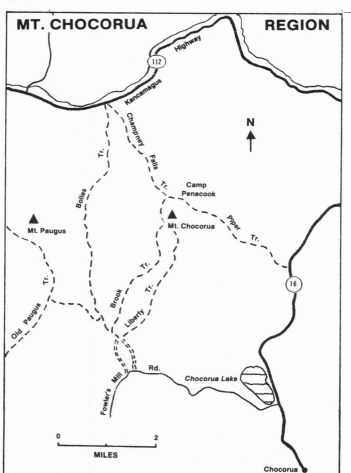

MT. CHOCORUA REGION

112 Highway
Kancamagus
Champney Falls
Tr.
Bolles
Tr.
Camp Penacook
Tr.
Piper
Tr.
▲ Mt. Paugus
▲ Mt. Chocorua
Tr.
Brook
Tr.
Liberty
Tr.
Old Paugus
Tr.
16
Fowler's Mill Rd.
Chocorua Lake

N

0   2
MILES

Chocorua

Legend says that chief Chocorua was shot on the mountain that bears his name, or leaped to his death there to avoid capture. At first friendly with the early settlers of this area, the Indian left his son with a family named Campbell, where the boy apparently ate some food left out to poison foxes. Chocorua held the Campbells responsible for his son's death and took his revenge on the women and children of the family, only to be hunted by his former friend and the other English settlers.

Not long after the Indian chief's death, settlers' cattle died of a mysterious ailment; local lore attributed the herd's failure to a curse Chocorua placed on their land. But years later, a Dartmouth professor solved the mystery by discovering muriate of lime in ground water; something as simple as mixing the water with soap suds might have counteracted the poison's effect.

X *Fowler's Mill Rd. also leads to a Forest Service road that offers ungroomed trails for cross-country skiing in the White Mountain National Forest (recommended only for intermediate or expert skiers looking for backcountry experience; trails undergoing changes at this writing) or hiking Mt. Chocorua (with connections to other trails linking you to the Kancamagus Highway, Chapter IV). (Caution: Unless you're accustomed to strenuous hiking and backpacking, these trails are not recommended. The climb up Mt. Paugus, for instance, will take 7 hours; hiking Mt. Chocorua can be dangerous in windy or wet weather.)*

Renamed for the Indian chief who died at Lovewell's Pond, near Fryeburg, ME, Mt. Paugus was once called "Old Shag."

> A.B. Durand, founder of the American Academy of Design, memorialized this mountain in his oil, "Sunset at Chocorua," but fellow-landscapist Thomas Cole found it more the inspiration for thought than for painting. Climbing Chocorua in the fall of 1828, he wrote that the ascent was "both perilous and difficult" due to windfallen trees along the trail.

On the right side of 16 is state forest land, and about three miles down the road, you'll see Piper Trail Camping on your left. The famous ***Piper Trail*** to Mt. Chocorua begins here, leading to the summit and connecting with other hiking trails throughout the Sandwich Range. *Warning: Extensive areas of open ledge on Chocorua make it dangerous when wet or icy. To avoid crowds or in bad or threatening weather, we recommend the Liberty or Brook Trail, accessible from rte. 113 (see Chapter IV and AMC WHITE MOUNTAIN GUIDE).*

It takes approximately four hours to reach the summit via the Piper Trail (backpack #2). If it's a cloudless, windless day and you're an experienced hiker, you may want to climb via the Piper Trail, arranging to have your car driven to the head of another trail. Look for the sign to the trail at the campground above and cross an open field into the woods. Follow the logging road into the WMNF, cross the Chocorua River (actually just a brook here) about two miles on the Piper Trail, then climb to the cleared outlook at Carter Ledge. From here you follow a series of switchbacks, paving, and stone steps for another mile. Camp Penacook with open shelter, tent

platform, and running water is off a spur path to the left here.

The main trail turns sharp right as it climbs, with more steps and paving, to open ledges with spectacular views. Other trails join as you climb; follow yellow paint for the Piper Trail over open ledges to the summit. From here, you can look northward to Mt. Paugus, with Passaconaway over its shoulder, flanked by Tripyramid to the north and Whiteface to the south. Due north, Mt. Washington rises out of the Presidential Range, snow-capped fall through spring.

> Fall is a popular time to hike the Piper Trail, but spring offers delights as well: smilacina, checkerberry, and partridgeberry peeping out of last year's leaves; trilliums, pipsissewa, bellwort, and Solomon's seal flowering among the greenery; yellow-bellied sapsuckers, myrtle warblers, slate-colored juncos hiding among beech and fir trees or broad-winged hawks and merlins near the summit; in May, butterflies like the mourning cloak or the Compton tortoise. The summit is 500' above the timberline and as one hiker described it, as "big as a table top." Nevertheless, the views are worth the climb.
>
> As another hiker wrote: "Chocorua is not a very high mountain. . . but its splendid isolation and the sharpness of its pinnacle give one on its summit a sense of height and of exaltation far greater than that to be obtained from many a summit that is in reality far higher."

Ahead on the right side of rte. 16 is the Lovejoy Wildlife Preserve, and after another mile, hikers should look on the left for the White Ledge Campground, with trails that connect to the Piper Trail and Champney Falls Trail, leading to the "Kanc," page 146. Iona Lake is on your right as your drive through the scattered community that comprises **Albany,** settled in the early 1800s.

Today little remains of the early village beyond the Albany Town Hall and a huge boulder off rte. 16, that may be the largest erratic in this country. *Look for rte. 113 east, turn right and drive three or so miles to a dirt road on the left. Cross over the railroad tracks after another mile and a half, looking for **Madison Boulder.***

> An "erratic" is any rock that is significantly out of place. Madison Boulder is believed to have been moved by ice sheets from the ledges in Albany two miles north.

Several miles further along rte. 16, you'll see a sign for DARBY FIELD INN, 603/447-2181, whose dining room is popular in summer for its splendid sunset views.

> The first white man ever known to climb Mt. Washington was Darby Field from Exeter, New Hampshire. The Indians believed the mountain was sacred, so Field could convince only two natives to lead him there in 1642. On a second climb later that year, he and his companions carried away stones they thought might be diamonds, but in reality were just glittering crystals. Throughout the colonial period, the White Mountains were known as the Crystal Hills.

Before you know it, you'll come to the junction of rte. 112, the Kancamagus Highway, a scenic route west into the White Mountain National Forest, page 142. The "Kanc," as it's affectionately known, has no food or fuel along its largely undeveloped length; if you're interested in heading west here, make sure you have 32 miles worth of gas before you leave Conway.

Conway, Gateway to the Presidentials

The approach to **Conway** is a bit deceiving. At first you think you're coming into a quaint New Hampshire town. If a slowing of traffic hasn't made you aware of the popularity of this area, the outlet centers quickly will. Soon you'll be bumper-to-bumper on a strip that makes it hard to know where one town starts and the next begins. But as you enter Conway, it's still possible to imagine the setting that has made countless visitors want to begin their White Mountain explorations right here.

At one time, Conway was among the most populous inland towns in the state — settlers from southern New Hampshire came here for the good hunting, rich soil, and forests full of sugar maples and mast pines. Soon lumbering flourished; logs and masts floated down the Saco toward the sea. Later in the 19th century, Conway and the inns nestled among the mountains were "discovered" by writers and painters. More recently, winter sports and bargain shopping have attracted vacationers.

> "I do not think any approach to the White Mountains can be more beautiful that that of the Saco Valley. . . . Now, where is the scenery inferior to that of the Scotch Highlands, or the Lower Alps, or the Jura?" wrote 19th-century traveler Bayard Taylor in THE NEW YORK TRIBUNE.
>
> "It is here, at Conway. . . that the first enrapturing view of the White Mountains bursts upon the traveller like a splendid vision." Samuel Adams Drake, 1882.
>
> "The Conways afford that unusual combination of village communities with all the conveniences of modern life, and surrounded by fertile lands, yet located in an amphitheatre of bulwarked beauty." Wallace Nutting, 1923.

If you're tired of driving or if the traffic is backed up, consider a stop here. The Conway Village Chamber of Commerce, 603/447-2639, on your right has plenty of information to guide you — whether you're looking for a quiet inn, fishing on Conway Lake, or the best place to ski.

There are several inexpensive places to eat here as well. Open for breakfast and lunch, GRAMMY MacINTOSH'S VILLAGE CAFE, 603/447-5050, on your right across from the high school, is as eclectic in its menu as in its decor: hash and fresh eggs, potato pancakes, huevos, seafood salad, "East 58th Street" Reuben, quiche. CHECKERS RESTAURANT, 603/447-5524, a little further along on the left side of Main St., offers reasonably-priced Italian dinners (bay scallops with herbs, white wine, and cheese; spaghetti with hot sausages; or scampi), subs, and burgers for the whole family. *Open year-round for lunch, dinner,*

and take-out, though this restaurant shrinks in size in the winter, when its porch is closed.

Decisions, Decisions

The traffic light in Conway links several of our routes — and offers numerous choices. *If you turn right here onto rte. 153, you'll be heading southeast toward lovely mountain lakes and the smallest of the Mt. Washington Valley ski areas, via a winding two-lane road (see page 162). If you're heading toward the Presidentials (Mts. Washington, Adams, Jefferson, et al), proceed straight ahead through the light, then left, continuing north on rte. 16. (In the next few miles, traffic will be considerably more congested because of the outlet malls ahead).*

For bikers or anyone more interested in nature than in shopping, we recommend turning left onto the *West Side Rd.*, here at the traffic light in Conway. *Although traffic can be heavy on this road as well (since skiers and second-home owners have discovered this bypass to Bartlett), West Side Rd. is a largely scenic route that will give you a real feeling for what the area was like before shopping became as important as the outdoors.*

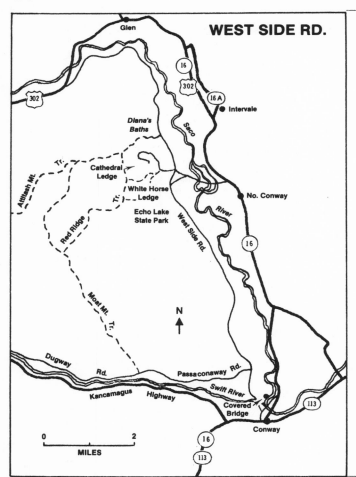

WEST SIDE RD.

Glen

16

302

16 A ● Intervale

302

Diana's Baths

Cathedral Ledge

Tr.

Attitash Mt.

White Horse Ledge

Tr.

No. Conway

Echo Lake State Park

Red Ridge

Saco

River

West Side Rd.

16

Moat Mt. Tr.

N
↑

Dugway Rd.

Passaconaway Rd.

Kancamagus Highway

Swift River

Covered Bridge

113

16

Conway

113

0   2
MILES

Sidetrip: ***Echo Lake State Park.*** Turning left onto the West Side Rd., you'll see some of the residential side of Conway and one of its two remaining covered bridges (under restoration at this writing). The road crosses the Swift River (brook and rainbow trout here) before moving out into the meadows of the Saco Valley. Pretty old farmhouses dot the landscape for much of the way. *Look for signs to Echo Lake State Park a little over 6 miles outside of town.*

Turn left into the park when you see the sign; there's a trail map at the entrance gate. Parking lot and restrooms are off to the right. Sand beach, picknicking.

Sidetrips: ***White Horse and Cathedral Ledges.*** Trails up these ledges are nationally known to rock climbers, which may explain why you see so many different license plates on cars in the parking lot at Echo Lake. It is not unusual for hikers to reach the ledges — only to find climbers with pitons crawling over the rocks to greet them. In fact, on one recent hike we encountered a climber who planned to sky-dive off the ledge.

AMC's ***White Horse Trail*** is a fairly strenuous climb (one and a half hours to the summit with connections to other trails) but is not dangerous unless very wet. Look for yellow (sometimes tan) blazes. *Echo Lake Trail* veers off to the right, while White Horse Trail continues about half a mile to the boulders at the south end of the ledge. After a steep climb, the trail meets a road to the right (used for logging at this writing), gradually ascending another half mile, circling around to the southwest side, where it connects with Red Ridge Link Trail. (This trail leads to Diana's Baths, a series of waterfalls and pools, near the West Side Rd. a bit further north.) For Red Ridge Link, follow orange blazes down a moderate grade. Or continue up sharply right for a steep .2 mile climb to the summit ledges with excellent views of emerald Echo Lake and the Conways. White Horse Trail descends through the woods and connects with Bryce Path up to Cathedral Ledge (an hour's climb).

The road heading east, across from the entrance to Echo Lake State Park, runs into North Conway, just above the EASTERN SLOPE INN. Unless you need to be in North Conway, we recommend continuing on West Side Rd. Look for the road on the left to Diana's Baths, after crossing Lucy Brook .7 mile past the entrance to Cathedral Ledge. Park on the gravel pullover and then walk along the road to a clearing just below the old mill site. **Diana's Baths** are a wonderful place to cool off and sunbathe, with Moat Mt. Trail leaving from the upper part of the clearing (Red Ridge and Attitash Mt. Trails lead from this trail further ahead).

". . .we came upon a fine cascade falling down a long, irregular staircase of broken rock. One of the steps extends, a solid mass of granite, more than a hundred feet across the bed of the stream, and is twenty feet high. Unless the brook is full, it is not a single sheet we see, but twenty, fifty crystal streams gushing or spurting from the grooves they have channelled in the hard granite, and falling into the basins they have hollowed out. It is these curious, circular stone cavities, out of which the freshest and cleanest water constantly pours, that give to the cascade the name of Diana's Baths. The water never dashes itself noisily down, but slips, like oil, from the rocks, with a pleasant, purling sound no single word of our language will correctly describe." Samuel Adams Drake from the HEART OF THE WHITE MOUNTAINS: THEIR LEGEND AND SCENERY.

Those going to ATTITASH SKI AREA or Crawford Notch should turn left from the park and continue on the West Side Rd. up to Bartlett. The road from here to Bartlett is narrow and without shoulders, but visibility is good. Still, bikers should use caution.

Those going through Conway on rte. 16 will have a sharp turn to the left, past the traffic light in the middle of town. For those interested in bargains, there's Conway Crossing Outlet Center on the left just past the light, then miles and miles more of outlets ahead.

It may seem hard to believe, but rte. 16 from Conway north is also one of New Hampshire's official bike routes, passing through some of the most beautiful scenery anywhere in these mountains on its 36 miles to Gorham. Although we know ski racers who pedal along here as part of their year-round training, we can't really recommend it as very pleasurable biking, except in spring before rte. 16 becomes clogged with cars again. *Rather than eating car exhausts, you're probably better off with back roads like West Side Rd.*

Outlet Fever

Crossing the Saco River on rte. 16, look to your left at the covered bridge. Malls and condos compete with mountain views along this stretch of road. *Rte. 302, the scenic road linking Maine's White Mountains with the westernmost peaks, joins rte. 16 in North Conway.*

You'll see Yield House on the left and the Mountain Valley Mall and the Gorham Outlet on the right, as rte. 302 merges with 16. At the next traffic light Settler's Green offers an incredible view of the Mt. Washington Valley, as well as a complex of condos, shops, hotel (under construction), and health club. If the prices seem high for Polo, Liz, or Calvin on the left, there's always L.L. Bean's Factory Store on your right before you come into the old downtown section of **North Conway.** *Glove Compartment Books has a map of the outlets in New Hampshire and Maine; $2.95 including postage and handling. Write Box 1602, Portsmouth, NH 03801-1602.*

Moses Randall settled in Conway at the beginning of the 1800s, and his great grandson built one of the first boarding houses in 1864. Although destroyed by fire at the turn of the century, it was rebuilt, eventually evolving into Hotel Randall with accommodations for 150. Burned again, the hotel was rebuilt once more, as the EASTERN SLOPE INN, complete with heated indoor/outdoor pool, tennis courts, health club, and restaurant.

Sooner or later — depending on the traffic — you'll come to the center of North Conway. Even before the outlets arrived, this was a favorite place to shop. Look for the League of New Hampshire Craftsmen on your left. Joe Jones and Carroll Reed have nice stores, selling sportswear and ski equipment. In recent years

EMS (EASTERN MOUNTAIN SPORTS) at the EASTERN SLOPE INN, 603/356-6321, has garnered quite a following among those interested in the outdoors. It now has nearly three dozen retail outlets.

In the 1930's, Carroll Reed, then a member of the White Mountain Ski Runners, broke his back at Wildcat, long before it was developed as a ski area. During his convalescence, he read about ski schools in Europe and decided to risk $1,000 to import an Austrian ski instructor to the Mt. Washington Valley. By 1939 there was a flourishing ski school, a lift up Cranmore — the skimobile — and the beginning of a new era for the White Mountains.

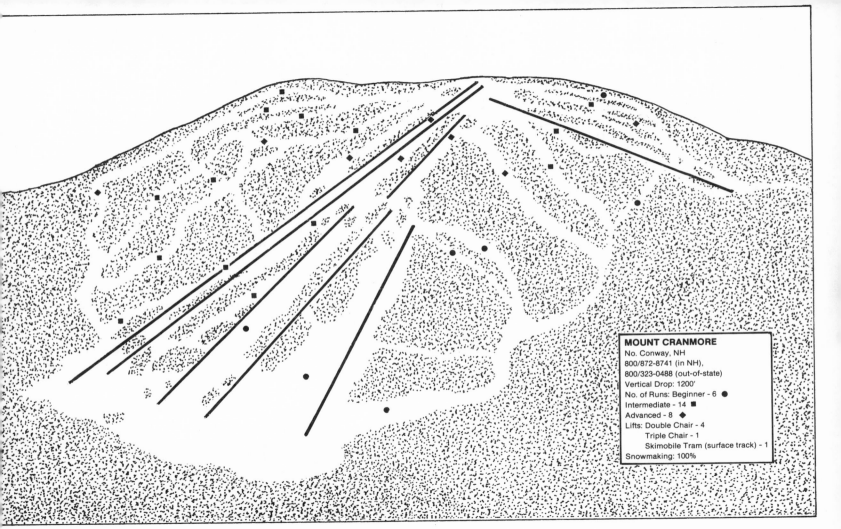

MOUNT CRANMORE

No. Conway, NH
800/872-8741 (in NH),
800/323-0488 (out-of-state)
Vertical Drop: 1200'
No. of Runs: Beginner - 6 ●
Intermediate - 14 ■
Advanced - 8 ◆
Lifts: Double Chair - 4
Triple Chair - 1
Skimobile Tram (surface track) - 1
Snowmaking: 100%

Breakfast lovers would do well to look for PEACH'S, 603/356-5860, on the left across from the Congregational Church, for breakfast and lunch. For moderate dining in North Conway, try HORSE-FEATHERS, 603/356-2687, on the right side of Main St., for Cajun popcorn, great burgers, and fries. The KOZY KITCHEN, where Minnie dishes out her own philosophy ("People are too busy today to be friendly") along with grilled cheese sandwiches, and the Five Cents to a Dollar Store on Main are reminders of the time North Conway was a sleepy mountain town.

Ski MT. WASHINGTON VALLEY

There are five working ski areas within minutes of the Conways — from KING PINE, southeast on rte. 153, to WILDCAT in Pinkham Notch. Among the oldest is MT. CRANMORE, 603/356-5543, on the east side of North Conway. There's a ski museum in a cabin just below the summit, with pictures of CRAN-MORE's early years.

As President of New York's Manufacturers Trust Company, North Conway native Harvey Gibson provided much of the financial assistance for ski development here in the 1930s. Using his banking influence, Gibson was able to pressure the Nazis to release famed Austrian Skimeister Hannes Schneider; he arrived at the North Conway train depot to a hero's welcome. Together Gibson and Schneider put Cranmore on the ski map.

Although its Skimobile (the only ride up a mountain where you can relax with your ski boots propped up above you) has been around for some time, CRAN-MORE has added new lifts and extended snowmaking — all part of a $7 million expansion effort. There's also an annual triathlon here in February that combines downhill racing, tennis, and swimming for teams of four to a dozen; call 603/356-5543 for information. Not surprisingly, the mountain has seen a large surge in the number of skiers recently — from 71,000 to 116,000 in just one year (1987) — which has meant long lines for some lifts, although many trails have been rerouted to avoid crowding in the future.

With both sides operating, CRANMORE is a pleasant intermediate mountain, although for long runs, you need to handle expert slopes near the top. In contrast, ATTITASH, page 123, over in Bartlett offers longer intermediate runs, while WILDCAT, page 106, gives even novice skiers an almost three-mile schuss down its mountain. Experts will want to try WILDCAT's more advanced slopes. Jackson's BLACK MT., page 98, the oldest of the five, and Madison's KING PINE, page 162, which just celebrated its 25th birthday, are more family-oriented mountains — ideal places to introduce youngsters to this exciting winter sport.

Although lift tickets and special rates vary from mountain to mountain, there are five-day passes available for these and four other New Hampshire ski areas, allowing you to choose from over 250 trails and 60 lifts. Contact

"Ski the Whites," Box 10ME, North Woodstock, NH 03262 for further information.

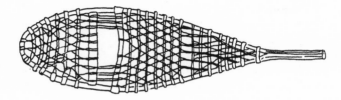

Even if you're not skiing, there's plenty to do in the valley in winter: ice skating in the Conways or Jackson (many area shops rent skates), local ice hockey in front of the train station in North Conway, ice fishing, or snowshoeing in the White Mountain National Forest. *To try this last sport, you can rent equipment from EMS, Joe Jones, or International Mountain Equipment in North Conway, and Kancamagus Highway Snowshoe Rental in Conway; warm hunting boots or mukluks are needed, as well.*

The Appalachian Mountain Club keeps some huts open in winter, while offering workshops and lectures on cold weather adventures, 603/466-2727. In addition, both ATTITASH and WILDCAT have Outward Bound winter programs for skiers who like to rough it. *Call ski areas for further details.*

"In the winter of 1876, finding myself at North Conway, I determined to make the attempt to ascend Mt. Kearsarge, notwithstanding two-thirds of the mountain was shrouded in snow, and the bare shaft constituting the spire sheathed in glittering ice. . . . I was up early enough to surprise, all at once, the unwonted and curiously-blended effect of moonlight, starlight, and the twilight of dawn. . . . The mercury stood at three degrees below zero in the village, when I set out on foot for the mountain.

. . .The ascent proved more toilsome than I had anticipated, as my feet broke through the frozen crust at every step. But if the climb had been difficult when in the woods, it certainly presented few attractions when I emerged from them half a mile below the summit. I found the surface of the bare ledges, which now continue to the top of the mountain sheeted in ice, smooth and slippery as glass.

The cold was intense, the wind piercing. . . . All the scrubby bushes growing out of the interstices of the crumbling summit — wee twig and slender filament — were stemmed with ice; while the rocks bristled with countless frost feathers. . . go down I must. But how? The first step on the ice threatened a descent more rapid than flesh and blood could calmly contemplate. . . . Seating myself. . . using my staff as a rudder, and steering for protruding stones in order to check the force of the descent from time to time, I slid down with a celerity the very remembrance of which makes my head swim, arriving safe, but breathless and much astonished, at the first irregular patch of snow." From THE HEART OF THE WHITE MOUNTAINS, Samuel Adams Drake.

For those visiting the mountains in warmer weather, the North Conway Railway Station was built in 1874 in the heyday of grand hotels. Although the last commercial train departed in 1971, the Conway Scenic Railroad, 603/356-5251, now runs 11-mile excursions through the valley. A ski train it's not, but to those nostalgic for the sound of a train whistle or kids who've never seen a steam locomotive, it's worth a ride. *May – October; admission, except for children under four.*

North Conway Arts Jubilee

Summer visitors to North Conway can also enjoy a wealth of entertainment under the stars. *July – mid-September; most programs charge admission, except for the free pops concert in August. Evening events are held at Mt. Cranmore or Grand Manor Antique and Classic Car Museum, Glen, page 96; call 603/356-9393 for details.* This summer festival began five years ago when it was rumored that the area might lose its highly profitable Volvo Tennis Tournament. A dozen businesses each contributed $2500; already the program has doubled from a three-week series to six-weeks.

Just past the EASTERN SLOPE INN, you'll see signs for Echo Lake State Park. *If you haven't been there, turn left on River Rd. (with connections to the West Side Rd., pps. 87-89, Diana's Baths, picnicking at the lake, biking, or hiking).* There's yet another mall ahead on rte. 16, then some attractive country inns. Long popular, THE SCOTTISH LION, 603/356-6381, ahead on the left, offers specialties of the British Isles, like steak and mushroom pie, beef Wellington, Highland game pie, salmon Kedegree, and delicious oat cakes; there's an import shop next door.

Attracted by the beauty of these mountains and the number of guest houses, so many 19th-century artists came here that a form of landscape painting is called "The White Mountain School." Benjamin Champney, the founder of this school of painting, wrote about this town: "... .we had heard incidentally of North Conway, and. . . . We decided to go there at once. We had interviewed Mr. Thompson of the Kearsarge Tavern, and he had agreed to take us in for the magnificent sum of $3.50 per week with a choice of the best rooms in the house. It was the middle of August and not a guest in town. . . . We were made to feel at home at once, with a generous table of good, old-fashioned cooking."

"I have known [North Conway and Intervale] so long, and so intimately that every corner and every stretch of view is dear to me, and I am proud to consider myself almost a native, and part owner. . : . A large slice of my life has been passed there, and I shall always do battle in its praise."

For some old-fashioned resort flavor, look across the road for signs to STONEHURST MANOR, 603/356-3113. A fieldstone 1872 English country manor reborn as an inn, this was once the home of the Bigelow (carpets) family. Dine here on gravlax or lobster ravioli, chicken Pernod, veal Oscar, fish poached in court bouillon, rack of lamb. *Open year-round; reservations requested; "Thursday Candlelight Dinner" specials*. On the north side of town, WILD-FLOWERS GUEST HOUSE, 603/356-2224, to the left, is an unusual example of late 19th-century architecture.

> Built under the direction of Boston architect Stephen C. Earle, the cottage faces away from Main St. to take full advantage of morning and afternoon sun; the exterior combines board-and-batten with cedar shingling.

Peaceful Intervale

A half mile further north on rte. 16 is an information center — and behind it, a broad vista of this beautiful valley. *Intervale,* as this settlement is so appropriately named, has a number of snug, attractive inns nestled up against the mountains. To sample them, turn right on rte. 16A, which connects with 16 again a few miles north. This country road makes a pleasant excursion — with the added advantage of avoiding congestion on 16.

Sidetrip: **Intervale Village.** *Turn right onto rte. 16A, the second right after Hurricane Mt. Rd., then follow Intervale Rd. to where it rejoins rte. 16, just past Dundee and Thorn Hill Rds., both of which are back roads to Jackson.* After the clutter of outlet strips, it's pleasant to see little development beyond inns, a cemetery, antique shop, art gallery, and mineral shop.

Based here in Intervale, field biologist Karen Nielsen offers nature programs for a wide variety of audiences. For guided nature walks or weekend workshops, contact OTTER BROOK WILDLIFE PROGRAMS, Box 168, Intervale, NH 03845, 603/356-5045.

THE NEW ENGLAND INN, 603/356-5541, took in early travelers to the mountains, then catered to painters of the White Mountain School of Art in the 19th century. Today it serves as a center for cross-country skiing, while offering classic New England fare to diners (cranberry pot roast Shaker style, chicken pot pie, or broiled swordfish). *Open for dinner nightly from 6 pm.*

Across the stream (actually the east branch of the Saco, where you'll find brook trout) is RIVERSIDE INN bed and breakfast, 603/356-9060 — a more modest establishment with an ambitious kitchen. (If you've had too much to drink, don't go to the bathroom here — the wallpaper is like a funhouse mirror and will distort the perceptions of a teetotaler). *Open for dinner year-round.*

Back on rte. 16 at *Glen,* auto buffs will enjoy The *Grand Manor Antique and Classic Car Museum,* 603/356-9366. Not only can you see one of only two dual cowl Phaeton 1927 Cadillacs ever built or "Bonnie & Clyde's" Ford, you can also listen to old-time radio shows in the parlor. *Open daily 9:30–5; fee. Car rentals and sales in addition to museum.*

Jackson, One of ESQUIRE's Top Four Ski Areas

In half a mile, rte. 16 turns right toward Jackson, the pre-eminent cross-country ski area in the White Mountains, while rte. 302 heads straight into Bartlett and Crawford Notch. We recommend a visit to Jackson — not only for skiing and hiking (there are close to 100 miles of cross-country trails in the area and 7 mountains within sight of town) — but also for its small-town flavor.

Although spectacular growth in condos and second homes has brought many "flatlanders" to Jackson, the town remains the kind of place where people care about each other — whether residents rally together to save the Wildcat River from a proposed dam project or to raise money to help a local family pay their doctors' bills. "People keep an eye on you when you first move here," says Bill Zeliff who's been running the CHRISTMAS FARM INN for the past 12 years. "But once you prove you're okay, they'll really stand by you."

A half mile on your right in Glen, you'll pass Storyland, 603/383-4293, with rides and changing child-sized exhibits from fairy tales; and Heritage New Hampshire, 603/383-9776, a journey back three centuries. *Wheel-chair access. Both places are pricey, but may be just what kids sick of sitting in a car need. Open Memorial Day to mid-October.*

After a mile and a half, you'll see the one-lane covered bridge to **Jackson.** Turn right on rte. 16A for the village. NESTLENOOK INN, a bed and breakfast, 603/383-9443, is a farm-turned-inn. In winter, you can ski tour or sleighride; in summer, there's a full-scale equestrian program and hayrides. As you continue into the village past the fire department, look for Thorn Hill Rd. on your right.

"Jackson. . . differs from the Conways in that it is closely shut in and lacks broad meadows. One is always touching the hills and often climbing them, although the thoroughfare is not a mountain grade," wrote one visitor. Today 65 percent of Jackson lies within the White Mountain National Forest.

A little way up Thorn Hill Rd. is a Victorian-era home designed by Stanford White. THE INN AT THORN HILL, 603/383-4242, serves some of the best food around (and that's saying something in this village of inns!). The menu is updated often with a half dozen specials: lightly-garlicked scampi with sun-dried tomatoes and angel hair pasta, pork tenderloin roasted with apples, or sirloin with green peppercorns and pecans; the wine list and service are on par with the cuisine.

Before you know it, you'll find yourself in the center of town. On your right is THE WILDCAT INN & TAVERN, 603/383-4245, popular for lunch and dinner as well as its apres-ski entertainment. The Jack Frost Shop and Ski Touring Center on the left is the starting point for most cross-country trails, as well as the anchor store for Nordic and Alpine ski gear.

Jackson hosts a 10K cross-country international early in the season, giving American skiers a chance to participate in world-class action. *For information on skiing here, contact the Jackson Ski Touring Foundation, 603/383-9355; 24-hour snowphone 603/383-9356. The Foundation maintains 146 km. of trails (half are double tracked) that connect with another 61 km. maintained by the AMC. Updated cross-country maps available from the Foundation.* The inns here are within easy access of ski trails, if not directly on one.

After a day of gliding over the well-groomed trails, you might enjoy a sleigh ride. Besides sleighs for rent at NESTLENOOK, Horse Logic Enterprises, 603/383-9641, has a 30-passenger sleigh available every hour (and a smaller version on the half-hour) from the Wentworth Resort Touring Center. *Wednesday – Monday, noon–4pm; 7–9:30pm.*

Sunny Black Mt.

If you're interested in skiing BLACK MT., 603/383-4490, or sampling other local inns (one of which can give THE INN AT THORN HILL a run for its money), *take rte. 16B to the left of the Jackson Grammar School, the middle fork in the roads here.* This is a scenic road with pretty old homes. Look for CHRISTMAS FARM INN, 603/383-4313, on your right as you climb the steep hill.

> The front part of the red house at CHRISTMAS FARM INN was built about 1778; this small "saltbox" was originally the home of the Rufus Pinkham family, then became a storehouse, and eventually the local jail. The large barn nearby boasts hand-hewn beams and pegs.

Begin dinner here with snails in garlic, herbs, and puff pastry; or duck, Japanese mushrooms, and cream served over pasta. In addition to mixed greens, the inn also has an unusual wild rice salad. Salmon is prepared differently each day; tenderloin of pork is cut into a fan and served with a sweet potato and red onion pancake. *Open year-round; reservations required.*

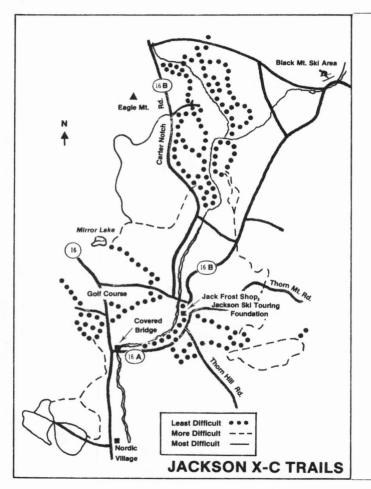

JACKSON X-C TRAILS

Least Difficult ● ● ●
More Difficult - - -
Most Difficult ——

16B continues a steep climb, then levels off along a ridge with incredible views of Mt. Washington before winding down past Black Mt. Meadow. Ahead is the comfortable WHITNEYS' INN JACKSON, 603/383-6886 (or 800/252-5622). Veal or duckling are always good choices here, as well as broiled schrod, grilled salmon, or rack of lamb (the latter only with 24-hour notice). *Open for dinner Sunday – Thursday 6–8 pm; Friday – Saturday 6–9. Reservations requested.* Although she no longer runs the inn that bears her family's name, Betty Whitney and her husband really started the ski boom in Jackson; photos at WHITNEYS' show hardy early skiers, clad in wool and using wooden skis.

At WHITNEYS', bear right and BLACK MT. will be on your left. With its southern exposure and natural protection in a bowl of mountains, BLACK MT. may be bearable even on the coldest, windiest days. From its beginnings 50 years ago, this "gentle giant" of a mountain has had a reputation as a friendly, family place to ski. *"Keep Skiing in the Family" packages allow Mom, Dad, and the kids to ski weekdays all day for under $40 total (non-holidays); two-day weekend passes are also reasonable, while weekend passes are interchangable at three other Mt. Washington Valley areas, and five-day tickets can be used at any major mountain in New Hampshire. Ski school, rentals, youth program, nursery; all the usual ski area amenities.*

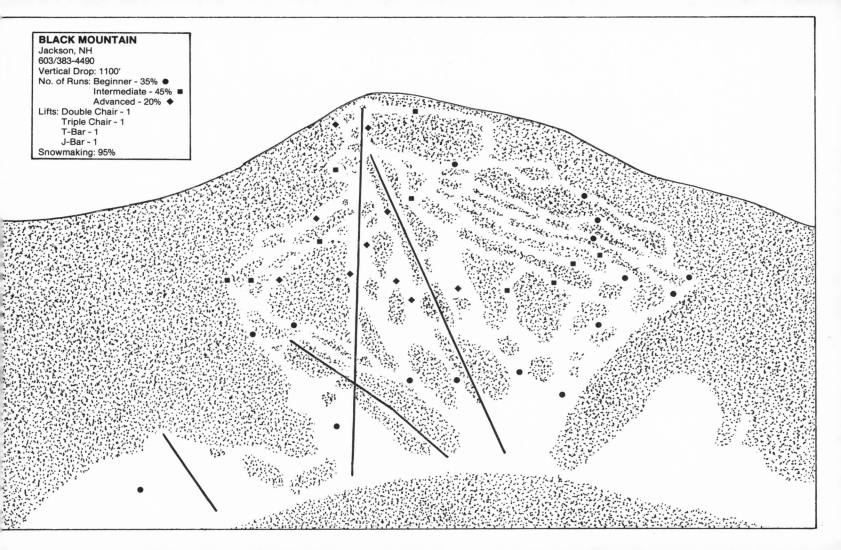

BLACK MOUNTAIN
Jackson, NH
603/383-4490
Vertical Drop: 1100'
No. of Runs: Beginner - 35% ●
　　　　　　 Intermediate - 45% ■
　　　　　　 Advanced - 20% ◆
Lifts: Double Chair - 1
　　　 Triple Chair - 1
　　　 T-Bar - 1
　　　 J-Bar - 1
Snowmaking: 95%

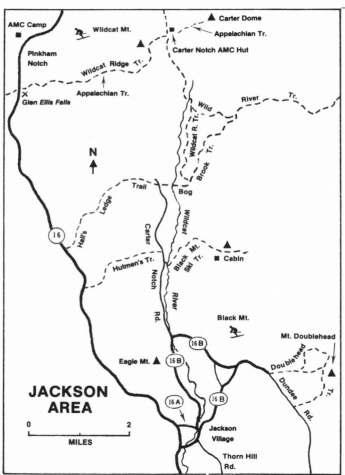

JACKSON AREA

0 ———— 2
MILES

"None of us knew anything about how to use skis," when the sport first began in Jackson, says Betty Whitney, who is still cross-country skiing today in her eighties. She and her husband bought one of the area's most popular ski farms in 1936 and hooked 75 shovel handles to an overhead cable to haul skiers up the hill.

For years the head of BLACK MT.'s ski school, Jackson's Arthur Doucette also remembered a very different sport from the one enjoyed today: the first classes were held at the Eagle Mountain Golf Course outside Jackson. Ski pants were made of wool serge (called Warburton), parkas were of windproof bird cloth, while ski sweaters were hand-knit. The first skis were of solid hickory, maple, or ash with poles of bamboo. Boots were all-leather (single lace-up); later iron toe-plates were added with a steel spring on the heel. A two-hour lesson cost $1.25 in the early days.

*Continue southeast on Dundee Rd., just past BLACK for a family hiking loop up **Mt. Doublehead.** Four miles; 1776' vertical rise. Allow three and a half to four hours to hike this loop, most of the day if you have young children with you. In less than half a mile, you'll see the start of your climb at Doublehead Ski Trail on your left. But keep driving another half mile, parking off the road, and looking for a new path on the left. (Walk back to Doublehead Trail to "warm up" for the climb.) After a half hour up this narrow ski trail, the old path forks right, leading to a col, or dip, between North and South Doublehead. This path is considerably steeper than the trail (but nothing children can't handle).*

Midway up is a spring; later a cabin will appear out of spruce woods on Doublehead. An outlook has been cut to reveal Mt. Washington, Lion Head above Tuckerman Ravine, and Huntington Ravine.

> "This is the cabin all of us dream about at one time or another when the real world becomes too much for us. It should be preserved and cared for not only by the forest service but by those who use it without permit or fee for daytime shelter or overnight lodging." Daniel Doan, hiker and author, 1983.

The trail to South Doublehead begins at the junction south of the cabin, descending through evergreens, then rises to lookout ledges with blueberries to pick in July and August. As you explore these ledges a little, you'll see Mt. Kearsarge North and Jackson village below. Looking east, you'll face Baldface Mt., Evans Notch, and Kezar Lake in Maine; west, you'll see Wildcat's summits, Carter Notch, and Carter Dome. *Descend on the new path, looking for two small cairns. The trail is steep but easy to follow, becoming better defined as you pass the larger spruces. Logging roads connect this trail with Dundee Rd.*

To return to Jackson, drive back on Dundee Rd. the way you came. Or if you're in the mood for a pretty drive and/or a serious climb, the Carter Notch Rd. can be reached by returning to WHITNEYS' and proceeding northwest on 16B, then turning north at the fork onto the Carter Notch Rd. For those heading toward Intervale and points south, continue along 16B the way you started, driving southeast to 16A.

Carter Notch

Back in Jackson, drive over the stone bridge spanning the Wildcat River.

Sidetrip: **Carter Notch Rd.** Turn north on 16B, just past the river. Drive up the steep hill with the WENTWORTH RESORT buildings to your left. (You may want to stop for a cool swim in the river.) In less than a mile, you'll see EAGLE MOUNTAIN HOUSE, 603/383-9111 or 800/527-5022, a newly-renovated turn-of-the-century hotel.

An hour's hike from the parking lot behind this hotel will take you up Eagle Mt. itself (1615'), with a marvelous view to the south; allow another 45 minutes to an hour for descent. (Cairns mark the trail.) *After about two miles, 16B turns right across a bridge. You want to continue straight, following the Wildcat River to the upper end of this steep valley. The road turns to gravel after the last house, then narrows after the log cabin on the left. Where the asphalt stops, several trails come in: Hutmen's from the left and Black Mt. Trail on the right.*

Sidetrip: **Black Mt. Trail.** This WMNF ski trail offers fine views of Mt. Washington, Wildcat, and Carter Notch, as well as connections to East Pasture Ski Trail. Allow close to two hours to reach the top.

Follow the dirt road into the woods and uphill to the Black Mt. cabin. Continue to the left of the cabin to a fork .3 mile, then bear left a short distance to the knob of this mountain.

Toward the end of the narrow gravel section of Carter Notch Rd., there are more trailheads: on the left, Hall's Ledge (marked by cairns, then yellow blazes) which leads toward rte. 16 at the Ellis River with views of Mt.

Washington, Boott Spur, and the Gulf of Slides; to the right are trails leading to the Notch itself.

Sidetrip: **Carter Notch AMC Hut.** Although somewhat lengthy, the hike up the Notch does end at a hut, where you may spend the night if you want — just be sure to reserve space in advance; allow six to seven hours for the round-trip.

> Because of its cold north wind, Carter Notch has a climate much like the summit of Mt. Washington. The hut here, built in 1914, is one of the oldest and the only one where smoking is prohibited.

Continue driving to a fork where you may park your car; walk a quarter mile to a turn-around past a cottage on the left and look for signs to Bog Brook Trail (WMNF) and Wildcat River Trail (AMC), which are the same for most of the first mile. (Follow blue ski club tags.)

Follow the east bank of the Wildcat, bearing left at the junction of Bog Brook and Wildcat River trails. Look for yellow ski tags here, continuing to climb the Forest Service road. In another mile and a half, you'll come to Bog Brook itself, where the trail angles left at the junction of two streams, then right for 10-15 yards along a narrow embankment between both brooks.

> Boreal chickadees can often be seen flitting among the treetops as you climb Carter Notch. The massive jumble of loose rock, or talus, visible to the right is known as the Rampart. There are ice caves here as well, among the boulders.

Real climbing begins about where Wild River Trail comes in from the east, shortly before the trail crosses Wildcat Mt. and ascends northwest. You know you're getting close to the notch when you start seeing campsites in the ever-

greens; the trail gets more rugged, climbing over boulders and roots as you approach the notch.

Continue past a spur trail to the Rampart. You'll see the long, low-frame barracks that are the kitchen, dining room, and hut quarters. Down from the earthen platform in front of the hut is a pool fed by a larger pond.

> Beavers, those inveterate builders, once plugged the pool's outlet here, raising the water level, but apparently the lack of leafy trees in the Notch discouraged them before their project was completed.

The perfect blue pond is stocked with trout. From the pond, you can see Mt. Wildcat to the west, with Carter Dome's round summit to the east. *From Carter Notch, overnight hikers can go on to Carter Dome, climb the lettered peaks of Wildcat on the Wildcat Ridge Trail to rte. 16 south of Pinkham Notch, or take 19 Mile Brook Trail to rte. 16 north of Glen House.*

Back on rte. 16A in Jackson, you'll see THE WENTWORTH RESORT HOTEL, 603/383-9700, a large complex of restored Victoriana with modern condos. *Swimming, tennis, 18-hole golf course.* THE PLUM ROOM here gives anyone a chance to sample the charm of a "grand hotel." Brie en croute, prosciutto and asparagus, fresh pasta, Caesar salad, filet mignon with seafood, and Saltimbocca are prepared New American style. *Reservations required; dinner nightly.*

Beyond the golf course is the Wildcat Country Store, currently vacant, but beckoning to resourceful entre-preneurs who don't want to leave these mountains. On the left is THE THOMPSON HOUSE EATERY, 603/383-9341, with inexpensive but inspired fare. For lunch, try one of the cleverly-named sandwiches (i.e. "Speared Tom" which translates into turkey with asparagus, red onion, melted Swiss, and Russian dres-sing), a salad of fresh Maine crab, or a frittata sea-soned with vegetables, cheese, and herbs. Summer-time coolers here include sangria, cranberry sparkler, or champagne freeze. *Open in summer only.*

If you stayed on rte. 16 without visiting Jackson, you'll cut through the WENTWORTH Golf Course, before joining up with 16A west of town. Anyone prefer-ring to head to Crawford Notch, Bretton Woods, and the incredible vistas and hiking that rte. 302 offers should return to Glen, turning right onto 302; then skip to page 121.

Rte. 16 North

As you continue west through town, 16A rejoins 16 north. This is the way to WILDCAT, Pinkham Notch, Mt. Washington and its Auto Rd., eventually to Gorham and Berlin, then finally to Errol, the Umbagog Lakes and into Maine. Outside Jackson, the road climbs, dips, and turns through pines and birches, passing a few old places and numerous condos nestled among the trees.

On the left about a mile from the intersection is the studio/gallery of David Baker, a long-time local whose paintings can be found over many a mantle — even far from these mountains. If there's an open sign on the gallery door, you might enjoy a conversation with him on the state of the arts, or just his own work.

Several miles further north you'll see WILDCAT condos on the right and THE DANA PLACE on the left, 603/383-6822. This 100-year old inn is popular throughout the year, but makes an especially nice place to gather with friends after cross-country skiing.

After entering the WMNF, rte. 16 adds a lane here and there as it climbs the mountains. There are occa-sional picnic spots along the way on both sides of the road. *Bikers will be grateful for the small paved shoul-ders on either side.* Almost four miles north of THE DANA PLACE is another picnic area, fairly large, opposite *Glen Ellis Falls.* This may be the most beauti-ful waterfall in the state that's so easily accessible.

As you drive under the shadow of Mt. Washington and Wildcat Mt. looms ahead, you'll know you're in *Pinkham Notch,* the widest of these White Mountain passes. This notch is named for Joseph Pinkham, who in 1790 arrived from the seacoast on a sled pulled by a pig. *There is a long northbound passing lane; the pull-overs here are worth your stopping, for the fine view southward down the Ellis River Valley is otherwise missed by those driving north.*

Porky Gulch

A little more than a half mile north of Glen Ellis picnic area (and also on the left) is a cluster of board-and-batten buildings, which comprise the Appalachian Mountain Club's hiking headquarters. The largest building is the *Joe Dodge Center,* a modestly-priced hostel that must seem like the Ritz Carlton to trail- and hut-weary backpackers. Among the "luxurious" appointments here are thermopane windows with locks, thermostats, bureaus, and individually-controlled lights over each pillow. *Numerous trails, some of them for skiers, connect with Pinkham Notch's Joe Dodge Center; this is also the site of many fine AMC workshops, lectures, and seminars year-round. 603/466-2727. The packroom here is open 24 hours a day for hikers who need a shower or just a place to stop and rest awhile.*

> The first road through Pinkham Notch was begun in 1774, but it wasn't until after the development of the WILDCAT SKI AREA in 1958 that the road became the wide thoroughfare it is today.

Joe Dodge, a modern legend among outdoorsfolk, spent a good deal of time in Pinkham Notch, which he called "Porky Gulch" for numerous porcupines who lived here as well. Dodge not only expanded AMC's hut system in these mountains so that no one is ever more than a day's brisk hike to a shelter, but was also a driving force behind the weather observatory on Mt. Washington. He was as famous for his colorful use of language as he was for his many accomplishments, however. (It is said that people would go to Pinkham Notch Camp just to listen to Dodge's oaths.) Nevertheless, this woodsman, ham-radio operator, weatherman, and skier (who pioneered the spring races at Tuckerman Ravine) left "about as many friends as there are trees in New Hampshire."

> Former hutsman and a friend of Joe Dodge's, Bill Whitney reminisced about their early days in Pinkham Notch: "Many a night we killed a dozen porkies. We clipped the noses for the 25 cent bounty, which was put in our meager kitty. In the spring, we would collect the bounty from the town clerk in Gorham, buy strawberries and cream, then go [back to Pinkham] and make what we called a porcupine shortcake."

One of the best trails up Mt. Washington leaves from the Pinkham Notch Camp. While we don't recommend Tuckerman Ravine to everyone, it is a fascinating and challenging trail. *Unsuitable for younger children or anyone not in excellent physical condition. In late spring and summer, expert skiers hike up Tuckerman to ski down the headwall. Recently, plans to carry skiers up Mt. Washington on the Cog Railroad were thwarted. While some skiers have been helicoptered in, the Forest Service discourages any skiing in Tuckerman, except by hikers.*

Sidetrip: ***Tuckerman Ravine Trail.*** This demanding, four-and-a-half or five hour one-way hike offers some of the best views of Mt. Washington, making it the most popular climb here. *Hikers should check with AMC personnel on weather conditions and camping restrictions, or purchase shelter tickets before starting off. From behind the Trading Post at Pinkham Notch Camp, the trail follows a tractor road, well-graded from the notch to the top of the headwall at Tuckerman — a steady, but not too steep — climb: crossing a bridge over the Cutler River at .3 mile; climbing a side path 20 yards for a good view of the Crystal Cascade. At .4 mile the Boott Spur Trail heads left for fine views. The Tuckerman Trail uses several long switchbacks, then heads west, crossing two brooks and eventually reaching the Hermit Lake Shelters. These AMC lean-to's are available to the public in warm weather; tickets can be purchased at Pinkham Notch Camp. Restricted use camping ONLY.*

"We are asking anyone who rides or flies to the top of Mt. Washington not to ski onto the snowfields above the Ravine or into the Ravine itself," says Mike Hathaway, Forest Supervisor. His closure order in April 1988 makes it illegal for any skier to enter the ravine or the snowfields *except* by Sherburne (ski) or Tuckerman Trails from Pinkham Notch.

Look for Boott Spur to the south; Lion Head, the cliff on the north. Caution is advised beyond this point; there is avalanche danger in the spring, rock slides after the snow has melted. The Snow Arch, sometimes formed by snow melt, can be extremely *dangerous* — do not go anywhere under it.

Until a Boston boy was killed when the Snow Arch collapsed on him, this was a popular place to picnic. "How can I hope to describe to you the rich surprise of entering this cold, crystal cabin, fashioned by a mountain and hardened there by the winter storms," wrote Rev. Starr King.

The Tuckerman Trail climbs into the upper bowl, before the steep ascent up the headwall. At the top is the junction with the Alpine Garden Trail, page 113, with summer-flowering plants that bloom nowhere south of the Presidential and Franconia Ranges. At the top of the plateau, Tuckerman Crossover is a straight shot to the Crawford Path, page 132, and the Lakes of the Clouds Hut. The Tuckerman Ravine Trail turns sharp right, ascending steep rocks marked by cairns and paint, and continues up Mt. Washington's cone to the Auto Rd., page 110, just a few yards below a parking lot near the summit. After this workout, you deserve a nice ride down. The Cog Railroad, 603/846-5404, sells one-way tickets, but since so many people drive up the Auto Rd., you may want to arrange to be met at the top.

On rte. 16 less than a mile beyond the Joe Dodge Center, you'll see the entrance to WILDCAT MOUNTAIN SKI AREA, 603/466-3326; 24-hour ski phone, 800-522-8952 in NH or 617/965-7991 in MA. This mountain is known for its long trails and incredible views of Mt. Washington. The majority of skiers here are considered expert because of the number of challenging trails, but even so, WILDCAT offers enough gentle slopes and such an exceptional ski school that beginners and intermediates should feel comfortable here, too.

One of the first ski areas to open in November, WILDCAT is also usually the last to close in the spring, thanks to its high elevation and proximity to Mt. Washington (which seems to create its own weather).

A $3 million expansion has meant new lifts to the summit, increasing capacity eventually to 8500 skiers per hour. 2100' vertical; 90 percent snowmaking. Separate novice area with its own triple chair; ski school, race programs, all usual amenities. "Ski for Fitness" aerobic outdoor workout. "Toofer" the price of one on Wednesdays, reduced rates Sundays; other special packages include a "Special Escape" combining lodging with lift tickets.

Every spring the New England Patriots "work out" on skis at WILDCAT as part of a fund-raiser for the National Handicapped Sports Association.

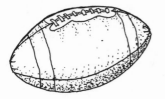

Even if you're not a skier, WILDCAT may be worth a stop. In summer and fall, sightseers can take an unforgettable ride to the summit in a two-person gondola. The views toward the Presidential Range defy description. And just a little ways north on the right is a quarter-mile nature trail leading to Thompson Falls, with a fine view of Mt. Washington and Tuckerman Ravine from the top of this long series of cascades. *Trail begins from the parking lot at Wildcat Ski Area.*

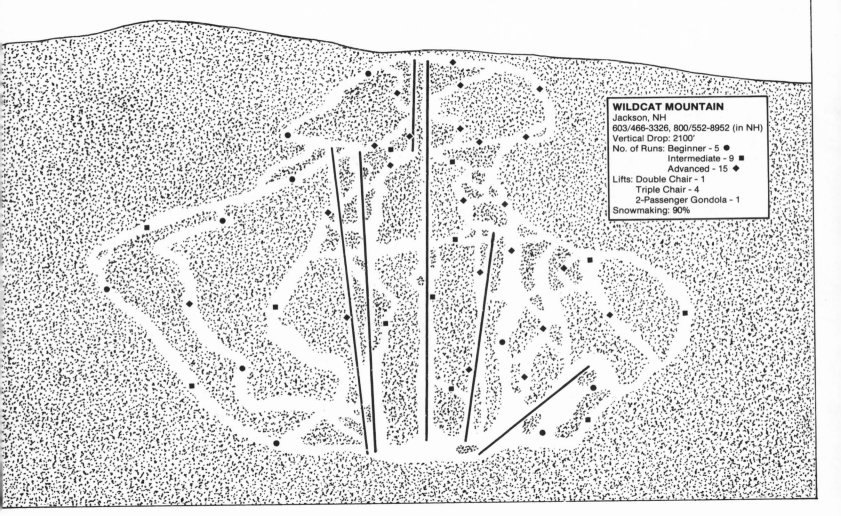

WILDCAT MOUNTAIN
Jackson, NH
603/466-3326, 800/552-8952 (in NH)
Vertical Drop: 2100'
No. of Runs: Beginner - 5 ●
Intermediate - 9 ■
Advanced - 15 ◆
Lifts: Double Chair - 1
Triple Chair - 4
2-Passenger Gondola - 1
Snowmaking: 90%

The Northeast's Highest Peak

Less than two miles north of WILDCAT, rte. 16 brings you to **Mt. Washington State Park** on the left. *Open mid-May to mid-October; no overnight facilities. Summit building has a post office, snack bar, souvenir shop, and restroom facilities.* The Auto Rd. on the left, 603/466-3988 or 466-2222, and the Cog Railway on the other side of the summit are both privately owned; *open, weather permitting, when the park is. Fee.*

No matter how you choose to climb **Mt. Washington** — in your own car, if your brakes are in good shape, or in a shuttle van, if not; by foot; or on the cog railway — this trip up New England's premier mountain is well worth your time and/or money. From the 6288′ summit, you may not able to see forever, but on a clear day Canada, New York, and the Atlantic Ocean are visible.

> Phineas T. Barnum, standing atop the old observation tower on Mt. Washington, reportedly called the vista "the second greatest show on earth!"

The road up this peak first opened in August, 1861, making the Glen House (the third version of which is located across rte. 16 from today's Auto Rd.) the most popular resort in the White Mountains. Today, vans shuttle tourists up the mountains from Glen House.

> When the ski craze hit these mountains, the Auto Rd. up Mt. Washington and Tuckerman Ravine became sites for spring skiing and races. Easter Sunday, April 16, 1933 saw the first race down the headwall at Tuckerman. Dubbed the "American Inferno," this event was so hazardous that it soon became better-known as a "suicide race;" the first year, only one skier managed to get all the way down, through driving rain and very heavy snow. In 1938 Toni Matt, one of the world's most brilliant skiers, schussed the headwall in one long dive that left the 400 spectators gasping for breath. But perhaps the best example of how dangerous skiing Tuckerman can be occurred in April of 1947 when 17-year-old Brooks Dodge (Joe's son and then Eastern Downhill Champion) was halfway down the course just as an avalanche began. Dodge let his skis run straight for the bottom and managed to outrun the sliding snow.

You may be surprised to read the thermometers here that measure temperatures in the valley and atop New England's highest mountain — there's often a 40-degree difference between the two! *Cafeteria; souvenirs. "Stages" leave regularly from 8:30–4:30 in season, one-and-a-half-hour guided tours for $14 per adult and $9 per child, allowing passengers a half hour at the summit.*

> In the 1870s the Glen House accommodated as many as 500 guests a day at $4.50 each for room, board, and transportation to the train in Gorham. Tolls up the Carriage Road were two cents a mile by foot, three cents a mile by horseback, five cents a mile by carriage. Auto "stages" were first used in 1912; gasoline-powered Thomas Flyers, Knoxs, Peerlesses, or Chandlers were later replaced by Packards and Pierce Arrows.

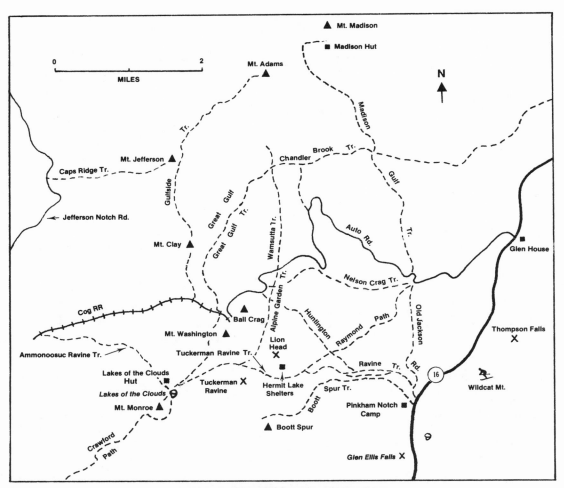

THE PRESIDENTIAL RANGE

An amazing engineering feat in itself, the Carriage or Auto Rd. has inspired all sorts of "firsts," but as you drive this road, remember how difficult it must have been (and often still is) to climb this mountain on foot.

Darby Field from Exeter, New Hampshire was the first white man to reach the summit in the 18th century. Later, early settlers Abel and Ethan Allan Crawford made trails up Mt. Washington, often leading famous visitors, or pioneering scientific expeditions. Not until 1816 was a map of Mt. Washington published, but ever since, this mostly snow-clad peak has attracted all sorts of people — some of whom have added to our understanding of the world around us; some who, unfortunately, have lost their lives.

In 1855 a 230-pound woman won a $1000 bet by walking to the summit and back in one day; she also danced all evening at the Glen House on her return. On another occasion, a tall, raw-boned man from Maine broke a record by running down the Carriage Rd., wearing a tall beaver hat. In 1896 Freeland O. Stanley and his wife made it up the 8-mile road in one of his own Steamers; their record time was two hours and ten minutes, despite frequent stops for water to fuel the auto's engine. As you may remember from Chapter I, Florence Murray Clark of North Woodstock drove a team of sled dogs up to the summit in March, 1926 — the first woman to accomplish such a feat.

Rev. Jeremy Belknap led the first group of scientists up Mt. Washington; they accurately described the headwall at Tuckerman but estimated that the mountain itself was at least 10,000 feet above sea level.

For many people, the most lasting impression of Mt. Washington is its weather. It may snow on the summit in mid-July; in winter it may be the coldest inhabited spot in the US. WMTW employee Lee Vincent describes his winter stay on the summit: "It's so cold in the building that I've had to close the doors to the transmitter room, turn on all the electric heat including the oven and. . . sit wrapped in a blanket." The highest wind velocity ever recorded on earth was measured here in 1934: 231 mph. Fifteen feet of snow is the winter norm.

A Road Through the Clouds

If your car is in excellent shape, the **Mt. Washington Auto Rd.** is probably the least expensive way up the mountain for a family or group — unless you'd rather hike. *Toll: $10 per car plus $4 for each adult (children 5–12 for less). Mid-May through mid-October, weather permitting; 7 am–6 pm. Drivers are advised to use low gear both ways; brakes, water, and gas should be checked before going up. Large towed trailers, pickup campers, and motor homes are not permitted on the Auto Rd.*

However you go up the Auto Rd., you're bound to get a real sense of this mountain's height. The first four miles pass through fairly thick woods with few open vistas. It's possible to pull off in places for a little hiking; two miles from the base look for trails on the left (Raymond Path goes to Tuckerman Ravine; Old Jackson Rd. leads to Pinkham Notch Camp). Your more ambitious passengers might want to hike up Nelson Crag Trail and be met at 5.3 miles up, or at the summit. *While this is a steady climb with some sharp ascents, you do get an unusual view of Pinkham Notch about a mile up the trail. Because most of Nelson Crag Trail is above treeline and very exposed to the weather, it (like all trails up Mt. Washington) should NEVER be attempted without adequate protection: backpack #2 (see introduction). This trail crosses the Alpine Garden Trail and Huntington Ravine Trail before climbing the rocks to Ball Crag, 6106', and the summit.*

Just past the two-mile point, you'll also see the Madison Gulf Trail leading across Great Gulf to an AMC hut in the col between Mts. Madison and Adams, the second-highest peak in New England. Great Gulf is the largest cirque, or bowl-shaped valley scoured out by glacial action, in the White Mountains; its headwall rises from 1100' to 1600' and is bounded by slopes of Mt. Washington on the south and Mt. Clay on the west.

The name of the cirque on the side of Mt. Washington probably came from a casual comment made by Ethan Allen Crawford, who in 1823 lost his way in cloudy weather, only to find himself at "the edge of a great gulf." The first trail was blazed here in 1881.

The views from the wall of Great Gulf are some of the best in these mountains; unfortunately, the section of trail on the headwall of Madison Gulf is also one of the most difficult (not recommended in wet weather or after spring run-offs; hikers should not carry heavy packs here, start late in the day, nor use this trail for descent). *The AMC allows about four hours from the Auto Rd. to Madison Hut, but because the ascent of the headwall can be so tricky, it's wise to give yourself an extra couple of hours. Hiking parties frequently fail to reach the Hut from this trail before dark because of the headwall.*

Two and a half miles from the base, you may notice that the trees seem smaller (they are!). Near the four-mile post, where the road turns sharply, the nature of the woods changes.

> In the lower altitudes, deciduous trees predominate: beech, maples, yellow and white birch. As you climb, evergreens begin to take over: white pine, balsam, and spruces with mountain ash as the only deciduous tree. At timberline, all the trees are stunted and twisted. Although "krummholz" trees may be as much as 100 years old, they never grow more than two or three feet in height.

Around 4000 feet, you'll see what's known as "krummholz" (literally "crooked wood"): balsam and black spruce growing in low, dense, tortured forms. You'll also have your first really dramatic view from here. Great Gulf is below with Mt. Clay to the far left, then Jefferson, Adams, Madison, and Pine. Beyond the Presidentials, the Angdoscoggin River Valley opens up with the Mahoosuc Range behind, ending at Grafton Notch in Maine.

Beyond this point is the Chandler Brook Trail on the right (connecting to Great Gulf Trail). From the five-mile marker, you can see Sunday River's whitecap in Maine, and closer to the east, Moriah, Imp, the Carters, then Carter Dome. There is a turnout ahead, with the first Auto Rd. view of the summit; looking southeast across Pinkham Notch you can see Wildcat (easily distinguishable by its ski trails), then the long ridge that is Pleasant Mt. and further southeast Sebago Lake — these last two are in Maine. Over Wildcat's southern shoulder are Mt. Doublehead and the pyramid-shaped Kearsage. Nelson Crag Trail crosses the Auto Rd. here; beyond the trail are the upper walls of Huntington Ravine with Boott Spur, part of Tuckerman Ravine, forming the jagged lower horizon.

If you're planning on hiking Mt. Washington sometime in the future, it may be wise to note the small emergency shelters located along the last two and a half miles of road.

Just past the 6-mile mark is the Wamsutta Trail, leading to the Lakes of the Clouds Hut and southern trails from Great Gulf. *Hikers may enjoy the novelty of hiking* down *to an AMC hut.*

Diapensia

> Tall poles that appear every now and then along the Auto Rd. help workmen find the road and culverts under the heavy snows that accumulate here. If you drive this road in spring you may still see snow; near the upper end of the Cutoff Rd. drifts may reach 25'.

This is the highest range of krummholz; the most prominent vegetation are mosses, sedges, lichens, heath, and rush.

Across the road on the left is the **Alpine Garden Trail,** well-worth your descent to the grassy lawn if you're here mid-June through mid-July. Plants grow on the slopes of Mt. Washington that cannot be found south of the St. Lawrence or Nova Scotia; most grow at lower elevations in places like Alaska, Greenland or Arctic Eurasia. Care must be taken not to step on these fragile plants — UNDER NO CIRCUMSTANCES pick them. *A close-up lens on your camera can bring these rare flowers home with you.*

> The best time for flowers at the Alpine Garden is late June or early July. Pink-magenta Lapland Rosebay, tiny pink Alpine Azalea, and white-petaled Diapensia are most frequently found here. Look for Mountain Avens in wet areas; in the US, these plants are found only on this summit or atop the Franconia Range. The rarest plant in the Alpine Garden is the Dwarf Cinquefoil, protected by its small size and inconspicuousness (you may see a few hiding in late snow).
>
> The grass found on Mt. Washington's higher elevations is Bigelow Sedge, which grows by adding cells at the bottom rather than the top — allowing it to live through the harsh winters here with the barest of protective snow covers. Diapensia has a different way of surviving — its habit of growing low to the ground in dense clumps seems to protect it from the wind. A 75 mph gale at 6 feet above ground is little more than 33 mph at 6 inches, explaining why plants are shorter near the summit.

Watch out ahead for a hairpin turn. At mile 7 the road climbs into the Cow Pasture, where dairy cows that were the milk supply for the summit hotel grazed a hundred years ago.

The pull-over at mile 7 is a good place to wait for hikers from the Nelson Crag or Huntington Ravine Trails, if they don't want to walk the last mile; or to walk down to Alpine Garden, if you didn't before. The view here is superb, though it will be better still ahead.

The Auto Rd. passes through Home Stretch Flat, named by tired hikers grateful that the summit was close by, then parallels the Cog Railway (see Bretton Woods, page 135) before swinging east with views of Alpine Garden, Huntington and Tuckerman Ravines. After a sharp right turn, the road comes to an end.

> Henry David Thoreau climbed Mt. Washington in 1858 and found the hiking a little rough. Descending the headwall of Tuckerman Ravine, he crossed a patch of snow and tore his fingernails to save himself from sliding down too rapidly. Later, he sprained his ankle so badly that he could neither sleep nor walk.

The Top of New England

While in the past visitors could spend the night atop Mt. Washington or gab with the editor of a newspaper published here, today only the park's visitor center is open to the public. ***The Summit Museum*** offers excellent booklets about Mt. Washington at reasonable

> The water tank at the summit is for cars, whose radiators are apt to boil over on the way up, rather than for people. 550,000 gallons of water must be pumped up the mountain every summer.

prices: whether you're interested in survival techniques, the geology of the mountain, or alpine flora. From the platform here, you have almost 180-degree visibility. Starting from your left are the Presidentials (Mts. Clay, Jefferson, Adams, Madison), Berlin and the Androscoggin River Valley, then Umbagog and Rangeley Lakes. Although no longer open to the public, Tip Top House has the best view to the west: the Mount Washington Hotel and the wide Amoonoosuc Valley, with the Rosebrook Range as its western wall. Cherry Mt. is discernible because of its fire tower and Vermont's Green Mountains appear in the northwest.

In many ways, today's summit is all business. WMTW, which beams ABC programs and serves as a cable relay point, generates all the electrical power at the summit; in winter its snowcat brings up supplies and personnel for the station and observatory.

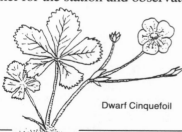

Dwarf Cinquefoil

> The first Mt. Washington Observatory had nothing to do with science; it was a 40-foot tower with an 8-man elevator for tourists. The first temperature readings here were taken by hotel employees.

Early attempts to establish a scientific station at the summit were futile, although observers did spend the winter of 1870-71, recording the coldest temperature on record here: 59 degrees below zero. The present observatory, started in 1932, is held in place with large chains; scientists within study everything from cosmic radiation to the physics of icing.

"To sample the world's worst weather spend a winter on Mount Washington. At least, the mountain can dish up the worst combination of cold, wind, and blowing snow to be found at any permanently inhabited place on earth," said Charles F. Brooks, Harvard professor and Observatory president. Bradford Washburn, former director of Boston's Museum of Science and conqueror of Mount McKinley, had to agree: "With the exception of some isolated peaks in the Arctic and Antarctic, Mount Washington has the most severe weather in the world."

Copp Country

Back on rte. 16, after inhaling the scent of overheated brake pads, you'll be grateful for gentler grades. Bikers who've made it all the way from Conway will be in top form by now. And there are lovely sights north of Mt. Washington, even if less dramatic.

Almost two miles north of the Auto Rd., you'll see signs for Great Gulf Wilderness on the left. There's good trout fishing from the West Branch of the Peabody River here. Hikers might want to keep their eyes peeled for the Imp Trails on the right: *the first is .7 miles north of Great Gulf, the second is another .3 miles further.* This is a loop, connecting with trails to Middle Carter Mt. Allow five hours for the 6-mile hike; 2275' vertical. (The hike up Imp is, by itself, only two and a half miles and is recommended for the views.)

Sidetrip: **Imp Trail.** Park in the picnic area on the left side of 16, across from the second sign for Imp Trail. Climb from the northern end to the lower ledges of Imp Profile, cross the rim of Imp Brook's ravine, where you'll see North Carter Trail, and descend an old logging road to the southern Imp trailhead, a quarter mile from your car. This trail is steep as it approaches the ravine, but rewards you with a vista that sweeps from Wildcat to North Carter, as well as the melody of a waterfall below.

The early settlers here, Hayes and Dolly Copp, carved a settlement out of the wilderness. Dolly named Imp Profile, clearly visible from her cabin door. A hard, unyielding man, Hayes built a wagon road here so that mail coaches and stages could bring civilization into the mountains, Like the Crawfords and other settlers, the Copps welcomed travelers to their home, charging 75 cents a night for bed, board, and stabling a horse.

> Known for her pipe-smoking as much as the homespun cloth and maple sugar she made, Dolly Copp declared on her golden wedding anniversary, "Hayes is well enough, but fifty years is long enough for any woman to live with any man." Selling their farm, Dolly moved to Auburn, Maine, while Hayes lived out his days in his childhood home of Stowe, also in Maine.

On the northern edge of the White Mountain National Forest, the Dolly Copp Picnic Area and Campground, another mile north, also on the left, make a good stop — whether you're ready to eat, fish, camp, or just refill a canteen. Backpackers and hikers may want to look on the right in another mile or so just before the bridge over the Peabody for trailheads. Besides the Stony Brook and Carter-Moriah Trails here, there are connections to Imp Shelter (4.1 miles) and Wild River Rd. (8.7 miles).

> One man — Paul Jenks — oversaw the placement of 5000 AMC trail signs here in the White Mountains.

Sidetrip: **Mt. Moriah.** Standing out from other mountains here, Moriah looks like a northeastern sentinel, offering views of the Mahoosucs in Maine as well as the Presidentials in New Hampshire. Because this is a 7-hour hike (3100′ vertical and almost 10 miles long), you are advised to try it only if you're spending some time camping nearby or staying in Gorham. But if you have time, you will be rewarded with wild raspberries, the ruins of a blacksmith shop, a sphagnum bog, and more incredible views.

Park off the road on the east side of 16; the trail begins as a road for two camps and a house. Follow Stoney Brook for three and a half miles, then take Carter-Moriah Trail north up the mountain. Return the way you came. There are steep stretches and slippery mossy ledges, as well as boggy ground (usually with plank walks — be sure to plant your feet firmly on these logs, unless you want to wade in the bogs). From the summit, 4047′, you can see Carter Dome south, the Presidentials southwest, the Mahoosucs to the north, North and South Baldface to the southeast.

Midway Between Montreal and Boston

In another two miles, rte. 16 brings you into **Gorham,** the northern gateway to the Presidentials. Settled in 1836 by Mainers, this community has long attracted visitors to the mountains, beginning with the completion of the Atlantic and St. Lawrence Railroad.

Sited at the confluence of the wide Androscoggin and the smaller Peabody Rivers, Gorham is surrounded by mountains: to the northeast Mt. Hayes, whose summit is exposed ledge; east of 16, the towering Carter-Moriah Range; due west Pine Mountain, the northernmost of the Presidentials, with Madison, Adams, and Washington behind it.

> Before the turn of the century, silver ore was mined from Mt. Hayes, lead from the valley below.

Today, Canadians will see signs pointing them to Old Orchard Beach and hear French names pronounced in flat New England accents. *Rte. 16 turns left at the stop sign, joining rte. 2, through most of town. If you're interested in Maine's mountains, a right on rte. 2 east will take you to the Evans Notch Rd., page 75, and eventually on to Bethel, page 61.* There's a White Mountain Information Center on your left, and an old railroad depot (1907), complete with vintage steam locomotive, outside what is now the Gorham Historical Society Museum, 603/466-5570 or 2208. Open by chance; donations welcome.

Although the town boasts over 14 restaurants (including chains and fast-food outlets), we have to say our favorite is SALADINO'S ITALIAN RESTAURANT AND BODEGA, 603/466-2520, 152 Main St. We liked the option of buying gourmet picnic items: chocolate bisconi, imported cheeses, mineral water, salads, sandwiches (even dinners that need only to be warmed). The place is squeaky clean and simple; there's scampi, chicken or veal parmigiana, lasagna, Italian or meatball sandwiches, or soup, bread, and salad bar. Espresso and capuccino are a nice way to end lunch or dinner here.

Gorham to Errol

At the traffic light past SALADINO's, rtes. 2 and 16 go their separate ways. While it may be something of an oversimplication, hikers should head west on rte. 2, if they haven't gotten their fill of mountains; fishermen ready to catch a salmon will want to continue north on 16. Rte. 2, a major route between Maine and Vermont, skirts the northern edge of most of the National Forest, going through Randolph and Jefferson, then Lancaster, page 167, and into Vermont (or north on rte. 3 to even more of the WMNF). Because we have mentioned so many hikes already — with even more to come — we recommend rte. 16 for somewhat different scenery and adventures.

This route runs along the Androscoggin River — a sparkling stream for canoeing and fishing — then continues almost due north to Thirteen Mile Woods for camping and hunting, and passes through Errol on its way to the Rangeley Lakes of Maine. From Errol, rte. 26 (described in Chapter V) leads you west to one of the most rugged mountain notches, Dixville, with its elegant resort and skiing — both Nordic and Alpine. Or you can head east through Maine's Grafton Notch and eventually to the popular southern coast.

Turn right to continue on rte. 16 toward Berlin *and* Errol *and rte. 26.* You'll probably smell the pulp mill to the north, even before you see it. This stretch of road is hardly lovely, but we read in a 1930s WPA Guide that the scenery here was disappointing back then, too, so this seems a logical place for commercial and industrial development. *Bikers who weren't put off by Conway's traffic might want to continue north here; there is a rural loop east of the pulp mill at Berlin.*

About three miles north of the traffic light, you'll see Cascade Flats below the highway on the right, where many of the millworkers live. Other workers, mostly French Canadian and Norwegian, live on the other side of the mills, in frame houses ascending Mt. Forist.

In the 1940s, there were 700 sawmills in New Hampshire; today that number has declined to 200. The state now has TWICE the volume of wood "on the stump" as it did then; unfortunately, many of the most important commercial species (white pine and red oak) are still cut too heavily.

Wood Pulp City

The huge smokestacks of the James River Corporation's pulp and paper mills dominate the landscape — and depending on the winds, their eminence dominates the senses. Even the peaks of the Mahoosuc Range lose competition for your attention.

The lumber industry was started in **Berlin** in 1852 by a group of businessmen from Portland, Maine, and there was little doubt as to where to put the mills. The Androscoggin is compressed through a narrow gorge here, resulting in a tremendous force for powering the mills; it falls 400 feet in less that 6 miles. The river also served as a highway for timbermen shipping cut trees to the mills and finished logs downriver to Maine. Today, the James River Corp. is the largest employer in Coos County.

We recommend bypassing Berlin, taking a bike route along the east side of the river for a more scenic route.

Just before entering downtown, rte. 110 turns off to the west, toward Groveton, while rte. 16 turns north, heading into the middle of this busy city. It's just as fast to turn right onto the James C. Cleveland Bridge, and travel north on the east side of the river. Keep the James River Corp. plant on your left, and you won't have too much trouble winding through the millworkers' homes — whether by bike or car.

Since World War I, Berlin has been pronounced BERlin, with the emphasis on the first syllable to distinguish it from the German city, for obvious political reasons.

At the first flashing light after the bridge, go straight on Unity St. past the Eastern Depot, snake around the plant, bearing left, and keeping the mill in sight on your left. A little further ahead you snake left again to a stop sign, then turn right onto Hutchins St. with the plant still on your left. Turn left, then right once more by NAVE Public Storage and Logging Supply; after passing a cemetery and quonset hut, the route straightens out and is easy to follow for the remaining three or four miles, until you come to the airport sign.

Although only two lanes, this road has paved shoulders part of the way. When they disappear, the traffic does too. Besides the views of Berlin, which looks very nice from here, there are only farms and lumberyards to distract you. The woods on the right, just after the paved shoulders end, belong to a beagle club — no hunting here! Another two and a half miles further north, you'll see a fish and game range on the left. In winter, this is snowmobile country (look for tracks to the left further north). *Another mile or so past a gun shop and grazing cattle, you'll see the airport sign where you should turn left over the Androscoggin into* **Milan.**

Milan North

If you're interested in a camping site, rte. 110B passes by state forest land on the left. There are a dozen primitive campsites here as well as impressive views of the Randolph Range to the south, and the low hills of Canada to the north.

For those continuing north on rte. 16, turn right after the bridge in Milan. The road surface worsens to the north, so we can't recommend this route for bikers. After the old-fashioned farming village of Milan, the landscape all the way to Errol has a northern aura to it — a flat, uninhabited valley, punctuated by pointed fir trees. Moose-crossing signs are serious here (the last time we drove this stretch we saw two separate animals, eating calmly beside the road).

You'll pass a Boise Cascade tree farm, then less than two miles from Milan, the Pontook Reservoir appears. *Parking on right by dam. Restrooms, water, telephone.* There are rainbow trout in the river; pickerel and hornpout in the reservoir. Canoeists planning to paddle the Androscoggin might want to leave a car here (you should bring your canoe ashore before the dam).

The vegetation changes as you continue north: lichen covers bark, while deer moss dangles from trees. In winter, look for snowmobile tracks on the left as you drive north of the recreation area. Also glance back occasionally for glimpses of the Presidentials, now far behind you.

Four and a half miles past the reservoir, you'll see a sign for **Thirteen Mile Woods,** jointly managed by the state, Boise Cascade, and the James River Corp. *Camping and fires by permit only.* This is a beautiful stretch, seemingly untouched by civilization. Only a logging or telephone repair truck remind you that people must live somewhere nearby.

Shortly after passing the Errol town line, a bridge crosses the river on the right. Snowmobile tracks lead off to either side here: to the east, the trail leads to rte. 26; west, it goes by several cold-water ponds to Signal Mt. with its tower. There are also several pull-overs along the river, where you might want to stop and tailgate or fish, although a full-fledged picnic area appears two and a half miles north of the bridge.

Another couple of miles north is the Mollidgewock Campground along the river, a good place to launch a canoe. And ahead through the balsams and hemlocks, you'll begin to see signs of civilization — starting with a sign proclaiming the village of **Errol.** The town has one place to eat, simply called THE ERROL RESTAURANT, 603/482-3352, and a combination gift and sports (spell that g-u-n) shop, as well as a motel. On the east end of town (just past where rte. 16 heads north to Rangeley, Maine), SACO BOUND, 603/447-2177 or -3002, will rent you a canoe or a kayak. *From town, you can go west on rte. 26 toward Dixville Notch, page 172, or head east into Maine through Grafton Notch, page 177.*

302 — CUTTING ACROSS THE HEART OF THE MOUNTAINS

Rte. 302, which comes into North Conway to link up with 16, offers an historic route that remains largely uncommercial from Glen west. For skiers, this road leads to both ATTITASH and BRETTON WOODS. Fishermen will find numerous streams and ponds within the White Mountain National Forest. Bikers have far less traffic to contend with than on 16, and hikers will delight in countless trails up the Presidentials or into the Pemigewasset Wilderness. Without any of that, we highly recommend this route for its beauty.

302 diverges from 16 at Glen, page 96, and heads west. It is accessible in the summer from the Kancamagus Highway via Bear Notch Rd. (closed in snow), or from the West Side Rd. in Bartlett, making it an attractive alternative for shunpikers impatient with outlet mall traffic.

Glen is about as commercial as it gets on this section of 302, offering gas stations, a reasonably-sized grocery store, state liquor store, and a hardware store. There is also a large choice of restaurants here (as many in Glen as you may encounter on the rest of the route to Twin Mountain). On the right just past the junction with 16 is GLEN CORNER, 603/383-9660, a clean and efficient place for breakfast or lunch year-round, and dinner in the summer. A model train clatters above you as it circles the room; the waitress is prompt with coffee and keeps your cup filled.

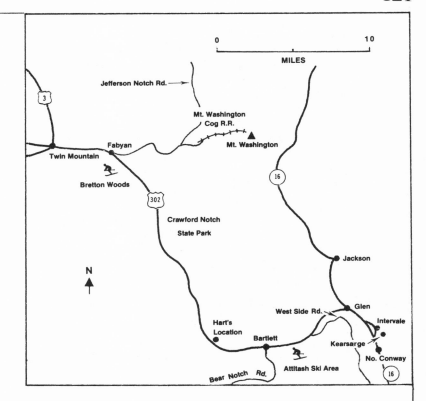

ROUTE 302

For those who like boisterous informality, big screen TV, good beef, an impressive salad bar, and lumberman-sized drinks, the RED PARKA PUB, 603/383-4344 is the place to go. Look for the RED PARKA sign down the hill from the liquor store. After crossing the Ellis River, you'll see another popular spot on the right, MARGARITAVILLE, 603/383-6556. *(Handicapped access; one step).* Since this Tex-Mex restaurant does not take reservations, it may be necessary to wait for a table, but the bar with its variety of beers as well as Margaritas helps the time pass quickly. Excellent hamburgers, chicken and avocado salad, deep-fried catfish, or Mexican chicken wings, plus carefully prepared regional standards: flautas, fajitas, burritos, tostadas, and tacos.

Without question one of our favorite places to dine here (or anywhere else in the White Mountains) is THE BERNERHOF INN, 603/383-4414, just across Rocky Branch on the right. Currently expanding, this old reliable restaurant focuses on seasonal foods with a European flavor: in summer, a fish terrine or a Chevre cheese tarte might be offered for starters; in the fall, you can enjoy a hearty, tomato-based seafood soup seasoned with aioli and homemade croutons. Veal is delicious here, but entrees also include tender roast lamb presented in a semicircle of slices around a mustard/mint sauce, fettucini with winter vegetables, fondue Bernese, or salmon served with shrimp in wine and scallions.

Note to the handicapped: We have indicated where a facility is clearly equipped for the special needs of the handicapped — usually state visitor centers. Many restaurants will say they have handicapped access, only there may be a "step or two" between the parking lot and the dining room. Needless to say, this can be very frustrating to those in wheelchairs. Because handicapped access remains subjective, we suggest that you call ahead, asking specifically: 1) How many steps are there between the parking lot and the dining room; and 2) How wide are the doors to the dining room and rest rooms?

The Maine Independent Living Center (MILC), in Augusta, 207/622-5434, has put out a directory of handicapped-equipped inns and restaurants throughout the state. Each establishment in the directory was personally inspected, with the needs of the handicapped in mind. Unfortunately, there were only two places reviewed in our area of coverage, and neither warranted mention in this book. MILC plans to issue a more complete directory in the fall; there is no handicapped access directory in New Hampshire.

The wine list offers a wide range of California and Austrian vintages; desserts are as tempting as the rest of the menu (ice cream topped with Kirsh, meringue stars, and cherries; or puff pastry shells filled with ice cream and topped with chocolate sauce). The small dining rooms seem elegant in their simplicity. *Reservations required; cooking school on the premises.*

A half mile further, the West Side Rd. comes in on the left, and The Covered Bridge Shoppe is on the right. The Saco River flows swiftly here (and should not be attempted in this area except by expert canoeists). Further along on the right, down below 302, are the riding rings and jumps for the Mt. Washington Valley Equine Classic, a major riding competition held every summer.

ATTITASH, Where the US Ski Team Trains

Next, you'll see ATTITASH SKI RESORT, 603/374-2368 or outside NH: 1-800/258-0316 (snow report only), a modern complex of condos, chalets, inns, and restaurants. In winter, the road is apt to be crowded here, but thanks to a limited lift-ticket policy, the slopes shouldn't be. *Weekend and holiday tickets may be reserved through Ticketron: 1-800/383-8080.* Terrain that meets very specific conditions makes ATTITASH one of two places in these mountains where our Olympic skiers can train. *Ski and race camps for juniors and adults; Outward Bound mini-courses in winter: 1-800/341-1744 or 207/594-5548. Atomic Ski Giveaway every Wednesday; ski shop, ski school and children's program, nursery. Interchangeable mid-week, non-holiday packages (children 12 and under can ski free with certain restrictions when a parent buys a 5-day ticket).* In summer, those who like thrills can cool off on the waterslides or Alpine Slide here.

Another two and a half miles brings you into **Bartlett**, a refreshingly rural change from the highly developed towns to the south. Yankee directness is evident at the Bartlett General Store, where a sign warns: "All shoplifters will be cheerfully beaten to a pulp." *In the middle of town, Bear Notch Rd. goes off to the left, leading to the Kancamagus Highway (Chapter IV); it's important, however, to know that this road is not maintained in winter.*

> The summer of 1826 saw a terrible drought in the mountains, broken at the end of August by torrential rains. The Saco River rose 24 feet, flooding all the valley land between Crawford Notch and Conway. In Bartlett trees, pigs, sheep, even a house were swept away. For some years afterward, the mountains remained naked and gray.

Modest bed and breakfast inns and ski dorms accommodate seasonal visitors, who expand the town's 1700 year-round population to 8000. THE NEW BARTLETT HOTEL, 603/374-2319, is the largest building in town, with 40 turn-of-the-century rooms. HEBERT'S, located here in the hotel, specializes in fresh seafood.

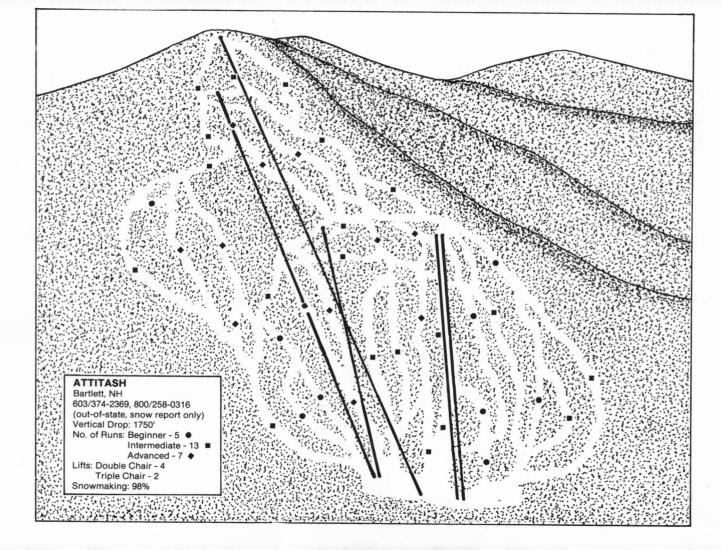

ATTITASH
Bartlett, NH
603/374-2369, 800/258-0316
(out-of-state, snow report only)
Vertical Drop: 1750'
No. of Runs: Beginner - 5 ●
Intermediate - 13 ■
Advanced - 7 ◆
Lifts: Double Chair - 4
Triple Chair - 2
Snowmaking: 98%

North of town, 302 quickly enters wilderness with pretty views to the right. Except for an occasional campground and store, like Silver Springs on the right, the only signs of civilization here are the highway and railroad, which cuts through the notch high above. Shortly after entering *Hart's Location* township and the National Forest, look for Sawyer Rock picnic area on the left; then Mt. Tremont and Rob Brook Trails in another mile.

About a half mile past the bridge with an old trestle bridge to the right, 302 begins to climb and scenic vistas appear. There are numerous places to pull over and look or park for hiking. **Nancy Pond Trail** is on the left across from a good-sized parking area on the right by the railroad tracks. An 8 1/2 mile round-trip past some falls and several ponds for trout fishing, the dam makes a popular destination for a day hike and a fine place to picnic. *The trail leaves the valley by a complex combination of logging roads, climbing steeply to the falls after a couple of miles. Next, the trail gets very steep and can be rough going, although it eventually flattens out through lovely woods, some of the last stands of virgin forest left in the White Mountains.*

The "Nancy" of the Nancy Brook and Pond was a serving girl to Col. Whipple, who lived outside Jefferson in Revolutionary days. She was in love with a farmhand, who was in love withher earnings. More generous than wise, Nancy entrusted him with her life savings, which he stole. Despite December snow and a biting wind, she followed him two days later, only to meet her death here in the Notch.

Continue past a bog, Nancy Pond, Little Norcross Pond, and finally Big Norcross Pond to a natural dam at its far end. From here you can look west across the Pemigewasset Wilderness to the Franconia Range. While the trail continues into the wilderness with connections to other trails, we recommend returning the way you came.

A mile north is THE NOTCHLAND INN, 603/374-6131, long an outpost of civilization here. The public is welcome for dinner any evening at 7:30 as long as you let the Bernadins know you're coming. Although Pat cooks primarily for overnight guests, her meals are worth planning a trip around: there are two choices of soup, three appetizers, and entrees ranging from sausage or seafood in puff pastry to roast veal, deliciously light sole or catfish, stuffed tenderloin or Cajun-style chicken. The dessert cart includes chocolate mousse and fresh fruit tarts; wine and coffees accompany each meal. Whether here for the night or just for dinner, guests can relax in front of an open fire in the living room (an old map of the mountains is painted on the floor showing important points of interest — including this inn); hiking and cross-country trails are within an easy walk on the property.

Crawford Notch

One of the loveliest of mountain passes, Crawford Notch takes its name from the family who settled here and kept the first inns. Abel and his son Ethan Allen Crawford were legendary figures, whose hospitality and exploits served as anecdotes in the writings of famous 18th-century travelers. But the first man through Crawford Notch was Timothy Nash, out hunting moose. Supposedly he climbed a tree to get the lay of the land and saw instead a break in the mountains. Reporting to Governor Wentworth on his discovery of a land route from the coast to the rich Connecticut River Valley, Nash was challenged to prove his story by leading a horse through the narrow, rugged notch — somehow he did so and won himself a township.

> "...the wind comes down through the narrows of the Notch with such violence that it requires two men to hold one man's hair on," according to Ethan Allan Crawford. But he also said, "I have never found it to blow so hard here [in the valley] as to equal this, yet it has blown so hard as to take loaded sleighs and carry then several rods to a stone wall, which was frozen... so firmly that it was impenetrable, and there the sleigh stopped."

In 1792 Abel Crawford had built himself a hut in the notch, later moving south, just across from THE NOTCHLAND INN. With his son Ethan, Crawford cut the first trail to Mt. Washington and advertised it in newspapers. Hawthorne, Emerson, Starr King, Daniel Webster, English travel writer Harriet Martineau, geologist Sir Charles Lyell, Franklin Pierce, and Henry David Thoreau stayed either with Abel or his sons.

Nearby, look on the right for the **Davis Path** (*permit needed for hiking*) built by Abel Crawford's son-in-law when he took over the tavern here. Fifteen miles long, crossing Montalban Ridge, the early sections of this trail make a good all-day family outing, with several natural stopping points en route. *Begin the Davis Path at the suspension bridge a quarter mile north of NOTCHLAND INN, crossing through private land. Continue straight east, ignoring other paths which lead to homes here. After about .3 mile the trail joins an old logging road, then .8 mile from 302 meets Davis' carefully-graded bridle path, ascending the steep ridge. At 2.3 miles from the highway, the trail forks left to climb* **Mt. Crawford,** *a bare, peaked summit with splendid views of the notch, valleys, and surrounding peaks. From here the main trail takes you through pleasant, gently rolling terrain for a mile and a half to a path to* **Resolution Shelter** (*an open camp for 8*).

> Resolution Shelter is so well protected that a group overnighting here in the Great Hurricane of 1938 thought they were dealing with just another steady rain.

CRAWFORD NOTCH STATE PARK

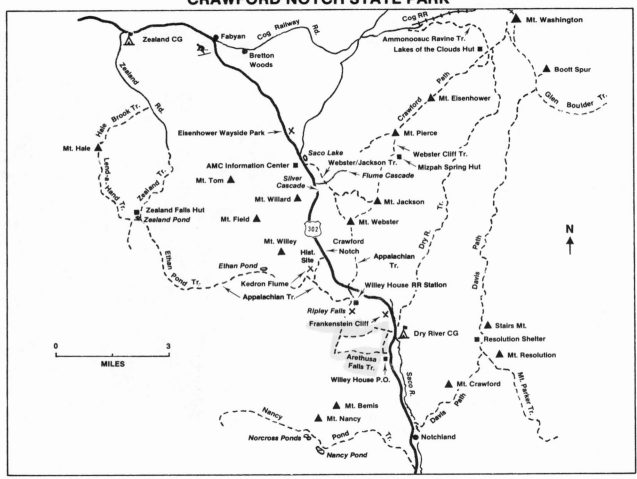

*Turn right on the Parker Trail for a half mile to the open ledges on Mt. Resolution's summit. The Davis Path leads on more steeply to the top of Stairs Mountain and eventually to the "top step" of **Giant Stairs** with a wonderful view.*

> Like the precipitous steps that a drunken giant might make, Giant Stairs was favored by 19th-century romantic poets as a place of inspiration.

While prepared, experienced hikers might want to press on to Glen Boulder, Boott Spur, Lakes of the Clouds Hut, and eventually the Mt. Washington summit, we recommend returning the way you came. The round-trip to Giant Stairs can take 6 or 7 hours.

The U-shaped valley that is Crawford Notch was cut into the rock during the Ice Age. Under conditions then prevalent here (now present in Alaska and Greenland), more snow fell every winter than melted in summer. For centuries snow accumulated — reaching a depth of thousands of feet in the notch. From its own weight, the snow turned to ice and crept slowly from higher to lower elevations, tearing rock from ledges, carving out ravines, hollowing out cirques, and smoothing the sides of cliffs — all at the rate of a few inches or feet each year. Crawford Notch is a fine example of a cirque — a half-bowl valley, scoured by glacial action.

> Pioneers expected the first snowfall here in Crawford Notch around November first; it stopped snowing about the first of April, with an average of 6 feet falling yearly. When Abel Crawford and his in-laws, the Rosebrooks, first settled in the Notch, winter snow made the 12 miles that separated them impassable, except by sleigh. One year the snow was so deep, the Rosebrooks couldn't get to the mill for 6 weeks.
>
> "To appreciate fully the necessity there was for. . . shelter, one should pass through the Notch in the depth of winter. The roads are then buried beneath the snow, piled up in drifts to a great depth. This is continually blown about by the wind so as to render impassable a well-beaten path. The traveler has frequently, shovel in hand, to work his way through the mountains," wrote Benjamin Willey in 1856.

Two Falls and a Flume

Past the Crawford Notch General Store and Camping are pullovers on both sides of 302. Before you know it, the road has entered the state park with perhaps more beautiful falls, hikes, and scenic vistas than any other part of the White Mountains. Look for **Arethusa Falls** ahead on the left, a popular, easy hike. *A paved road leads uphill to a parking area. Beyond the railroad tracks is a cottage, known as the Willey House Post Office. Look for the trail on the far side of the tracks to the left of the cottage.*

Frankenstein Cliff, named for a White Mountain painter rather than that character Boris Karloff portrayed on film, dominates the northern view along the railroad tracks above 302. *It's possible to climb the trail to the falls in street clothes, but we recommend hiking shoes and comfortable clothing if you plan to do the three-and-a-half to four-hour loop around the cliff.*

The trail descends gradually to Bemis Brook, which can be crossed on boulders. As the path gets rough, you can see the falls, the highest in New Hampshire at just over 200 feet. *Those prepared for a more strenuous workout can continue through the spruces to the Arethusa-Ripley Falls Trail toward the cliff, swinging left over a ridge and up between trees lining a small stream on the right. Turn north again as you cross the brook and climb more steeply to a right fork a mile above the falls. The trail to the right goes to the cliff, descending easterly to a glacier-smoothed dome. Skirting the north side of the ledge, the trail gives various views of the cliff (the best view comes about a half hour past the Arethusa-Ripley Falls junction).*

Not only can you see the head of Arethusa Falls and tiny cars on 302, but the vista of the White Mountains also sweeps beneath you. *On your way down, the trail can be hard to find. Avoid the straight, easy path. Keep to the right, descending among ledges between small maples and beeches. There are switchbacks here in the hardwoods, faintly marked with axe blazes and faded yellow paint (you want to go north under more cliffs). The descent is steep before you turn right and scramble over rocks. The gravel can be dangerous — be careful! In the final descent you walk through open woods and then under the girders of Frankenstein Trestle. The trail forks right at a sign down a moderate grade for a half mile back to the parking area.*

There have been approximately 100 fatalities among hikers in the Presidential Range. The first occurred in the late fall of 1851 when a young Englishman, Frederick Strickland who was staying at Notch House, decided to climb Mt. Washington, even though snow covered the slopes. He apparently fell several times, because the search party found his body badly mangled and scratched, lying face down in a little stream.

About a half mile ahead, you'll see Dry River Campground and Trail on the right (leading through Oakes Gulf for a 7 or 8-hour hike to Lakes of the Clouds Hut). Then in another half mile, a picnic area appears on the left before the bridge.

Through-hikers, people walking the Appalachian Trail its entire length from Maine to Georgia or vice-versa, find the steep pitches of the White Mountains here in New Hampshire and Maine among the hardest climbs they have to make. Nevertheless, many people have hiked the entire 2100 miles in less than a year. Grandma Gatewood through-hiked when she was in her seventies; Warren Doyle has hiked the AT seven times (sometimes wearing a headlamp at night).

You'll see signs for the Appalachian Trail with connections on the east side of 302 to a 6-hour hike up Webster Cliff (see AMC White Mountain Guide for the trail that eventually leads up to the Mizpah Spring Hut). On the west side of the highway, the Appalachian Trail leads past Ethan Pond to Zealand Pond for excellent fishing.

In .2 miles, look for **Ripley Falls** parking on the right. A 20-minute hike each way, this 100-foot cascade is a cool place to relax on a hot day.

At Willeys

A mile further north on 302 brings you to the **Willey House Historical Site,** where an avalanche of mud wiped out one family of pioneers. Mt. Willey, northwest of Kedron Brook (and behind the buildings here), still shows the scars of that massive mud slide. *Snack bar and general store, New Hampshire Made Products, and State Tourist Center behind the parking area on the left. Additional parking on the right where the Saco River broadens.*

The same drought/deluge of 1826 that wreaked havoc in Bartlett and the rest of the valley brought about terrible devastation here at Willey's. From the diary that Ethan Allan Crawford is said to have dictated to his wife Lucy: "We were awakened by our little one coming into the room and saying, 'Father, the earth is nearly covered with water, and the hogs are swimming for life.' I arose immediately and went to their rescue. . . . What a sight! The sun rose clear; not a cloud nor a vapor was to be seen; all was still and silent excepting the rushing sound of the water as it poured down the hills. . . . The whole intervale was covered with water a distance of over two hundred acres of land. . . . The water came within eighteen inches of the door in the house and a strong current was running between the house and the stable."

Although worried about his neighbors, the Willeys, Ethan could find no way to reach them. Later, he swam out to a traveler on horseback, who had found the Willey home deserted — with only a dog to greet him. Apparently frightened, the Willeys had left the safety of their home. "There came a large slide down back of the house in a direction to take the house with it, when within ten or fifteen rods of the house, it came against a solid ledge of rock and there stopped and separated, one on either side of the house, taking the stable on one side, and the family on the other." Eventually, a search party discovered the terribly mangled bodies of the Willey family, buried by the slide. Had they remained at home, ironically, they would have survived.

Children tired of sitting in the car may enjoy a walk around the pond and the wildlife exhibit across the highway from Willey House Site. There's also a short, somewhat challenging hike up to **Kedron Flume** that leads from picnic tables behind the buildings on the left side of 302. Allow one and a half to two hours for a round-trip; 600' vertical. *The hike is easy for the first .2 mile to the railroad tracks, then it steepens, turning to the left as it climbs. Continue through beech woods to spruces, where the trail bends, then dips into a ravine at Kedron Brook.* In addition to a brook pouring down a narrow sluice, this hike rewards you with an outlook across the Notch to Webster Cliff and the Presidentials' southern peaks behind.

Be careful of wet, slippery rocks at the flume; use caution descending the steep slope — gravel tends to roll underfoot.

Even if you never leave your car or bike, there are impressive views from Willey's. To the right are the cliffs of Mt. Webster, named for Daniel; Mt. Willard looms ahead on the left. *The grade steepens with a passing lane. In another .7 mile, there's a parking area on the left. Look to your right for Silver Cascade and the Flume Cascade — especially impressive after spring thaw.*

As you leave the park, you'll see more parking and trailheads. To hike Mt. Willard — a rewarding summit on a clear day — look for the trailhead on the left, behind the railroad tracks. Nearby is the Crawford Depot, now an AMC Information Center. The Webster/ Jackson Trail goes off to the right. Children might enjoy the very short walk along this last path to **Elephant Head,** a gray ledge with veins of white quartz that, indeed, does resemble a pachyderm.

Fishermen may prefer to use the small parking area below **Saco Lake** on the right — look for brookies here where the river begins. And hikers will appreciate the **Crawford Notch Hostel** past the depot on the left. *Inexpensive self-service lodging year-round; reservations encouraged. Hikers need to bring their own food and sleeping bags; the hostel provides stoves and cooking equipment. For information on this and other AMC hut schedules, write Reservation Secretary, Pinkham Notch Camp, Box 298, Gorham, NH 03581.*

Two-tenths of a mile ahead on the left is the Crawford House Site, where Abel Crawford's son Thomas kept an inn, known as Notch House, later to be replaced with Crawford House, one of the many huge Victorian inns in this area. Across 302 is the Crawford Path, part of the AT and blazed in white. Probably the oldest footpath in continuous use in the country, the trail can be dangerous in places if the weather is bad. Don't attempt the Crawford Path without a compass, foul-weather gear, and a good map. Be especially careful on the ledges below Mt. Eisenhower and on the cone of Mt. Washington past Lake of the Clouds Hut.

The footpath up Mt. Pierce was cut by Abel and Ethan Allan Crawford in 1819; later Thomas converted it into a bridle path for horse travel. A cutoff today leads to the Mizpah Spring Hut (approximately an hour-and-a-half's hike into this shelter). To the southern end of Mt. Eisenhower takes close to three hours; four to Mt. Franklin's summit; nearly five hours to Lakes of the Clouds Hut; and 6 hours MINIMUM to Mt. Washington's summit. This trail is recommended only **for experienced, prepared hikers.**

The flat ridge here makes for excellent biking. In another mile and a half, you'll see Eisenhower Wayside Park with several picnic tables, but no camping. Pointed firs are mixed with deciduous trees along this route. About a mile and a half past the wayside, look for a sign showing you all the Presidential Range.

In November, 1807 English travel writer Edward Augustus Kendall, Esq. visited the White Mountains. Coming south from Conway, he took the "new turnpike" from Crawford Notch to "Briton's Woods" in the shadow of Mount Washington.

Briton's Woods

Soon you'll catch a glimpse of bright red roofs and a huge gleaming white building. THE MOUNT WASHINGTON HOTEL, 603/278-1000, is almost as impressive as New England's highest peak just behind it. Recently purchased by a Boston development company, this palatial 225-room "grand hotel" will be winterized, modernized, and hopefully restored to its former elegance. At present the 2500 acre resort in **Bretton Woods** offers plenty of summer-time amenities: tennis, golf, horseback riding; dining by reservation, big band orchestras. Open May – October at this writing.

At one time as many as 50 railroad cars a day would bring guests here to while away their summers, far removed from the hectic pace of Philadelphia or New York. In 1944 the hotel hosted the Bretton Woods Monetary Conference, that established the American dollar as the standard of international currency exchange. There's a small museum in the hotel's conference room.

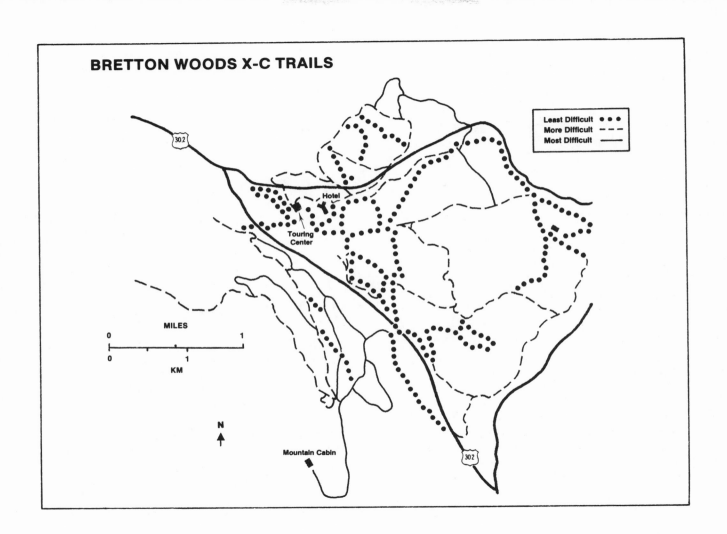

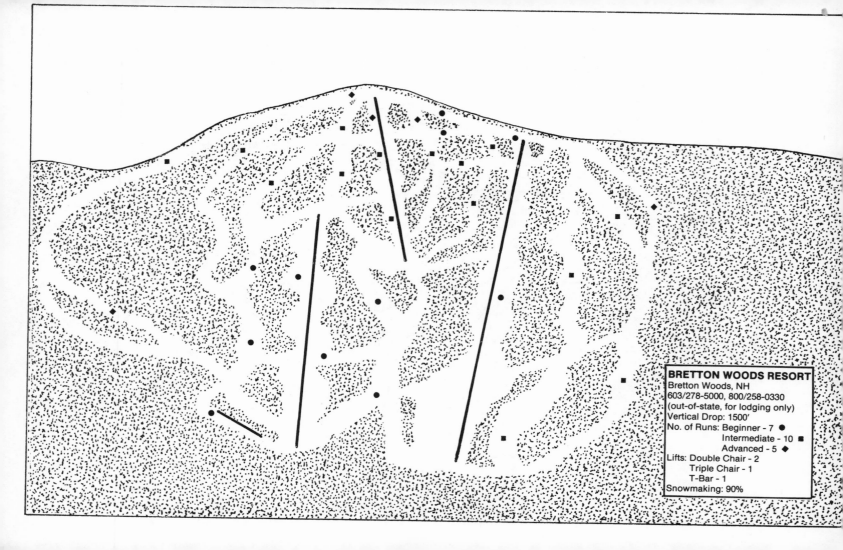

BRETTON WOODS RESORT
Bretton Woods, NH
603/278-5000, 800/258-0330
(out-of-state, for lodging only)
Vertical Drop: 1500'
No. of Runs: Beginner - 7 ●
Intermediate - 10 ■
Advanced - 5 ◆
Lifts: Double Chair - 2
Triple Chair - 1
T-Bar - 1
Snowmaking: 90%

On your left is THE LODGE AT BRETTON WOODS, 603/278-1500, a more contemporary inn for year-round dining and lodging. DARBY'S RESTAURANT here serves fresh swordfish, chicken teriyaki, brook trout almondine, veal picatta, or filet mignon daily. Then a half mile further north on 302 is the BRETTON WOODS Ski Area, 603/278-5000 or 1-800-258-0330 (outside NH, lodging only). One of the largest cross-country facilities in the East, BRETTON WOODS has three interconnected trail systems with 100 km of trails, most of them double-tracked, as well as a low-key downhill facility.

90 percent snowmaking on a largely intermediate mountain. Limited ticket policy with advance ticket sales weekends and holidays; rentals. Children five and under ski free at the T-bar anytime; frequent skier program and plenty of special rates, including senior's and beginner's rates. Night skiing downhill and moonlit cross-country tours; 50-meter biathlon range. Usual lodges, snack bars, nurseries and ski schools.

Railroading was not yet 30 years old when Campton's Sylvester Marsh petitioned the New Hampshire legislature for a charter to build a track up Mt. Washington. Despite great ridicule, Marsh only became more determined. In 1865 he organized the Mt. Washington Steam Railway; every piece of equipment and supplies had to be hauled by oxen from Littleton. Two years later, the first track was laid; in 1868 the trestle known as Jacob's Ladder was built. In 1869 Ulysses S. Grant became the first US president to reach Mt. Washington's summit, via Marsh's Cog Railway.

On the right, you'll see signs for *The Cog Railroad*. If you haven't been to the Mt. Washington summit before, you may want to try this 19th-century mode of ascent (some hikers ride up, then walk down). *Allow three and a half to four hours for the round-trip on the Cog; expensive. Call 603/846-5404 for information or reservations. Operates May – October, weather permitting.* For committed, experienced hikers who'd rather walk than ride, the base of the Cog is also a trailhead.

Just beyond the Cog Railway Rd., you can get a bite to eat at FABYAN'S STATION, an old train depot turned into an attractive restaurant, 603/846-2222. Railroading paraphernalia and wonderful old prints of the Presidentials line the walls; woodstoves warm the room. Cleverly-named sandwiches, juicy burgers, crisp salads (like spinach with apple slices and bacon) are lunch offerings; shrimp wrapped in bacon for starters or scampi for an entree, along with steaks or veal and pasta dishes, make for casual evening dining.

Sidetrip: **Toward the Cog.** *Turn right by the trestle bridge to the Cog Railroad. You'll pass townhouses on the left and plenty of ski trails. In a couple of miles, you'll see fishermen by the bridge (both brook and rainbow trout here). Further ahead, look for the Jefferson Notch Rd., — hikers may want to turn left, as will anyone heading north to rte. 2. You can hike the Caps Ridge Trail up Mt. Jefferson, and if you'd like to make a loop along Castle Trail, leave a second car in Bowman, several miles east of the Jefferson Notch Rd., off rte. 2.*

Caps Ridge Trail. While Jefferson Notch Rd. does much of the climb for you, this is still a demanding hike straight up the western shoulder of the mountain; vertical rise is 2715′ with some difficult footing in the upper sections. The ridge itself is above tree level and very exposed, so be prepared; only older children should attempt this hike because of the distance between steps. Allow a good three hours one-way to Jefferson's summit, another two if you want to push to Mt. Washington.

From the Cog Railway Rd., turn left on Jefferson Notch Rd. driving between three and four miles north to the trailhead on the right with a parking area nearby. This is a steady climb with some scrambling over rocks, which may be slippery in some places. One mile up is an outcrop of granite on your right with views of where you'll be hiking. 100 yards ahead is the link with the Castle Trail for those wanting to return that way. Caps Ridge continues to climb, reaching the lowest caps in another half mile, around 4400′. The trail is open from here on with splendid views of the Great Gulf. (There is a shortcut to Castle Trail on the left in another .6 mile, but this is a very rough trail.) Caps Ridge continues east to Jefferson's summit; go down about 40 yds. for the Six Husbands Trail, leading to a junction with Gulfside Trail toward Mt. Washington, and Castle Trail which is narrow and rocky from here (return to the link trail, mentioned above).

Sidetrip: **Cog Railroad.** As you continue east on the Cog road, you'll see places to park for other trails, then the base parking area at the Railroad.

Old Peppersass, the original locomotive on the Cog Railroad, has been retired to the parking lot, but little else about the Cog has noticeably changed. On its initial run, a Boston JOURNAL reporter wrote: "I stopped the train myself on descending with one thumb and finger, with no more effort than if I had been taking a pinch of snuff." Today the Cog remains the world's slowest, but safest, railroad.

Several trails leave from here (see map, pg. 109.) The Ammonoosuc Ravine Trail (close to four miles, allow four and a half to five hours) begins behind the Cog Railroad Gift Shop. In combination with parts of the Crawford Path, this is the shortest route up or down. *Don't attempt this trail without backpack #2 (see introduction); unsuitable for younger children. Because of fragile plant life on the mountain's upper elevations, hikers are asked to stay on trails.*

For those taking the slow trip up, *there's a museum, snack bar, gift shop, even overnight cabins. Because soot can leak into the train, you may want to bring a handkerchief or Kleenex along, so you don't have to breathe the black smoke.* Patience is required for the Cog, but the views are well worth your effort. Wildflowers, lichens, and ferns provide interest on the first leg of the trip up to Waumbek Tank. Then the valley opens up behind. To your right is the Ammonoosuc Ravine, where the river begins; on the left, you'll see Burt Ravine, named for the editor of a daily summer newspaper, AMONG THE CLOUDS, that used to be published from the summit.

> "My name is Bill," says a youth with a soot-blackened face, "I'll be your brakeman for today." If you're on one of the trains going to the top of Mt. Washington, you soon realize why this crewmember/guide looks like an old-time minstrel performer. Don't worry though, all the soot will blow off when you reach the summit.

As your train continues toward Halfway House, 4000', the Presidentials become more distinct on the left, and you may see hikers on a trail there. Lakes of the Clouds Hut appears along the skyline on your right. If it's spring or even early summer, you may see patches of snow here in the higher elevations of Mt. Washington. The vegetation becomes shorter, as the train climbs.

Perhaps the most exciting part of the Cog ride begins at Jacob's Ladder, where the grade is as steep as it is anywhere. Try standing in the aisle — your body will form an acute angle from the floor.

> The normal grade for most railroads is two or three degrees; on Jacob's Ladder, it is 37 degrees.

As the last twisted trees disappear and only lichens, grasses, and blaze marks color the landscape, you get a good view of both Jefferson and Adams on the left, then the Mt. Washington Observatory on the right.

> Under the leadership of surveyor Bradford Washburn, former Director of Boston's Museum of Science, the precise elevation of Mt. Washington's summit has been established at 6288.176'. Perhaps more important to most of us, the survey led to a new map of the mountain. *Available for $7.95 from the AMC or Museum of Science.* Ten years in the making, the map was made possible through aerial photos and surveys, as well as field work and laser sightings.

The crew may stop the train to switch tracks in what may be the most complicated railroad ritual going: 9 switches to transfer track a few feet so that a train going up can't collide with one coming down. Stone cairns stand like lonely sentinels, enlivened only by passing hikers. Huge, billowy clouds meet you at eye level. By Gulf Tank, you can pick out Madison's peak on the left. Then the rocky plateau of the summit, made even more bizarre by its collection of weather equipment, appears.

At the summit, you may only have 15 minutes to admire the views, if trains have been delayed on the day of your visit. Nevertheless, the sights are breathtaking, and in the summer, restrooms, a snack bar, a museum, and even a post office are open.

Back on rte. 302 heading west, you'll see Cherry Mt. Rd. on your right. This sometimes narrow road becomes a snowmobile trail in winter and leads to hiking trails up Cherry Mt. The Dartmouth Range (Mt. Dartmouth, 3727', and Mt. Deception, 3671') on the right side of the road has no trails.

> Deception was named by one of the Crawfords' lady guests who, on attempting to climb this mountain, found it a more difficult hike than its appearance had originally led her to believe. Her female companions did reach the summit, however, and described a delightful view of the valley.

Zealand

We recommend that hikers continue driving a little further on 302 to Zealand Rd., on the left just past **Zealand Campground.** *Tents and trailers; picnic facilities.* The Ammonoosuc and Zealand Rivers as well as Zealand Pond are good for trout-fishing; in addition, there are numerous hiking trails in this area. One exhilarating day-hike, that includes lunch at an AMC hut, climbs up Mt. Hale. *If you can, leave a car two and a half miles down Zealand Rd. on the right by the Hale Brook Trail sign, and continue another mile or so to the Zealand Trail parking area. (For those without two cars, the distance is relatively short between these two trailheads; a cool-down walk along Zealand Rd.'s relatively flat surface will be a pleasant way to end a good workout.) On a hot summer's day, this hike is very refreshing, especially if you wear a bathing suit under your clothes for swimming at Zealand Falls.*

The Zealand Trail begins easily enough, following a railroad grade, with a bypass that's a bit rougher. Returning to the grade, the trail approaches a stream that will become the Zealand River. *Continue on the west bank to the first of several brook crossings at 1.5 miles.* The trail passes through an area where beavers have diverted water into broad pools.

> In June, the magenta blooms of rhodora add color here. Look for insect-eating sundew plants along the water's edge.

At 2.3 miles from the trailhead, the A-Z Trail enters left, while Zealand Trail skirts Zealand Pond, a nice place to fish. In .2 mile, there's another junction; continue straight ahead on Ethan Pond Trail to Zealand Falls Hut, approximately two hours' hike from the trailhead. The trail becomes steep just below the hut.

There are lovely, icy pools for summer bathing at **Zealand Falls**, and the hut makes a nice place to picnic. From the porch, you have a marvelous view through Zealand Notch to Mt. Carrigain. *Open summer and fall with his and her bunkrooms and "crappers," not unlike latrines at summer camps.* The two-and-a-half mile **Lend-a-Hand Trail** connects the hut with the summit of **Mt. Hale,** a fairly easy climb with some rough footing.

The trail diverges right or north from Twinway Trail .1 mile above the hut, climbing steadily and crossing a small brook several times. Eventually the grade eases, but footing may be difficult over brooks. After 1.5 miles, Lend-a-Hand brings you to a scrubby ledge area, then climbs. In .4 mile there's a nice view from the rock about 15 yards on the right. A half mile further the trail climbs another rocky pitch before continuing through dense woods to Hale's summit.

> Hobblebush, easily distinguishable in spring by its pretty white flowers, is a hiker's friend. Its soft, broad leaves are nature's form of toilet paper.

Twin Mountain

Back on 302, you'll see another campground on the left. *Tents and trailers welcome; fishing and hiking.* Then in another mile, the road leaves the White Mountain National Forest. A stoplight ahead signals your arrival in downtown **Twin Mountain.**

> Your compass may only confuse you on the Lend-a-Hand Trail; many of the rocks here are magnetic.

Looking across Zealand Notch you may be able to pick out Whitewall Mt., burned to bedrock by a forest fire in 1886 along with 12,000 acres and much of the logging industry outside Lincoln. In 1903 another fire devastated 10,000 acres in the Zealand Valley; the growth you see here may seem miraculous. Between Carrigain and Washington, you can spot Mts. Lowell, Anderson, Nancy, and Bemis beginning at Carrigain Notch. Then past the Pemigewasset Wilderness are Mts. Willey, Field, and Tom with Jackson beyond.

Continue north on the loop from the summit to Hale Brook Trail for a two-and-a-half-hour descent to the first parking area. This trail is quite easy with good footing, passing through a birch forest much of the way.

Even at the intersection of rtes. 3 and 302, the only two important roads anywhere around, don't expect a traffic jam, for the town of Twin Mountain has chosen to remain undeveloped — no condos, upscale shops, or ski areas to attract "flatlanders." The views are the best thing about this area — a great spot for a quick look is from the bandstand, where many local weddings have taken place. The town also boasts an airport, a rarity here in the heart of the mountains.

You need to decide if you want to continue west on 302 through the interesting community of Bethlehem and on to Littleton and I-93, with connections to Vermont and Canada. Anyone who's hungry would be well-advised to stay on this route, as there is little more than a grocery store in Twin Mountain.

Or you can head north on rte. 3 for more hikes, another state park, the Connecticut River Valley, and eventually the North Country. Just turn right onto rte. 3 north, see Chapter V. We recommend 302 west or 3 south for people in a hurry, and rte. 3 north for those skiers, hikers, and fishermen who have the time to explore more notches, lakes, and resorts.

> Henry Ward Beecher, that 19th-century preacher so popular with the ladies, suffered horribly from hay fever and summered nearby in Bethlehem. He held his tent meetings here in Twin Mountain, where people came from miles around to hear him.

Sidetrip: ***Shortcut back to I-93 south.*** *Anyone in a hurry to drive south (or anyone who hasn't visited Franconia Notch with its Old Man of the Mountain and the state park there) may prefer to turn left on rte. 3 for a shorter route. You'll pass a store and motels, then cross the Ammonoosuc before seeing the airport on your left. There are plenty of gas stations if you want to fill up before re-entering the National Forest.*

Bikers will find little traffic on rte. 3, which is good because the shoulders need resurfacing. In close to two miles, Beaver Brook Picnic Area appears on the left, as well as a National Forest Information Booth a mile further on the right. Mt. Cleveland looms to the north, with a small wayside ahead on the left. *Summer visitors may want to tune in to 1610 AM for National Forest information.*

Approximately three miles past the last picnic table, you'll see Gale River Rd. on the right, which runs west to rte. 142 and the village of Franconia, see page 29. In another .3 mile, there's parking on the left with trailheads for hikes to Mts. Garfield or Lafayette via the Skookumchuck Trail. Franconia Notch State Park and Cannon Mt. are straight ahead for more biking, hiking, or skiing.

Those who continue west on rte. 302 will find excellent trout fishing on the Ammonoosuc. Not only does this swiftly moving river run cool even in summer, but it is also relatively undiscovered above Bethlehem. The state manages and stocks the river with brook trout.

The Little Resort of Bethlehem

As 302 turns north, the highway passes through a pretty valley, marred only by occasional signs of logging. The Bethlehem Flower Farm (*open in summer*) appears on the right, then the little town of **Bethlehem.** A sign proclaims this community the "Poetry Capital of New Hampshire," and for one week, when poets from all over the country are invited to town, members of the local writers' group tack up others' work to picket fences or bulletin boards.

It was hay fever that put this town on the map in the mid-19th century. Rhode Island's governor became the first developer here after the Civil War, then notables like Presidents Grant and Cleveland sought relief in Bethlehem from the misery ragweed and pollen can bring.

> "There is nothing [in Bethlehem] which merits notice, except the patience, enterprise, and hardihood of the settlers. . . a significant prospect of the White Mountains; and a splendid collection of other mountains in their neighborhood," wrote a traveler in 1803.
>
> Actually there was a tavern here in 1800 and a number of other public houses throughout the 19th century. At one time, in its heyday as a resort, the town boasted as many as 30 hotels.

Perhaps because of its name, Bethlehem has attracted more Jews than Christians, and even today there are three hotels for Hasidics, as well as an orthodox synagogue here. In summer you're as likely to hear a Brooklyn accent in Bethlehem as a Yankee "Ayuh," but the town is more bedroom community than anything else today.

Anyone ready for a little variety will find it here. In addition to the Ranger Station on 302 with its WMNF information, you'll pass a deli/pizza parlor, an inn for feminists, a newly-restored casino, tennis courts ready for playing as well as others badly in need of repair, antique/junk shops, and a bed and breakfast inn with bells that bear no resemblance to anything Paul Revere ever cast.

In addition to the antique stores along Main St. (some of which sell genuine bargains), there are several craft studios open year-round. Roland Shick turns, carves, and even inlays wood at Ironwood Studio, while Broken Tree Studio has both native and exotic hardwood creations for sale.

ROSA FLAMINGO'S 603/869-3111, on the left side of 302 serves dinner, but the S&S PIZZA AND DELI, 603/869-5579, offers three meals a day, starting off with homemade donuts at 6 am and ending up with home-baked pies until 11 pm. The newest and most upscale restaurant in this area is LLOYD HILLS, 603/869-2141. The main street in town offers motorists unparalleled views east or west. Outside of Bethlehem, 302 connects with I-93 before arriving in **Littleton,** page 36. From here you can head south on rte. 302 or to the North Country, Chapter V.

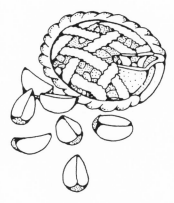

Chapter IV THE "KANC" AND THE SOUTHERN MOUNTAINS

The first three routes, described in previous chapters, offer a wealth of mountain views and explorations; however, they do not include some of the loveliest parts of the White Mountains. There is a largely non-commercial road (no gas or food is sold along its 34 miles), that connects the Saco River Valley with the Pemigewasset — the Kancamagus Highway (pronounced Kan-kuh-Mog-us, or simply called the "Kanc" by those who use it frequently). Not surprisingly, the "Kanc" or rte. 112, is considered by travel editors to be "one of America's five most scenic highways."

> Federal Forest Highway No. 8, as the "Kanc" was called when it was staked out, took 25 years to build. CCC workers started to carve the road through wilderness, but it was slow going. A supervisor reporting back to Washington in the 1930s wrote: "Quality of work: Excellent. Morale of workers: High. Progress of construction: Negligible."

There are also scenic routes through the southern ranges of the White Mountains, linking Ashland with Chocorua, and forming a pleasant loop with the "Kanc." Still other shunpikes in this chapter offer an alternate to the often-crowded rte. 16. Whether you're looking for charming colonial villages, dirt roads that seem unchanged since the early settlements, low-key skiing, or the newest wilderness area in the National Forest, you're sure to find it here.

RTE. 112, THE "KANC"

Open year-round, the Kancamagus Highway is a beautiful route through wilderness, once described as "unfit for human habitation." That perception has been turned to everyone's benefit, for residential development would have spoiled the unique communion with nature that can now be experienced here. Along rte. 112 are six well-equipped campgrounds, four picnic areas, and four scenic overlooks. Numerous hiking trails and fishing spots in the aptly-named Swift River attract those who are willing to venture further into the outdoors.

Bikers can make an enjoyable and challenging 40-mile loop, beginning on the "Kanc," climbing Bear Notch Rd., then heading east on 302, page 123, for four miles, before taking the West Side Rd., page 87, south back to Conway.

Named "the Fearless One" in Indian dialect, Kancamagus was a hot-tempered Indian chief. He was the last of the Penacook chiefs, leading a confederation of tribes in New Hampshire during the 17th century. Although Kancamagus tried to live in peace with increasing numbers of English settlers, he and his people were betrayed and humiliated by the people they had helped.

Major Richard Waldron of Dover invited the Penacooks to a feast and then seized a number of "guests," sending them to Boston in chains. The tribe fled north to Canada, seeking aid from the French; four years later, Kancamagus returned in a raid on Dover, where former "host" Waldron was chopped to pieces at his own table.

Start your drive just south of Conway, where you may find the north-bound traffic backed up, and be glad you can avoid it. Turn left or west; the **Saco Ranger Station** *is immediately on the right, and worth a visit. Open daily, year-round except Christmas and New Year's Day.* The rangers are knowledgeable about current conditions — which campgrounds are the most likely to be full or whether a snowy rte. 112 has been plowed recently — and have the information you need to individualize your visit to the White Mountain National Forest. *Free printed information and maps on hiking, cross-country ski trails, camping, flora and fauna, etc. Eagles View Nature Trail; selected publications for sale as well. Rest rooms.*

Some trees you'll see here and throughout the WMNF include pine, spruce, larch, alder, black cherry, several kinds of maples, white birch, and poplar.

As the road gradually eases out of civilization and into wilderness, rte. 112 passes an art gallery, a gift shop, and the SWIFT RIVER INN, 603/447-2332 (no meals served to the public). Following the usually turbulent Swift River, popular with white-water rafters as well as fishermen, the road passes from the bed of a glacial lake (Conway's meadows) through stands of birch, with plenty of places to pull over.

A little over a mile after entering the WMNF is a trailhead on the left for Loon Lake and White Ledge Trails. Soon you can see ledges from the road. About five miles past the Ranger Station is the Albany covered bridge, crossing the Swift River and connecting with Dugway Rd. leading back to Conway. *There is cross-country skiing near the bridge on WMNF trails (neither groomed nor patrolled, but no fee.) Covered Bridge Campground is on the right with close to 50 camp units; the smaller Blackberry Crossing Campground with a picnic area is just ahead on the left.*

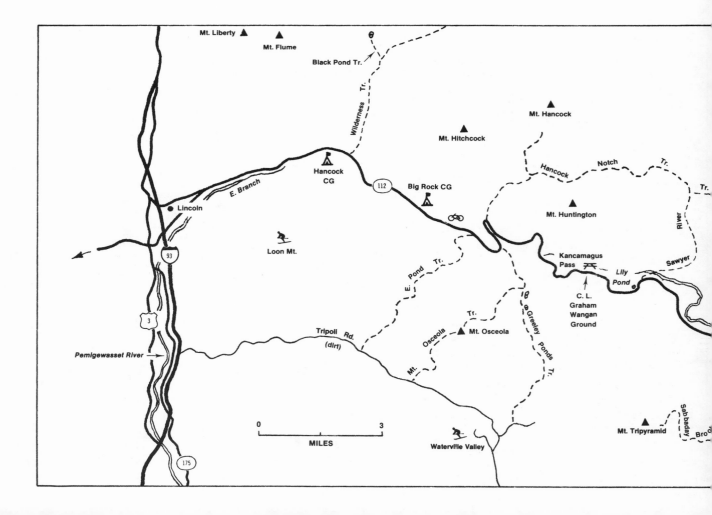

Mt. Liberty

Mt. Flume

Black Pond Tr.

Wilderness Tr.

Mt. Hancock

Mt. Hitchcock

Hancock CG

Hancock   Notch   Tr.

E. Branch

112

Big Rock CG

Tr.

Lincoln

Mt. Huntington

River

Loon Mt.

93

E. Pond Tr.

Kancamagus Pass

Lily Pond

Sawyer

C. L. Graham Wangan Ground

3

Osceola Tr.

Mt. Osceola

Greeley Ponds Tr.

Tripoli Rd. (dirt)

Pemigewasset River

Mt.

0   3

MILES

Mt. Tripyramid

Sabbaday Brook

Waterville Valley

175

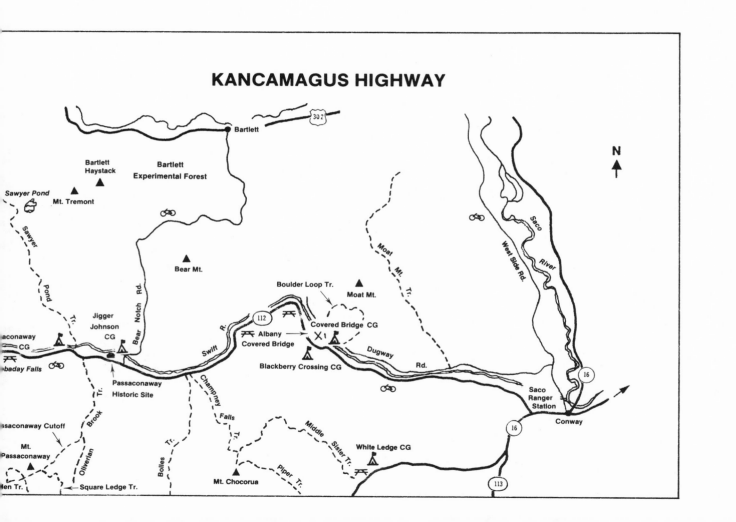

KANCAMAGUS HIGHWAY

N

Bartlett

30 2

Bartlett
Haystack

Bartlett
Experimental Forest

Mt. Tremont

Sawyer Pond

Bear Mt.

Boulder Loop Tr.

Moat Mt.

Saco River

West Side Rd.

Moat Mt. Tr.

Sawyer Pond Tr.

Bear Notch Rd.

Jigger
Johnson
CG

Swift R.

112

Covered Bridge CG

Albany
Covered Bridge

aconaway
CG

Passaconaway
Historic Site

Blackberry Crossing CG

Dugway

Rd.

16

baday Falls

Champney

Falls

Saco
Ranger
Station

Conway

aconaway Cutoff

Brook Tr.

Oliverian Tr.

Mt.
Passaconaway

Bolles Tr.

Middle Sister Tr.

White Ledge CG

16

len Tr.

Square Ledge Tr.

Mt. Chocorua

Piper Tr.

113

There's a loop trail that leaves the parking area on Dugway Rd. near Covered Bridge Campground. Although not a difficult hike, this three-hour loop is a bit of a climb, so proper hiking shoes, clothes, and back pack #1 (see introduction) are advisable. **Boulder Loop Trail** gives family hikers a wonderful view of the Passaconaway Valley with Chocorua's sharp peak beyond; spur trails leading up to ledges are more difficult and may not be suitable for young children. *Free pamphlet, available at the Ranger Station, is keyed to 16 different stops enroute.* A 30-foot rock, worn smooth by the ages and covered with lichen is one point of interest.

Moat Mt. Trail begins on the north side of Dugway Rd., further east. Because the trees along this ridge burned some years ago, the summits remain bare, offering marvelous views. The northern end comes out on West Side Rd. near the EASTERN SLOPE INN, 603/356-6321, making the Moat Trail an excellent hike for anyone spending much time in this area. *Allow 6 1/2 to 7 hours to hike the entire length to West Side Rd., see AMC WHITE MOUNTAIN GUIDE. Backpackers may be interested to know that Moat Mt. Trail also links up with the Attitash Trail.*

A half mile further west, you'll see a scenic area on the right, a popular place to swim in warm weather, even though the water's very cold. The best fishing spots are the farthest away from the highway and campgrounds, but fishermen who like to hike will be rewarded with large brook trout. *New Hampshire's Fish and Game Department keeps this river and its tributaries stocked; the time to fish here is from June 1st – July 31st.*

As you continue west, look for the trailhead on the left, connecting Champney Falls and Bolles Trails. A 9 1/2-mile loop to Chocorua's summit and a challenging all-day hike, the Champney Falls Trail makes an easy walk for .3 mile along Champney Brook to the falls — without venturing any further. *Experienced hikers may want to continue on Middle Sister Trail toward Mt. Chocorua, then take the Piper Trail to the summit, returning via Bolles Trail. Named for painter Benjamin Champney, the falls are most exciting in the spring.*

Painter Benjamin Champney was partial to this area, particularly Moat Mt.: "One learns to love its outlines and changing light and shade as the scene moves or when it is partly shadowed by the clouds, or, again, when the clouds pass over it in heavy floating masses, leaving some point visible, and others lost in charming mystery. It is a constant source of study and pleasure. In truth, Moat Mountain is perhaps quite as interesting as Mount Washington and its lofty brothers, which are seen at a greater distance."

Sidetrip: **Bear Notch Rd.** *Two miles ahead is Bear Notch Rd., closed in winter.* This 9-mile route to Bartlett follows Douglas Brook into the notch between Bear Mt. on the east and Mt. Tremont and Bartlett Haystack on the west. Sections of this road pass through an experimental forest, so you'll see more trees than mountains.

Bartlett Experimental Forest is a 2600-acre field laboratory for research in growth, culture, and composition of a northern hardwood forest — typical of those found in New England. Forest Service personnel have a chance to study different management techniques here — comparing "natural areas" where woods are left completely uncut versus moderate selection cutting, progressive strip cutting, or clear-cutting.

Cross-country skiers should look for the plowed turn-around areas on the west side of Bear Notch Rd., one mile north of the "Kanc." **The Upper Nanamocomuck Ski Trail,** east to west along the river, is fine for even novice skiers; this Forest Service Trail connects with loop trails nearby. *No fee; no grooming.*

Lightly-traveled, Bear Notch Rd. winds through a pine forest, with occasional views of Chocorua and other mountains. No picnic or camping facilities exist along here, but there are several parking turnoffs and trailheads.

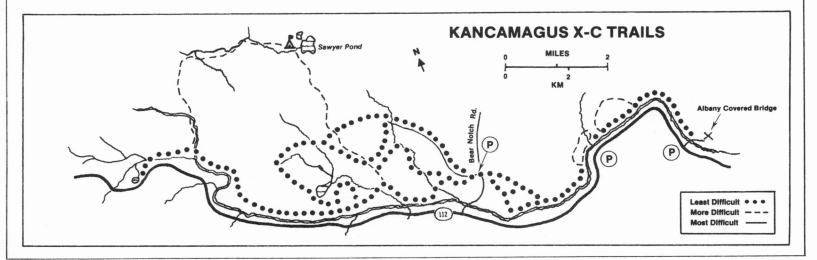

KANCAMAGUS X-C TRAILS

Sawyer Pond

N

MILES
0   2

0   2
KM

Bear Notch Rd.

Albany Covered Bridge

P

P

P

112

Least Difficult • • •
More Difficult - - -
Most Difficult —————

Passaconaway

Bikers may want to continue along the "Kanc," although the Bear Notch Rd. shortcut is another option for cyclists accustomed to hills. Just past this road is the Jigger Johnson Campground. *75 camp sites; trailer space*. Nearby is the **Passaconaway Historic Site and Visitor Center,** located in George House. *Open daily mid-June to Labor Day; weekends only from Memorial Day to mid-June and Labor Day to Columbus Day.*

There's a quick walk right here at the Visitor Center, **Rail'n River Forest Trail,** that's ideal for families or anyone who wants to know more about the mountains (don't let the ease of this loop or other tourists here dissuade you). *Half mile loop begins near the parking lot; wheelchair and stroller access*. Start off learning about overlogging and rebuilding forests. Walk an old railroad grade. Identify trees. Visit a swamp where plants thrive in wet, acid soil and beavers gnaw at trees. Get a good look at Mt. Passaconaway. Learn forestry practices, conservation, and ecology with this walk and the accompanying free pamphlet.

The white frame George House in Passaconaway was built by early settlers in 1810 and named after them, but it contains mementos of another family who lived here. For almost 40 years, Ruth Colbath placed a lamp in the window in case her husband came home. He did, eventually, three years after her death.

A half mile further west on the left brings you to the head of Oliverian Brook Trail, a four-hour hike to the summit of cone-shaped Mt. Passaconaway (via Passaconaway Cutoff, Square Ledge, and Walden Trails). Ahead on the right is the Sawyer Pond Trail, a two-and-a-half hour hike that's relatively easy, provided the Swift River is low and doesn't need to be forded. AMC maintains five tent sites and a shelter for 8 at Sawyer Pond, a good fishing spot.

There's another National Forest campground on the right side of 112, just ahead. *Passaconaway Campground has 33 camp units, with hiking and fishing, especially along Sabbaday Brook.* Across the highway on the left is a picnic ground and a trail which leads through the forest to the impressive **Sabbaday Falls.** For an easy half-hour walk along a graded path with several informational signs, you are rewarded with a picturesque narrow flume. *Fishermen should continue south on Sabbaday Brook Trail, which crosses the stream four times in the two hours it takes to hike along here.*

Look for Lily Pond another mile or two west on the right — and you might even see a moose eating here. With more than 1600 estimated moose in New Hampshire, it is likely that you'll see at least one somewhere in the White Mountains. Just ahead at the C.L. Graham Wangan Ground you can enjoy picnicking and fantastic views. *Comfort stations, fresh spring water.*

A wangan was a logging company store, selling goods to workers. Wangans, like J.E. Henry's in Lincoln, sold everything loggers needed, except liquor (forbidden because it interfered with productivity). Like many lumber "kings" who virtually destroyed the original forest here, Henry was a tough customer, presiding over payrolls with a gun on his hip — in case he needed to settle any disagreements over deductions (including workers' wangan accounts).

Kancamagus Pass

The road snakes through the Kancamagus Pass, the summit of a ridge where streams to the east feed into the Saco and those to the west feed in to the Pemigewasset. As 112 descends, you have more scenic overlooks: with views of Mts. Hancock, Hitchcock, and Huntington, named for a 19th-century geologist, on the right; to the left Mt. Osceola, Loon Mt., and the purple hue of the Kinsmans.

On the right, hikers will see the Hancock Notch Trail, and after the next hairpin turn, trailheads to the left. Greeley Ponds Trail, which leaves from the Wilderness Area parking lot and crosses several brooks (difficult spots are bridged), is an easy, short hike into a lovely scenic area, and continues into Waterville Valley.

Bob Henderson, who's plowed the "Kanc" since it opened, has learned to respect winter storms, which threaten to tear the "paper" off the birches here. "There's a mile or so just east of Kancamagus Pass that we call Breezy Lane; the winds gust up to 60 mph, and you just hope the wing plow holds you close to the bank."

Still heading downward, the "Kanc" passes a rest area (left) and then Big Rock Campground (right). *While this is a relatively small campground, trailers are welcome here.* Rte. 112 is said to have been built on the bed of the narrow-gauged East Branch and Lincoln Railroad. This logging track carried timber into Lincoln for manufacture into lumber, pulp, and paper.

Lumber baron J.E. Henry gave free rail passes to immigrants in Boston willing to work as lumberjacks. The back of their tickets read: "Lincoln, NH. . . is the headquarters of the J.E. Henry & Sons Lumber Co., one of the largest firms in the state. A good man can find work all year. A poor man better not go there, as such men are not wanted."

When Henry built the East Branch and Lincoln Railroad, track was laid in segments as needed. Housing for workers was moved by rail — making Henry the inventor of the mobile home!

Just beyond the campground is a large parking area and information booth. *Open daily mid-June through Labor Day; weekends only from Memorial Day to mid-June and Labor Day to Columbus Day.* For an easy hike to a trout pond, look for the **Wilderness Trail** north of the parking lot. The trail follows an old railroad bed along the Pemigewasset's East Branch, beginning to reclaim its reputation for brook and rainbow trout after years of pollution.

Cross the East Branch over a suspension bridge, bearing left onto Black Pond Trail after 2.6 miles. This trail leads three-quarters of a mile to the deep two-and-one-half acre pond bordered by Mt. Bond to the east and Mt. Flume to the west. Those who prefer to continue along the 10-mile Wilderness Trail will come to numerous campsites, several falls (one of the finest in this area), Franconia Brook, and numerous other trails — offering options for short or long trips, camping or day hikes, easy or challenging terrain.

From here on, the road follows the East Branch of the Pemigewasset, passing Hancock Campground on the left. You'll know you've left the WMNF, as signs of civilization begin again: resort condos and LOON MT., page 21, with an old logging train by its entrance. Just ahead is the very commercial part of **Lincoln**, with close to two dozen places to stay and a number of restaurants.

In summer, visitors may want to stop by the North Country Center for the Arts, 603/745-2141, in an old mill/mall. *Five stage shows, alternating with five musical programs from July 5 – September 3. Nine children's*

As you drive through Lincoln and continue south on I-93 through the Pemi Wilderness, you might ponder some of the dilemmas facing the Forest Service and agencies like the US Fish and Wildlife Service. Atlantic salmon and the bald eagle have returned to northern New England, thanks to over $10 million of private and public funding. Officials from the Fish and Wildlife Service, which administers this effort, hope to see migrating salmon in the East Branch of the Pemigewasset River by the year 2010.

Others, like LOON MOUNTAIN's president and general manager, Philip Gravink, are doubtful. Nevertheless, his recreation corporation is spending a quarter million dollars on an environmental impact study to see if LOON's plan to increase its skiers from 5500 to 12,400 will negatively affect such efforts. Expansion means drawing water from the Pemigewasset to make snow for LOON's slopes, and more human consumption of water comes at the same time sewage needs increase.

Presently, 94 percent of the town of Lincoln is state or national forest, and the 6 percent allotted for development is about as built up as it can be. Gravink, whose corporation pays out close to $200,000 yearly in taxes and provides a $315 million tax base through his employees, says that skiing is essentially a "clean" industry that gives more to the area than it takes — many local businessmen agree.

The public comment phase of the environmental study began in August, 1988. WMNF planner Geoffrey Chandler says, "Public opinion is very important. . . . We consider one thought-out letter, where people have laid out feelings in a very logical and rational manner, counts more than a petition with 100 names on it. "

theatre programs with matinees Wednesday and Saturday. Admission. For more information on this area, see pages 21-2.

To continue this loop, drive south from Lincoln on I-93 to the Ashland exit. For those who have not been in this section of the White Mountains, we recommend your reading Chapter 1.

THE SOUTHERN ROUTE

This lakeside section of our loop makes for a nice contrast to the mountainous drives further north. Combined with the "Kanc," it forms an interesting circuit, which can be driven easily in half a day.

Our suggested route starts in Ashland, near the geographic center of New Hampshire; turn east from I-93, Exit 24 onto rtes. 3/25. However, if you're coming from the north and are tired of the interstate, you can get off at Plymouth, Exit 25 and head southeast on 175 through Holderness, an attractive area, to our recommended route by Little Squam Lake.

From Exit 24, Ashland/Holderness, you enter the unpretentious hillside community of **Ashland** — a comfortable way to ease into rural New Hampshire. In the late 1700s, the landscape was dotted with gristmills and sawmills. Until 1868 the town was part of Holderness.

There is an air of completeness to Ashland, which has not only a modern shopping center and the usual strip of pizza houses and franchise fast-food places, but also a solid, old-fashioned downtown, with a mix-

ture of well-kept houses in the surrounding hills. One restaurant of note is THE COMMON MAN, 603/968-7030. With places in Lincoln and Concord as well, THE COMMON MAN is popular with locals and tourists alike for its daily specials, generous sandwiches, and homemade soups (this is one restaurant where they tell you the soup is a day old — *and* a day better.)

Connected to the restaurant is a deli offering fresh-baked goods and sweet-smelling spices, as well as its own specials; THE COMMON MAN DELI makes a good place to buy picnic fare. And next door is Out of Hand Gifts and Crafts, with a wide selection of well-made New England collectibles.

For the history buff, there is also the **Whipple House Museum,** 4 Pleasant St., *Open 1–4 pm, Wednesday and Saturday, July through Labor Day.* This early 19th-century brick house was the birthplace of New Hampshire's only Nobel Prize winner.

> Pathologist George Hoyt Whipple, whose research led to the cure of pernicious anemia, won the prize in 1934.

Rte. 3/25 turns left past THE COMMON MAN. Follow the Squam River on the right, past dairy bars, to a dam. **Little Squam Lake** has salmon, lake trout, both large- and small-mouthed bass, as well as other species waiting to be caught. Views of low mountains make a lovely backdrop to this shimmering lake, where you're likely to see waterskiing, sunfish and sailboats, even a seaplane landing. *Look for the public beach near the junction with rte. 175 in **Holderness**.*

The town of Holderness was founded in 1761 by Governor Benning Wentworth and 67 other Episcopalians, intent on establishing a rival to Puritan Boston as the hub of New England. Unfortunately for New Holderness, as it was then known, Boston had a few things more going for it, like a harbor and access to the sea, so the lakeside settlement didn't pose much of a threat.

New Holderness

Sitting on a peninsula separating Little Squam from Squam Lake, Holderness is a small resort colony, made up of several cottages, a motel, gift shops, antique dealers, a general store, and an ice cream parlor, SQUAM LAKESIDE FARM, 603/968-7227, with its take-out window and boat rentals. You'll see the Loon's Nest gift shop on the left and Smith Piper General Store on the right.

Our route bears left near THE STUDIO CAFE, 603/968-3003, a casual spot with an extensive menu: baked brie, nachos, red-hot chicken wings, potato skins, or fried zucchini sticks for starters; followed by salads, crepes, omelets, burgers, as well as both Italian and Mexican fare.

Gourmets may want to continue straight for a fraction of a mile to THE MANOR ON GOLDEN POND, 603/968-3348. This turn-of-the-century inn has its own pool, tennis courts, pontoon craft for lake cruises, as well as cross-country ski trails and ice-skating rink.

But you don't have to stay there to dine on elegant cuisine in the wood-paneled billiard room. Salads become interesting with the addition of peanuts and deftly-seasoned dressings. Shrimp with pink peppercorns and Pernod, duckling framboise, loin of lamb rosemary, poached salmon with caviar, pasta topped with lobster and fresh Parmesan, veal in a mushroom and truffle sauce, and a fine wine list draw Americans, Canadians, and Europeans here.

Rte 113 bears left, just west of THE MANOR, with the much larger *Squam Lake* on the right. Holderness today has an asset few other towns can claim: this lovely lake, aka Golden Pond, the location for the Hollywood movie of the same name. This body of water is the second largest in New Hampshire, but it's hard to tell by looking at it, for you can get only an occasional glimpse of parts of Squam from the road.

Squam is "an easy lake to get lost on," says Fred Rozelle, whose family has summered here for over 40 years. "If you've got a big boat with a big keel, there isn't any way to get it onto the lake, short of dropping it in by helicopter."

The lake has been described as sprawling out over the hills like a spider. The result is many islands and peninsulas, with no large open expanses of water. This keeps things quiet, as power boats can't build up a head of steam before running into something. The canoe is the preferred means of travel here. The same kinds of fish you find at Little Squam can be caught on Squam.

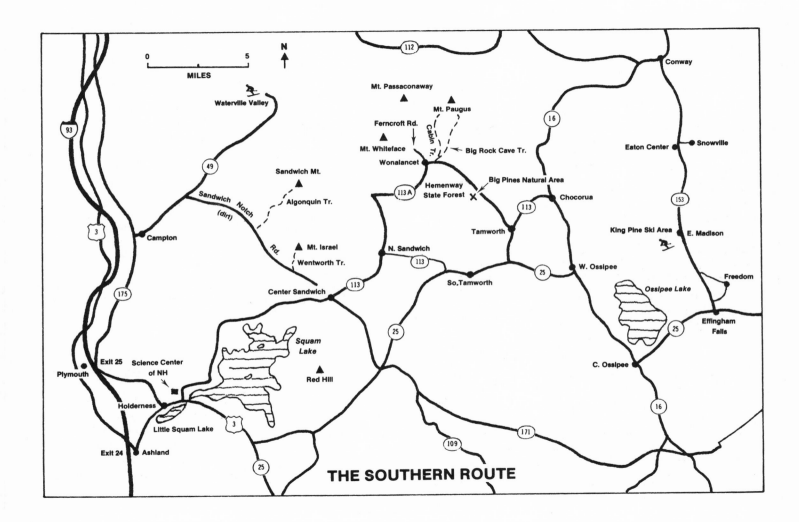

THE SOUTHERN ROUTE

While the water is pure enough to drink, don't even think about swimming in Squam Lake unless you live in one of the five neighboring towns or can disguise yourself as a loon. There are approximately 500 cottages around the lake, but they blend in so well with the landscape that the shoreline seems completely undeveloped. A real estate agent specializing in lakefront cottages would go broke in a hurry here, for these cottages pass from generation to generation. Most aren't for rent, either. All of this puts a damper on land speculation — leaving Squam wild; the loons and otters can swim in peace.

> On Squam, people get downright "loony": roping off loon nesting areas at the beginning of each summer, often putting half a dozen inlets and islands off-limits to humans. Residents have worked on a loon count for 15 years, and it's paid off. In 1984 there were 44 adult birds and 12 chicks, just about right for a lake this size; at three times Squam's size, Winnipesaukee has fewer loons.

Shortly after turning left onto rte. 113, look for the **Science Center of New Hampshire,** 603/968-7194, on the left. A 200-acre wildlife refuge with bear, deer, bobcat, and other native animals in enclosed natural communities, the Science Center makes an excellent place to learn about the woods, fields, ponds, marshes, and lakes in and near the White Mountains. *Open from May 1 – November 1 daily (weekend afternoons in fall and spring). Admission (children under four are free); frequent presentations. Statewide school program; TV series. Picnic facilities and gift shop.*

For the next five miles, the road meanders past driveways with many-named signposts. Only occasionally do you catch a glimpse of a huge lakefront "cottage," the lake itself, or a tiny island. ROCKYWOLD/ DEEPHAVEN CAMPS, 603/968-3313, on the right, the second largest resort in the state, is marked by a simple wooden sign. This exclusive adult camp in rustic surroundings has catered to proper Bostonians and other urbanites for years; many ex-campers have eventually purchased their own cottages or camps here.

> In the past, drinking at Rockywold was forbidden and a dress code was strictly enforced, even though the accommodations are very simple. You know you'd broken the rules if Mrs. Armstrong "forgot" to send you her annual Christmas card — her subtle way of letting you know that you weren't welcome here anymore.

Rte. 113 passes old farms and boggy areas that look as though a moose should be standing there waiting for you. Just over the Sandwich town line, you see mountains again and the road grade steepens. In about five miles are more mountain views. Look to the right for the fire tower atop Red Hill — an easy climb, offering 360-degree vistas that include the White Mountains as well as the lakes region.

Pretty old homes with their own special views become more and more frequent as you drive down a hill into *Center Sandwich*. Discovered by a hunting party in 1760, Sandwich was settled before the Revolution and remains one of the loveliest villages anywhere in New England.

Historic Sandwich

On the right as you approach the village, look for Country Elves Crafts in a little cottage, moved here from Tamworth. Then you'll see one of the focal points of the community, A.G. Burrows General Store, where you can buy picnic fare and find out whether or not the Sandwich Notch Rd. is passable. *Just past the store, you'll see Grove St., diagonally left. This street leads to the Sandwich Notch Rd., a delightful dirt road for shunpiking, picnicking, or hiking. This road is not maintained in winter, but makes one of the prettiest fall sidetrips we know.*

Sidetrip: **Sandwich Notch Rd.** Climbing up through the Sandwich Range and eventually linking up with rte. 49 in Waterville, approximately 10 miles away, page 11, this road is really one lane most of the way. If you meet another car, one of you will have to back up a ways and pull off the road. Hikers will be rewarded with trails, as well as woods and fields to explore en route. You're rarely far from the sound of water, as you walk or drive along this historic thoroughfare.

In the late 18th century, Sandwich was a trading center; the town appropriated $300 to build a road one rod wide from Center Sandwich through the notch and over the mountains to Thornton. Today's Sandwich Notch Rd. has changed little in 200 years.

Within the first few miles outside the village, you'll pass an old burying ground on the left and Chapman Nature Refuge on the right; there are lovely old homes and a gorgeous lake view as well. The Bearcamp River, a headwater of the Saco, meanders to either side of the road as stone walls appear and vanish. About three miles from Center Sandwich, look for the Sandwich town recreation area and Beede Falls with its Cow Cave. Legend says a settler's cow survived one winter here in this dank hollow, created by an overhanging ledge.

The spruce forests of Whiteface and Sandwich Mts. are attractive to the Canada jay, or moosebird, a gray and white cousin of the familiar bluejay. While these clever birds may steal food from a logging camp or a hiker's rations, they are found only where wilderness prevails.

In another two and a half miles, hikers should be on the lookout for the Wentworth Trail on the right, leading up Mt. Israel, with its fine views of lakes and mountains. A cross-roads will surprise you, before the road comes out into a clearing where hardy folk still live. The views are wonderful here. The Algonquin Trail, leading for 7 miles up to the summit of Sandwich Mt. (3993'), is on the right. The road turns to pavement again, descending eventually into Water-ville Valley.

Early settlers in Sandwich Notch planted Balm of Gilead trees, which look like poplars but make music with their heart-shaped leaves and whose buds were part of many home-made remedies.

Try to spend a little time, preferably on foot, exploring Center Sandwich. (One of the highlights of fall here is the fair in early October.) You'll discover fine antique stores, an art gallery, hand-woven treasures at Ayottes' Designery, and a wide range of crafts at Sandwich Home Industries, a League of New Hampshire Crafts shop, as you wander past colonial and Federal homes.

"All about middle New Hampshire are granite signposts. It is, I am afraid, no longer the custom to plant them, but a good many of the oldsters survive. . . planted five feet deep, so as to withstand the heaving power of frost." Cornelius Weygandt, 1934.

Rte. 113 turns left before an old granite signpost with its hand-painted notations. Open as an inn for over 100 years, THE CORNER HOUSE, 603/284-6219, serves wonderful lunches and dinners at reasonable prices. Ham and pepper soup, lobster-stuffed avocado, mussels casino are delicious introductions to a meal here. Shrimp served on rainbow-hued rotini; chicken Valencia with artichoke hearts, ham, and cheese in white wine sauce; raspberry-orange duckling; lobster and scallop pie; sirloin with dijon butter and rosemary are served with salad, homemade rolls or bread, a vegetable and choice of pasta, rice or potato. The biggest problem at THE CORNER HOUSE is finding room for chocolate Kahlua pie, dessert crepes, or hot apple crisp — you may want to finish with espresso or cappuccino instead.

A little past the restaurant is the **Sandwich Historical Society Museum,** 603/284-6269, with its collection of Americana that ranges from the town's early days through this century: an Indian dugout canoe, farm implements and tools, antiques, replicas of an old country store and post office. *Open June – October 1–5 pm (from 11–5, July and August); free.*

While a New Hampshire bike route, rte. 113 has its share of hills and very sandy shoulders; the surface is often in need of repair. Cyclists should exercise caution, as visibility is frequently limited and the road is quite narrow in places.

About three miles past the granite signpost in Center Sandwich, rte. 113 turns right toward Tamworth. Hikers may want to continue straight ahead on 113A to Mt. Whiteface (3985') and the town of Wonalancet. Recently, nearly 100,000 acres of White Mountain National Forest north of Wonalancet were designated as wilderness; some trails and shelters in this area are currently subject to relocation or removal. *Hikers should check with the Forest Service for updated information on this area.* Cyclists will enjoy the 12-mile sidetrip through Wonalancet into Tamworth.

Built in 1849, the attractive CORNER HOUSE was originally a one-story home, with a harness shop attached; later the inn was Victorianized.

Wonalancet's George Zink may well be the "father" of the newly-created Sandwich Range Wilderness. A retired science teacher who has battled timber interests in the southern mountains, Zink is literally a "tree-hugger." "I bring my grandchildren up here, and I hug trees. After awhile they say, 'Grampa, here's a good one,' and they hug it. Good indoctrination, I think."

"Ninety-nine percent of people go into the forest to climb a peak," Zink says. "They don't go in to see what wilderness is all about." From his own experience (often hiking every four days), Zink believes wilderness should be a place to experience solitude or to understand nature without the protection of civilization.

Sidetrip: ***Wonalancet.*** *Rte. 113A is also a bike route, but you'll worry less about traffic here.* Two miles east on 113A, you'll pass STAFFORD'S IN THE FIELD, 603/323-7766, a country inn shaded by ancient maples. The public, as well as overnight guests, may dine here; *reservations advised.* Mock turtle soup, bourride with aioli, braised pork with walnuts and apples, roast duckling in green peppercorn sauce are followed by southern buttermilk pie, chocolate sin, lemon curd tart, or delicious sundaes.

Rolling farmland, stone walls, and occasional mountain views make an interesting trip to ***Wonalancet,*** named for Passaconaway's son. Unable to keep peace with the English settlers, Wonalancet retired, seeking refuge in Canada and leaving his nephew Kancamagus in charge.

Wonalancet is famous for the Chinook Kennels, where the sled dogs that led Admiral Byrd to the South Pole were bred. Arthur Walden brought three identical yellow pups home from Alaska in 1917 — one of these dogs showed the natural strength necessary to pull a sled and had the ability to lead. Chinook's offspring displayed his fine characteristics, and a new breed was born. After the original Chinook and 15 of his line conquered the Pole, more kennels sprang up throughout northern New England.

Hikers should turn left on Ferncroft Rd. in Wonalancet for numerous trails up Mts. Whiteface, Passaconaway, and Paugus. Cabin Trail and Big Rock Cave Trail start from the left side of 113A as you head out of town. Continuing southeast, you will pass the Hemenway State Forest, a cool spot on a hot day, and Big Pines Natural Area on the right. The road crosses the Swift River, although this is not the same stream you saw along the "Kanc," with both brook and rainbow trout. Heading south to Tamworth, the "Chinook Trail," as 113A is also known, becomes a roller-coaster road with a rough surface and no shoulders. Cyclists need to be careful, because of poor visibility.

Those who turn right, staying on rte. 113, will pass White Mountain Kennels, then for the next few miles the Thompson Sanctuary on the right. While there is neither an access road nor sign, this 200-acre marsh and evergreen upland is home to snipe, ducks, hawks, owls, and warblers; otter, beaver, bear, deer, and up to five moose at one time have also been sighted here.

Sweet Country Roads of Tamworth

The road continues through thick woods, crossing the Bearcamp, an excellent trout stream, before reaching **South Tamworth**. A half mile ahead on the left, is the Bearcamp Natural Area. *At the junction with rte. 25 in Bennett Corner, turn left, staying on 113 and heading north to Tamworth.*

"There are sweet country roads in Tamworth. And roads deep in the woods, where sunlight glances off shining birches, to fall on rocks and glisten on ferns. Roads so narrow you can't turn around — but that is all right, you won't want to," wrote one visitor here.

The village of **Tamworth** is probably best known for The Barnstormers, 603/323-8500, the state's oldest theatre company. Originally a traveling troupe of players, the group today operates out of a good-sized theatre in the middle of town. *Old and new plays, as well as musicals, are performed June through late August by a professional equity company; admission.* Across the street is the TAMWORTH INN, 603/323-7721, an attractive old place for dinner or lodging.

Country Roads — 25 and 153

Rte. 113 leads east of Tamworth toward Chocorua and rte. 16, page 83. If traffic is heavy on 16, or if you're already familiar with this road into the heart of the White Mountains, we suggest heading south on 16 briefly to **Center Ossipee,** *page 82, then east again on rte. 25. This shunpike runs through almost forgotten towns like Effingham Falls, connecting with rte. 153 which meanders peacefully past more mountain lakes and even a ski area, eventually bringing you into Conway.*

From the junction of rte. 25 (the Ossipee Trail) with rte. 16, turn left and continue east, past **Ossipee Lake.** *Fishermen will find a public boat launch east of the lake; take the first left, after crossing the second bridge on rte. 25. There's good fishing for salmon and trout in the lake; the two smaller bays to the east offer perch and pickerel fishing. Parking fee at Ossipee Lake boat ramp.*

Continue east on rte. 25 along the southern end of Ossipee Lake for five miles to the village of **Effingham Falls.** Turn left here onto rte. 153. From 1820 until 1855 there were gristmills, sawmills, and woolen mills here, using the Ossipee River for their power. The town grew around the mills, but they lasted only a brief time. What remains is a collection of attractive 19th-century frame houses, mostly painted white.

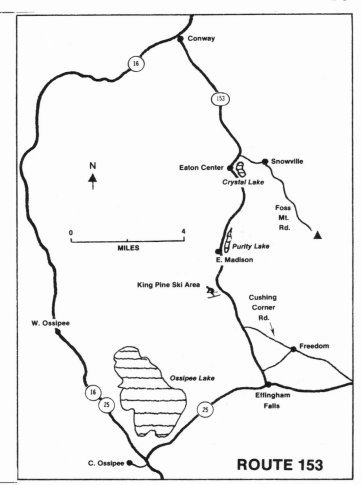

ROUTE 153

After driving a half mile north on 153, look for the road to Freedom on the right. In a mile and a half more, you'll find this attractive village situated among the hills, with several brooks and a 15-acre trout pond. In summer, the town doubles in size. The unhurried lifestyle of this community on the New Hampshire-Maine line draws urbanites from all over the country.

> "Nobody's from Freedom," says Peter Case, himself a refugee from New York City's fast lane. His neighbors come from the industrial parts of the Northeast. "The town I grew up in was like this — once," people in Freedom will tell you.

Hometown, USA

Freedom is a town of flagpoles, front porches, and picket fences. While we saw no brick houses, there seems to be at least one of every other variety here, many with ornate woodwork, lending an air of well-being to another former milltown. After passing the town hall, the pretty First Christian Church, and the Freedom Country Store with its soups and sandwiches, *turn right at the triangle-shaped heaterpiece, cross over the bridge at the waterfall, and explore the rest of town. On the left are more attractive houses, as well as FREE-DOM HOUSE BED & BREAKFAST, 603/539-4815.*

> Back in colonial days, wagons carting mast pines couldn't negotiate sharp-angle turns, like the one in Freedom, so intersections were built with Y-shapes rather than T-shapes, forming what are known as heaterpieces.

The bandstand is used during Old Home Week, when former residents return for a visit. (On this occasion in August, flags are displayed every three feet along the main street; half the folks in town dress up and march in the parade, which lasts maybe ten minutes, while the other half watches.)

Heading back across the river, turn right at the heaterpiece, and them immediately bear left onto Cushing Corner Rd. This road climbs a steep boulder-strewn hill until reaching the top of a long ridge, with fine views of the Ossipee Mts. to the west. Ancient stone walls crisscross the fields and woods. You will pass an old cemetery, and a mixture of lovely colonial farmhouses, with newer chalets — even a lilac farm in a perfect setting and Cabin Fever Antiques. *In about two miles the road ends at rte. 153, where you will turn right.*

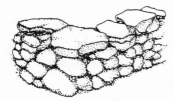

> "Stone walls are highways for red squirrels and striped squirrels and white-bellied mice. . . . Deer take even those walls that are shoulder high at an easy bound, showing white scuts like great jack rabbits. . . .Porcupines tumble over walls without regard for the bumps they receive."
> Cornelius Weygandt.

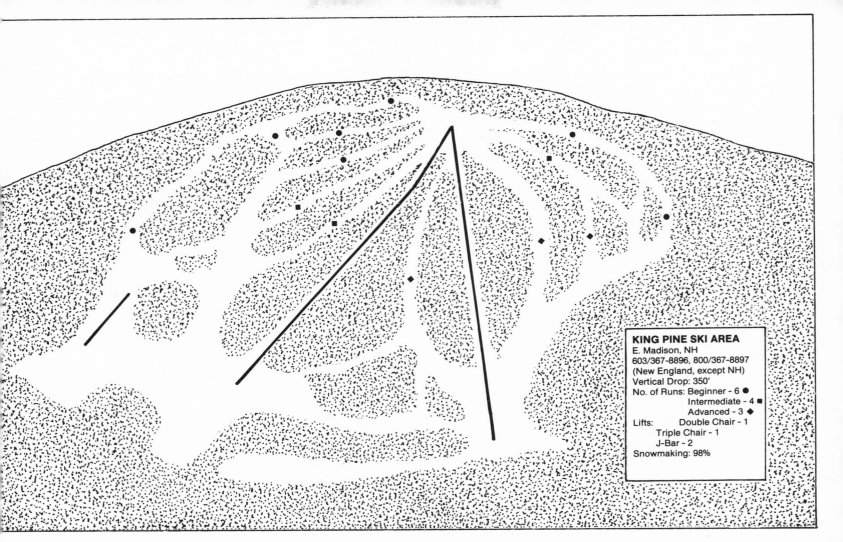

KING PINE SKI AREA
E. Madison, NH
603/367-8896, 800/367-8897
(New England, except NH)
Vertical Drop: 350'
No. of Runs: Beginner - 6 ●
Intermediate - 4 ■
Advanced - 3 ◆
Lifts: Double Chair - 1
Triple Chair - 1
J-Bar - 2
Snowmaking: 98%

For the next three miles, the road winds through deep hemlock woods, past more stone walls, climbing ever higher into the mountains, until you reach the neat white lodges and cottages of PURITY SPRING RESORT, 603/367-8896, in *East Madison.* This American Plan (three meals-a-day) family-oriented inn overlooks its own private two-mile long lake, complete with a tiny pine-studded island. In winter, the resort is popular with skiers using the KING PINE Ski Area, a half mile north.

On the left ahead, KING PINE, 603/367-8896 (or 1-800/367-8897 in New England but not NH), is not going to give KILLINGTON or WILDCAT much competition, with only 13 trails and four lifts, but it is a popular family mountain. For beginners and intermediate skiers, KING PINE makes a leisurely and inexpensive alternative to the more intense, crowded ski areas further north. There are three relatively steep, narrow trails for more advanced skiers. *Night skiing; limited lift policy. Rentals, ski school, nursery, snack bars and lounge.*

> "There are some lakes were we can go ice fishing and catch 100 perch in a day. But Wayne and me are waiting for the big one, we know he's down there," says Bobby Thompson, who likes to ice fish at Crystal Lake, where record trout have been caught. "Last weekend we had 50 or 60 visitors stop by to see us. It's mostly those skinny [cross-country] skiers. . . wondering what we're doing."

Crystal Lake

Continuing north, rte. 153 passes a mixture of housing which at best can be considered rural. Ahead are a series of beautiful trout ponds, including *Crystal Lake* three miles north of KING PINE. The pretty little village of *Eaton Center* hugs the west shore of the lake. Among the quaint buildings here is the INN AT CRYSTAL LAKE, 603/447-2120. An inviting lodge where Victoriana mingles with the owner's interest in geology (rock sculptures abound), this is a comfortable place that puts effort into its menu: German sauerbraten and chicken with brie may be the specials one night; roast turkey or shrimp steamed in vermouth the next. The Spinks sometimes eat with their guests and frequently entertain them with stories about Walter's boulder collection or Jacqueline's antiques.

At the intersection by the inn is Ridge Rd. which will take you up the hill to ROCKHOUSE MOUNTAIN FARM INN, 603/447-2880, a 400-acre working farm complete with barnyard animals. After passing the Eaton Village Store (an archtypical country store, old post office, coffee shop, and lunch counter) and some venerable cottages, you will come to the north end of the lake, where there is an inviting sand beach — reason enough to move here, for it is restricted to town residents only. Fishermen will find that the town does welcome augers and huts in the winter. *The lake continues to be restocked with brown trout; check local regulations about the number of "tip-ups" per fisherman.*

A traditional New England sport, ice fishing can be a challenging pursuit. Novices are advised to jig, or jerk, bait up and down — giving a "wounded" appearance to bait or lure. "Tip-up," or tilt fishing, with a simple rig and a flag that rises when a fish has struck, is useful for larger prey, like pickerel or trout. Once you have your tackle, you still need to chop through the ice. Ice augers with interchangeable bits and a skimmer to scoop out slush and any ice that refreezes at your fishing hole are as important as your bait bucket and gaff.

Dress warmly — in layers — and wear waterproof boots. Once you're a committed ice fisherman, you might want to invest in a small bobhouse and portable stove; you can rent them on some lakes where ice fishing is popular.

Snow's Village

For another picture-book village, cross-country skiing, and an opportunity for excellent dining, *turn right, by the Eaton town beach, for **Snowville** less than a mile down the road.* Settled in the early 1800s by people named Snow, the town consists of a dozen or so lovely colonial capes and Victorian frame houses lining the narrow country road.

The only store in town is Sleigh Mill Antiques, originally an 1890s carriage mill owned by Will Snow, where sleighs and old tools can still be seen. You'll also find a custom furniture maker and a lady who cooks old-fashioned barley candy in the same house where she was born.

In the middle of the village is Foss Mt. Rd. on the right. For spectacular views of the Presidential Range, turn here and go up the hill. Part way up Foss Mt., in a clearing on the right is a collection of barn-red buildings surrounded in summer by lush flower beds. This is the SNOWVILLAGE INN, 603/447-2818, a wonderful year-round country retreat.

Built in the early 1900s, SNOWVILLAGE INN was originally the retreat of Frank Simons, Harvard grad and political correspondent who divided his time between Washington, DC, Europe, and Snowville. Swiss innkeeper Max Pluss turned the home into an inn, after deciding the views equalled those of his homeland. Today, Austrian-born Trudy Cutrone Americanizes her native traditions quite comfortably here in the inn.

Guests who arrive just to eat are advised to have a reservation; however, the Cutrones (like many mountain innkeepers) will try to serve you without advance notice, if they have enough food. While dinner guests have only one choice of entree, it is carefully prepared. A basket of homemade breads, salad bar with only the freshest ingredients, and delicious soups make an encouraging introduction to a meal here. Veal or chicken picatta, baked haddock, peppered beef tenderloin, curried chicken with peaches are delightful entrees. Wine, dessert, and coffee round out your dinner. *Wine tasting, cooking courses, and other special events here. Cross-country skiing (rental shop on premises) and hiking from the inn.*

Further up the mountain, the landscape gets wilder and the road gets rougher; hiking is the preferred means of travel. The trek is worth it, for on the dome of Foss Mt. are blueberry barrens; if you are there in late July and August, you may want to bring your own bucket. Most of the mountain belongs to the town and is now a free park, and the panorama is also free.

*Retrace your steps back to rte. 153. Five miles to the north you'll come to the stoplight at rte. 16 in **Conway**. Ahead is the **West Side Rd.**, page 87; to your right is civilization with a capital "C." For those who have not yet visited the heart of the mountains, we recommend following one of the routes in Chapter III; if you've already done so, but want to continue to the North Country (in the next chapter), simply take the route you didn't follow before.*

Chapter V THE NORTH COUNTRY

Between the Presidentials and Canada lie a vast wooded tract, more of the White Mountains, two very different passes through these summits, and what to most minds constitutes "true wilderness." You can drive for hours and see fewer homes than you'd pass in a tiny village.

For fishermen, hunters, and many skiers this area will seem like paradise. However, like the more southerly ranges, the North Country is threatened — by logging, rather than by too much development or too many backpackers and hikers. Indeed, the very lack of trails in this area and the absence of conspicuous landmarks mean that fewer nature lovers actually know this area very well, leaving it vulnerable to timbering — as long as cutting is done out of sight, away from the roads.

There are numerous routes to the North Country. Anyone coming west from Maine need only reverse our directions in this chapter, returning east on 302 through the heart of the mountains, Chapter III. From Littleton and I-93, rte. 135 parallels the Connecticut River for excellent fishing and relatively easy canoeing. But our favorite trip north links the heart of the mountains with the North Country. From Twin Mountain, there's a good biking road.

Route 3 North

If you choose the northern route out of **Twin Mountain,** you'll pass an information booth on the left. Rte. 3/115 has wide paved shoulders for biking. Several miles outside of town, vistas open up.

Shortly after rte. 115 veers off to the right (leading toward Jefferson, Gorham, and Berlin), you'll see a fish hatchery on both sides of the road. *Open daily 8–4, contact New Hampshire State Fish and Game Dept. for information, 603/846-5429.* Nearby Carroll Stream is a great place to fish.

Bikers will find the grades pretty easy along this stretch of road, especially if you've done much biking in the mountains. (Shoulders do turn to gravel occasionally, but this is not a heavily-traveled road.) Your efforts will be rewarded with splendid views: mountains, a large erratic boulder, a bog on the right. You may have some tough biking, however, as you head into **Whitefield.**

Church spires welcome you to "the Friendly Town with a Beautiful Point of View" — determined that things will stay that way. For good reason: Whitefield is today exactly the delightfully old-fashioned kind of place that the Conways used to be. An old railroad depot has been converted into a bank and shops, but there's little commercialism beyond the needs of the people who live here. Nearby is an attractive state park for a picnic, bass fishing, and swimming.

Sidetrip: *Forest Lake State Park. Turn left by the Colonial Deli and filling stations onto 116 for a lovely drive to the park. Two miles out of town, you'll see a sign for KIMBALL HILL INN, 603/837-2284, up the hill on the left.*

The dining room here is open year-round Wednesday – Sunday 5–8 pm with honest New England fare: baked haddock, broiled scallops, and steak. The 180-degree vista, from the Presidentials off to the right through the Kilkenny Range to Vermont's Green Mountains off to the left, makes this inn worth the drive.

Continuing along 116, you'll see Burns Pond on the right, a nice spot to launch a canoe. Bikers will find paved shoulders and enough of a ride to deserve the swim that awaits. Soon you'll see the sign on the right at the road for Forest Lake State Park.

Drive through pretty woods past home construction. You'll see cottages on the left, just after the road enters Dalton township. Bear left to the entrance of the state park, two miles from rte. 116. Fee; handicapped access to both picnic area and beach. Changing rooms, life guard, playground. This lovely lake at the foot of Mt. Dalton is warmer than most streams or many other ponds.

> You don't have to be a backpacker to see some of New England's wildflowers. In late spring, the woods at Forest Lake State Park are full of lance-leaved violets, as well as trillium and ladyslippers.

Return to Whitefield, or continue along the Ammonoosuc to Littleton.

> New Hampshire's largest rainbow trout was caught at Mirror Lake in 1986 by Richard Dunbar of Whitefield.

Back in Whitefield, rte. 3 north takes you past the common with the town bandstand, then 116 goes off to the right toward the Weathervane Theatre *(6 different productions per season; 603/837-9322)* and THE WEATHERVANE COUNTRY INN, 603/837-2527 *(lunch and dinner Monday – Friday; dinner only, Saturday).*

Rte. 3 north of town passes near Mirror Lake on the left, an accessible trout pond. Just past the Lancaster townline, you'll see Blood Pond, surrounded by mountains on the left, and *Weeks State Park* on 430 acres to the right. *The mansion where Sen. John Wingate Weeks lived is open; mountaintop park on Mt. Prospect offers superb views in all directions from the tower. Open Wednesday – Sunday 10–5 in the summer, weekends only Labor Day to September 30; 603/788-4467.*

> When he was a young man, John W. Weeks was said to have rescued an old Lancaster woman from boys' pranks, even spending his lucky coin to buy her tea and crackers. According to local legend, she prophesied that Weeks would grow to manhood, loved and respected by all who knew him. Whether this "witch," as people believed, did indeed have the gift of prescience, or her words just before death so impressed the boy that he lived up to them, we will never know, but Weeks did later become Secretary of War and the Senator who persuaded Congress to buy up what is today the White Mountain National Forest.

America's First Carpet

Rte. 3 is like a roller coaster from here into **Lancaster.** This community, nestled between the Pilot and Presidential Ranges, on the meadows of the Connecticut River Valley, is the oldest in this part of New Hampshire, dating back to 1764. One of the first shire towns where Court was held in Coos County, Lancaster at first had no suitable place for judges to board.

An enterprising pair of pioneers, the Everetts, built an addition on their home to accommodate boarders. Everett rode the hundred miles to Portland to buy beds, looking-glasses, and metal wash bowls, while his wife sewed curtains and created what may have been the first American-made wool carpet (at that time, most rugs came directly from England and were very expensive). The judges called their rooms here "the finest in New Hampshire."

Today this remains a comfortable town, with a huge heaterpiece/common boasting the obligatory Civil War statue and downtown commercial area undergoing renovation. *If you turn right here, Rte. 2 will lead you east to Gorham, page 117, and a return trip south on 16.*

OLD SUSANNAH'S, 70 Main St., 603/788-2933, is the kind of place where three generations can still enjoy sitting down to eat together. Its menu offers potato skins, deep-fried pepper rings, lobster salad, deli sandwiches, spaghetti, seafood and steaks; the help bustles about in a friendly way.

Susannah Brownson, for whom OLD SUSANNAH'S was originally named, is remembered by a remarkable gravestone. Its inscription reads:

Widow Susannah Brownson
Was born August 3, 1699
And died June 12, 1802
Her duty finished to mankind
To God her spirit she resigned.

More churches than you see in most towns and interesting old homes line rte. 3 north. Look for the Lancaster Historical Society and museum in the Wilder-Holton House on the outskirts of town. There is a four-fireplace chimney as well as a collection of local memorabilia in this home that has served as tavern, church, and meeting place. *Open on Sundays from late June through early October when the flea market is in operation, or by appointment, 603/788-2530; donations appreciated.*

Lancaster has two covered bridges: one, built early in this century, crosses the Connecticut River to Vermont; the other, constructed in 1862, is on Mechanic St. east of the junction of rtes. 2 west and 3 north.

In the early days, New Englanders using covered bridges were charged tolls; usually the elderly were employed to collect money from travelers. To walk across a bridge might cost two cents, to ride a horse four cents, to drive a cart, sleigh, or wagon ten cents.

To the North Country

Rte. 3 to the North Country leads past some excellent fishing spots with wonderful views of the Connecticut River Valley and Vermont's Green Mountains. North of Lancaster, the road passes through a commercial area with fairgrounds on the left. The road surface is good here, with little to distract the driver. Bikers who want to cycle through Dixville Notch will find this is a good road for stretching their muscles. While not the most interesting route, the grades are not as steep as they will become, and the shoulders are paved most of the way.

Two miles north of the fairgrounds, rte. 3 comes to the small rural community of **Northumberland. Guildhall,** across the river in Vermont, is a pretty town with an inn.

In another mile or two you'll see a picnic wayside on the left. The road crosses railroad tracks, then you'll notice smoke rising from the James River Corp. plant. *Rte. 110 turns off to the east toward Stark, the Upper Ammonoosuc for trout fishing, and eventually Berlin, see page 119.*

Long an industrial town, **Groveton** became important when the Grand Trunk and Boston and Maine Railroads arrived here in the mid-19th century. Today a few pretty old homes remain testament to those glory days, though the lumber yard and American Legion Hall may be what you'll notice here. *Outside of town, the road narrows but again is little traveled.*

Fishermen might want to look for Bog Pond Rd. in Stratford four or five miles north. This road leads north to a good pond for brookies. You'll pass Burnside Cemetery on the left and a pretty Greek Revival home on the right. Working farms add interest along the road here.

Coos County has long been a rich agricultural area. In Lancaster, town salaries were, for years, paid in wheat. Groveton was known for sawmills, starch mills, then paper mills. Colebrook was an important potato-raising area.

Emerson's Country Store is on the left, then in several miles you'll find yourself in **North Stratford.** Some of the best trout fishing anywhere can be found north along the Connecticut River. Rte. 3 offers good access for both fishing and boating. *Canoeists will find fast water with rapids down to Guildhall; it is advisable to portage at Northumberland Dam, but you'll have 9 more miles of good paddling south to Lancaster. (The rte. 2 bridge there is a good place to leave a second car or ask someone to meet you.)*

All three kinds of trout are found in the northern Connecticut River. A 16-pound brown trout was caught here in 1975.

There's an interesting burying ground on the left, and in another half mile, you'll see a place to rent canoes. *Bikers will find paved shoulders most of the way.* Indians gave the early settlers here in North Stratford a hard time. Today, clear cutting is the concern, as the logged hills on the right past the general store and filling station show. In another couple of miles, rte. 3 passes the northernmost covered bridge, then some pretty farming country as you come into **Colebrook.**

> Named for one of the original grantees, Sir George Colebrook of Granada in the West Indies, this mountain town is as well known for the people who left it, as it is for those who settled here. A dozen Colebrook families founded Beloit, Wisconsin in 1846 and the college of the same name.

Route 26 East

Heading east from Colebrook, rte. 26 cuts through the narrowest of the notches at Dixville and a Maine state park at Grafton Notch, taking you to marvelous fishing and hunting country, while offering both hiking and biking opportunities. You can also enjoy an elegant meal at one of the last grand hotels in the mountains, as well as the chance to wander around our favorite historic village. *Experienced bikers might want to be met in South Paris, ME a day or two after heading east; there are bed and breakfast inns and campgrounds en route.*

Mostly a two-lane highway, 26 does occasionally have passing lanes and paved shoulders. While there are plenty of hills and some steep grades now and then, this route is little traveled west of Bethel. Because of the popularity of the Bethel area, you may have some traffic on holiday weekends east of town, but most of it backs up around South Paris/Norway, where several other routes funnel into 26 for the most direct way to the Maine Turnpike.

Turn east or right on rte. 26, just past the WILDERNESS RESTAURANT, 603/237-8779, in Colebrook. The road crosses the Mohawk River, another trout stream, on the outskirts of town, and passes a 9-hole golf course on the left. Rte. 26 is wide outside of town with wonderful views, but paved shoulders end a few miles east.

Look for the narrow notch ahead, as you pass the road on the left which leads to a fish hatchery. There's a picnic area on the right in another two and a half miles, but THE BALSAMS ahead in Dixville Notch is noted for its buffets, if you'd rather wait to dine in style. *About a half mile past the country store with motel and restaurant, look for signs to Coleman State Park, and turn left for the park approximately four miles north. There's a sportsmen's lodge and fly shack en route, as the road continues through this heavily-timbered area.*

Sidetrip: **Coleman State Park.** *Left on E. Colebrook Rd., then left again on Bear Rock Rd. to a large park on Little Diamond Pond. 30 tent sites, both stream and lake fishing (in addition to trout, you'll find salmon at Big Dia-*

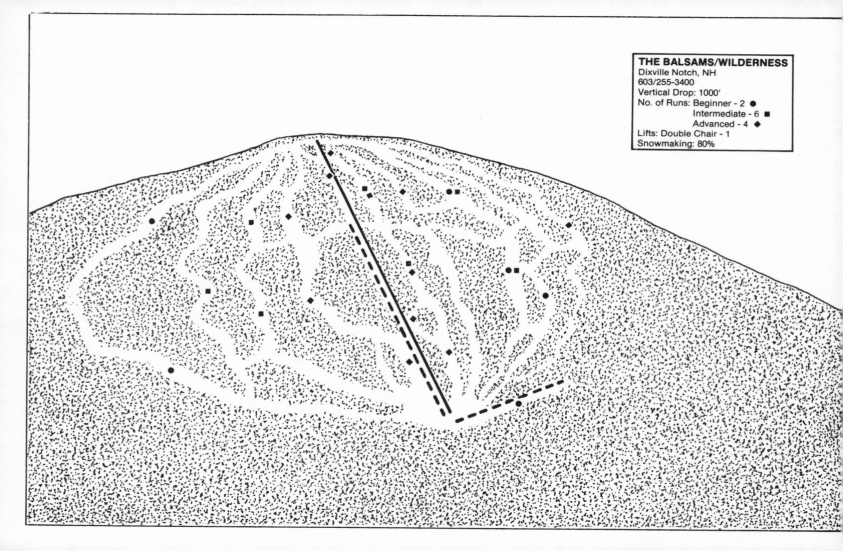

THE BALSAMS/WILDERNESS
Dixville Notch, NH
603/255-3400
Vertical Drop: 1000'
No. of Runs: Beginner - 2 ●
Intermediate - 6 ■
Advanced - 4 ◆
Lifts: Double Chair - 1
Snowmaking: 80%

mond Pond, just north of the park itself). Picnic facilities in the park; boat ramp at Big Diamond. Snowmobile trails connect this area with Colebrook in winter.

The Last of the Grand Dames

The road crosses the Mohawk River several times before a ski area is visible to the right, with funny, lumpy mountains to the left. *Near the Dixville town line, 26 adds a passing lane. Skiers should be on the lookout for Wilderness Rd. on the right, leading to THE BALSAMS/WILDERNESS SKI AREA, 603/255-3400 (snow conditions, 603/255-3951).*

This is one ski area where you won't be fighting for a place in line. The motto here is: "No crowds. No hassles. No exceptions." Guests at THE BALSAMS ski free; the terrain offers good intermediate skiing downhill and 40 km. (25 miles) of marked cross-country trails (most double-tracked). *An average 250″ of annual snow is backed by 80 percent snowmaking. Rentals; classes in downhill, cross-country, and telemarking. Usual ski area amenities, including NASTAR racing, nurseries, and lunchroom.*

> "Everyone has his favorite notch and mine is Dixville. It is the narrowest of the notches and the steepest, and on a dark night it is fearsomely lovely." Travel writer Eleanor Early, 1935.

There are impressive rock faces high up on your left. As the road enters this narrow notch, the grade steepens and you're in shadow — even at midday. On the left, look for the entrance to THE BALSAMS, 603/255-3400 (800/255-0600 out of state, 800/255-0800 in NH), an old-fashioned resort that bills itself as "The Switzerland of America." It is here in this hotel that Dixville's few residents vote, shortly after midnight every election day, so that their ballots can be counted before the rest of us awaken.

> Hay fever sufferers enjoy Dixville, as did the resort's founder Henry Hale who spent $11 million to create a lake, forest, and "Victorian dream" of a hotel.

It's possible to dine here without staying overnight; just stop by the front desk to get a meal ticket. The lunch alone consists of three huge "groaning boards," where the food tastes every bit as good as it looks. Choose between imported cheeses attractively arranged, salads that run the gamut from pasta to fresh radicchio, every kind of cold cut imaginable, then soups and hot entrees (veal cordon bleu, smoked shoulder with braised red cabbage, fresh sole in shrimp sauce). A waiter brings you a choice of breads, coffee, tea, or any cocktail you might like, but be sure to save room for dessert: chocolate-filled eclairs, white chocolate strawberries, mousses, cakes and pies — our favorite was a custard pie topped with nut-fudge confection.

For the past three years, UNH entomologist John Burger has been testing a biological pesticide, Bacillus Thruingiensis Israelnesis (BTI), on the black fly population in selected streams near THE BALSAMS. The human-biting black fly population has been reduced about 90 percent, he claims, but BTI is not something the average person can use to combat flies, because a formal permit from the state is presently required.

Hikers should look to the right at the entrance to THE BALSAMS for the **Sanguinary Ridge Trail,** a good way to work off a meal here. *While this trail does not climb Sanguinary Mt., the north wall of the notch, it does connect to other trails, giving you a choice between easy walks and real hikes. A hiking map is available at the hotel.*

By most standards, the mountains that form Dixville Notch are relatively low; there are only wooded summits. Sanguinary Mt. to the north takes its name from its blood-red color at sunset. Dixville Peak, 3482', is accessible only by snowmobile.

Starting from the trailhead by the entrance to THE BALSAMS, Sanguinary Ridge Trail climbs steeply for incredible views of Lake Gloriette and the resort. Then you descend east via a winding footpath with scenic lookouts to Table Rock and Old King cliffs, as well as vistas toward Errol and the Mahoosucs. Follow blue, then yellow blazes along this path, eventually reaching a flume and picnic area. Allow close to two hours from the hotel to the picnic spot.

Dixville Notch

Just past the resort, rte. 26 enters **Dixville Notch State Park.** Look for Table Rock parking area on the right. *This is a very steep trail, and rocks here can be slippery. We suggest you park at the picnic area ahead and hike back to the entrance of the resort (see Sanguinary Ridge Trail above).* In another mile, you'll see the Flume Brook Picnic Area on the left, with more trailheads here, and Cascade Brook Picnic Area on the right near the eastern edge of the park.

Clear Stream, which wanders to either side of the road, is a good trout stream. And this is true moose country, with more woods than clearings. As the valley opens up around you, canoeists may want to consider a water route into Errol, four miles east. *While the upper part of the river is too steep for canoeing, most of Clear Stream is easy. as long as you're on the lookout for fallen trees, which can completely block this river, not much wider than a canoe in places. You may have some riffles and small rapids, but nothing too challenging. The best place to take your boat out is a quarter mile past the rte. 16 bridge in Errol, where Clear Stream flows into the Androscoggin.*

Years ago Clear Stream was part of the log drive. Although trucks have virtually eliminated the need for streams clogged with wood, logging is still much in evidence here in the North Country.

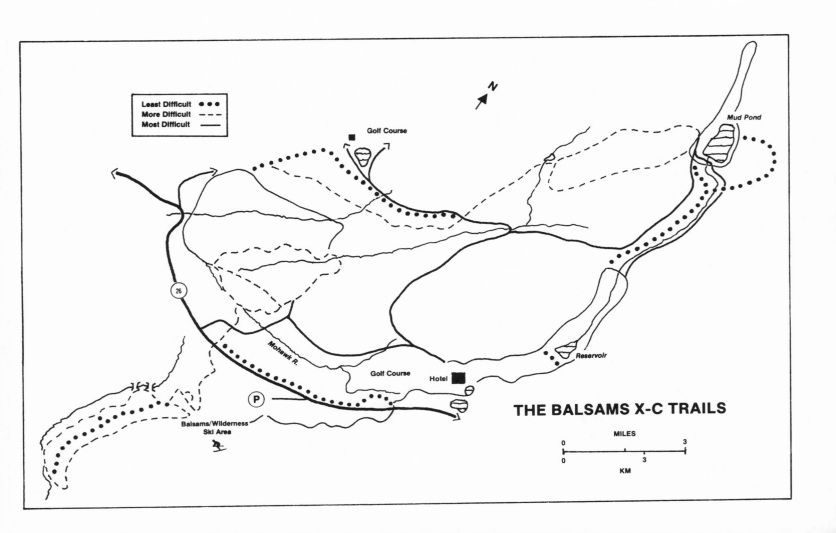

Least Difficult ● ● ●
More Difficult - - -
Most Difficult ———

N

Mud Pond

Golf Course

26

Mohawk R.

Golf Course

Hotel

Reservoir

P

THE BALSAMS X-C TRAILS

Balsams/Wilderness
Ski Area

MILES
0 3
0 3
KM

Just past the North Woods Gift Shop on the left, you'll enter **Errol** township. *The first road to the right is a snowmobile trail that runs north along Coarser Brook to Swift Diamond River, a trout stream. The trail branches off west by Nathan Pond Brook, which leads to several cold water ponds for more fishing, and eventually back down to THE BALSAMS. There is no fishing in Lake Gloriette at the resort. Continue north along this snowmobile trail to the Diamond River, heading west to Diamond Pond and Coleman State Park.*

Rte. 26 passes a well-maintained farm, as the surrounding hills become gentler. You're not out of the mountains yet, or even the woods, although the road crosses meadows from time to time. The "Errol International Airport" is close enough to Canada not to be a joke. In another couple of miles, you'll see signs for Old Orchard Beach, an odd sight so far from the coast of Maine, until you realize how many Canadians spend their summer vacations there. Rte. 16 is ahead on your right. An official state bike route for much of its length, rte. 16 leads south from Errol through Thirteen Mile Woods to Berlin, Gorham, and the Presidential Range of the White Mountains, see Chapter III.

If you're hungry, THE ERROL RESTAURANT, 603/482-3352, is popular with hunters, French Canadians, families, and everyone else. This unpretentious place offers charbroiled meats (with "no guarantee" if steaks are too well-done) and a wine list that includes "rum 'n coke." We recommend soup and a sandwich (the turkey is fresh) or a mooseburger (in reality, hamburger with provolone, onions, mushrooms, and special sauce); you can also get Sam Adams or several kinds of imported beers here.

A little ways past the restaurant on the left, just before the library, you'll see a children's fish pond — a good way to introduce youngsters to a great sport! You'll see SACO BOUND, 603/447-2177, for canoe rentals, as you continue east out of town.

> New Hampshire's settlers depended on moose for food, but their need for cleared land and, later, timber may have had as detrimental an effect on moose as aggressively hunting them. At the southern edge of the moose range, and the northern extremity for white-tailed deer, New Hampshire favors Bambi over Bullwinkle whenever it destroys its woodlands and drains its bogs.

On to Maine

Taking rte. 26 east from Errol, you begin a long climb up a steep hill (one of many) as you head southeast. Tree farms, rustic cabins, and rural homes appear occasionally. There are mountain views to the south, then five miles of moose country through the woods.

The road narrows about four miles east of town, as you descend the high ridge, with glimpses of Lake Umbagog and mountains to the left. In another two miles or so, snowmobile trails go off to either side (the one to the right leads back the bridge on rte. 16 south of Errol, page 120).

> Twelve miles long and a mile or two wide, the Indians called this lake "muddy water," though on a clear day it sparkles like a jewel between the mountains.

And before you know it, you're at Lake Umbagog (the Indian name is pronounced Um-BAY-gog). Known for fishing and boating, this wild, uncommercial lake offers anyone a chance to "get away from it all" and to see wildlife: in addition to moose, there are waterfowl and a few eagles. Fishermen will find brook trout from ice-out in early May until the water warms up; warm-water fishing is excellent here, as well. *Look for the boat landing on the left, about five miles outside Errol; there are campgrounds up the hill in another .4 mile, also on the left. Signs with information about camping and building fires are posted here in French as well as English.*

> Moose meat, much leaner than beef, is considered a true delicacy by those who have eaten it. In Maine, where almost half the male population hunts, it's been found that very little moose meat is left in the woods — most of it is eaten! Even with New Hampshire's very brief moose-hunting season, it's expected that as much as 15,000 pounds of moose meat will end up on tables there.

After another mile and a half, you'll be in Maine, passing through the tiny settlement of **Upton**. There's little here — just the general store which doubles as a

filling station, a few homes, and some old churches off to the left. The road to Andover also goes off to the left in another mile, if you're interested in climbing Baldpate or the Cascades.

The next four miles are beautiful with rugged evergreens relieved here and there by tamaracks and deciduous shade trees, a small burying ground or rock outcroppings. *Moose are common, so drive carefully. Six miles ahead, the road passes between Old Speck Mt., 4150', and Baldpate Mt., 3996'.*

Grafton Notch

One of the least commercial and most scenic of the notches, this state park provides plenty of opportunities to pull over for a better look. Shortly after you enter **Grafton Notch State Park,** you'll find a map on the right to help you get your bearings and decide what you want to do in the next 6 miles. The Bear River, which flows through the park, is a trout stream (both brookies and rainbows here).

> Grafton was originally a lumbering town, although little evidence of that community remains today. When the supply of pine and spruce was exhausted, people moved on. What seems amazing is how beautiful this area has become once again, thanks to state efforts.

Look for Spruce Meadow Picnic Area on your right a mile and a half further. *Numerous picnic sites in a lovely setting.* Rock ledges jut out behind small trees, and the Appalachian Trail crosses the road a little further south. A mile past Spruce Meadow, also on the right, is a good-sized parking area by a bog. *Trail maps; trash receptacles.* From here, you can climb Old Speck, 4180′, via Eyebrow Loop. *Part of the AT, Old Speck Trail is blazed white; Eyebrow is blazed orange and is extremely slippery in wet weather.* With a fire-tower at its summit, this mountain offers a full 360-degree view on a clear day: to the southwest is Mahoosuc Notch; southeast, Sunday River Whitecap; east, Dresser and Long Mountains; northeast, the twin peaks of Baldpate. Allow 6 hours round-trip for this strenuous hike.

> A group of third-graders at a nearby school in Maine recently visited Grafton Notch State Park in the fall:
>
> "We gathered into groups, and prepared for our hike to Table Rock. Before setting out, we snacked on apples to gather energy and strength. Monica enjoyed walking over the bridges and logs on the trail. The bridges were made from wood for us to cross over wet places. Erica liked to look at the leaves because they were changing into all different colors. . . . On our way, Rachel studied a caterpillar climbing up a spruce tree. The caterpillar was white. Jay watched a partridge fly toward a big tree. He also saw a chipmunk scurry behind him. Amy noticed the interesting way Mother Nature formed the roots of trees to look like steps. Warren liked how the rocks were different shapes and sizes. He noticed one rock as tall as a person. As we approached the top of the mountain, we stopped to rest. . . and waited for the tail end of the line to catch up."

We recommend the short, but somewhat steep 900′ climb to **Table Rock** on a southwest peak of Baldpate. Along this spectacular hike, you are rewarded with an excellent outlook and a large slab-cave system (allow close to two hours for exploration). *Take the trail to the right of the parking lot, cross rte. 26, walking briefly through the woods beside a marsh until you reach a log bridge .1 mile.* **Table Rock Trail** climbs gently for .3 mile above the marsh, then steadily up to a rocky, moss-covered boulder patch at .6 mile. After switch-backs along rocky ledges, you enter a deep ravine between two rock faces; at the top of this ravine, bear

MAHOOSUC & GRAFTON NOTCHES

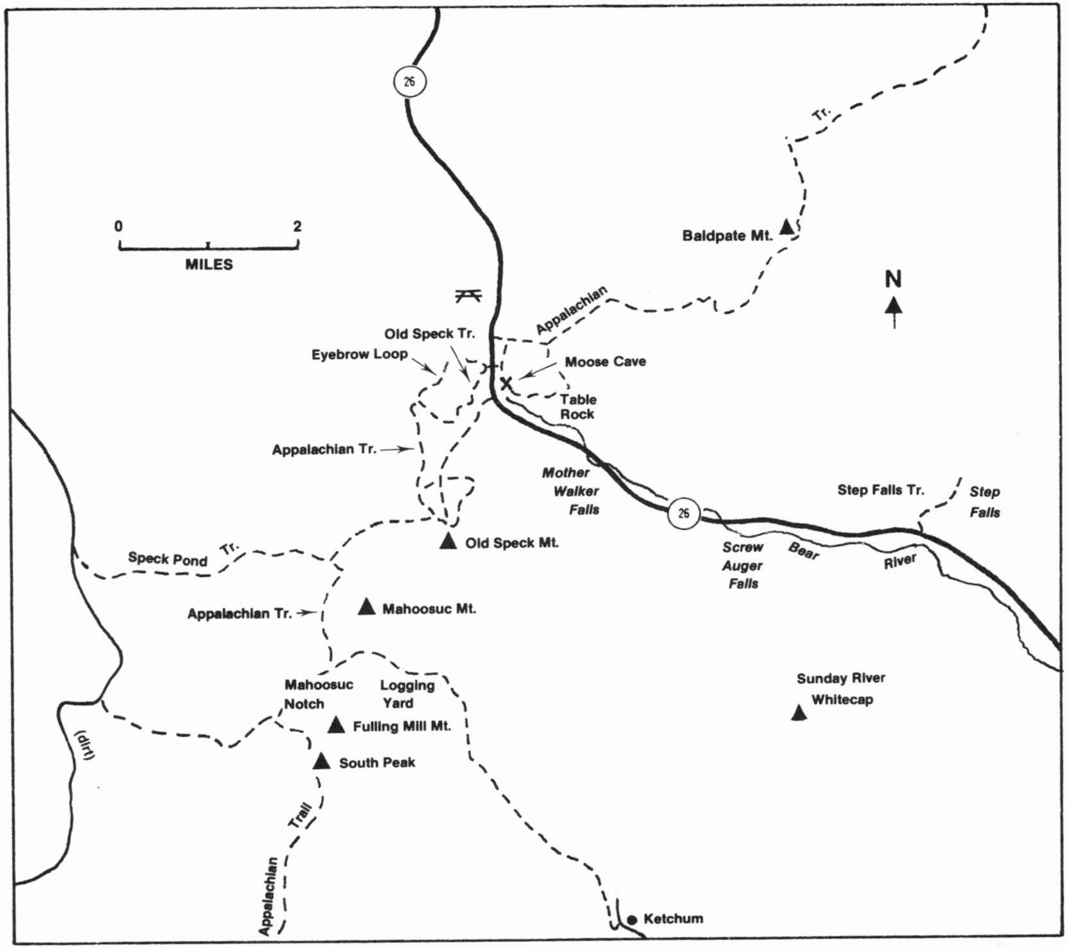

0 — 2
MILES

26

Baldpate Mt. ▲

N
▲

Old Speck Tr.
Eyebrow Loop →
Appalachian
Moose Cave ←
X
Table
Rock

Appalachian Tr. →

*Mother
Walker
Falls*

26

Step Falls Tr.
*Step
Falls*

Speck Pond Tr.

▲ Old Speck Mt.

*Screw
Auger
Falls*

Bear

River

Appalachian Tr. →
▲ Mahoosuc Mt.

Sunday River
Whitecap
▲

Mahoosuc
Notch
Logging
Yard
▲ Fulling Mill Mt.

▲ South Peak

(dirt)

Appalachian Trail

Ketchum ●

right, climbing less steeply to the outlook (.8 mile) and the base of ledges that form Table Rock (.9 mile) where the caves begin. Be careful as some caves are quite deep; a fall could result in a serious injury. The trail continues south around the bottom of Table Rock (look above for the rock that resembles a shark's fin). At a mile, follow a blue-blazed trail to Table Rock (20 yds. left). Continue along the blue-blazed trail right about .5 mile to AT. If you want to go on to Baldpate (1.5 miles further), head east (right); to return to the parking lot, go left (west).

Another .7 mile east on 26 brings you to **Moose Cave** on the left. *Hikers on the Appalachian Trail will find it .6 mile south of Old Speck Trail.* The quarter mile loop can be fun even for young children, who may not understand why anyone would want to eat moose. Older, more sophisticated youngsters may doubt that any hunter could hoist such a huge beast out of the crevice. *A trail to the right leads to Table Rock, above, but the gorge here is interesting as well.*

A little further south, the road passes a much longer, V-shaped gorge, known as **Mother Walker Falls,** near enough to the road for you to hear them. *Nature walk and geological exhibit.*

Mother Walker and Screw Auger Falls may be the only gorges in Maine with their own "natural" bridges, formed out of rock.

Another mile further, look for a parking area with picnic tables. **Screw Auger Falls Gorge** was cut out of the rock here by the Bear River: 120′ long and 9′ wide, exposing granite and pegmatite. The "Jail" above the picnic area, .4 mile west of the falls, is a large pothole which offers fun and exercise to anyone who wants to wiggle up and "escape." *To reach the "Jail" from below, go into the woods 250–300 yards east of the bridge and walk south to the brook, which you can then follow upstream to the falls, looking for the pothole on the north (right) bank.*

The last waterfall in this area is **Step Falls,** managed today by the Nature Conservancy, and best reached from Screw Auger. *The other access to the falls is outside the park, with no place to park. From the pools above Screw Auger Falls, a half-mile path leads east of rte. 26 to another series of cascades, draining the southeastern slope of Baldpate. You'll hear this 200′ waterfall before you see it.*

In another mile the road leaves the park, entering a valley dotted with old farms and apple trees. The church on the left, three miles further, is an interesting mix of architectural details. A town office and the Bear River Grange let you know that you're in **Newry.** *Rte. 2 joins 26 just south of town.* Look for the Riverside Rest Area on the left for picnicking next to the wide Androscoggin River, or the Sunday River Rd., on the right, if you're here in ski season.

Paved shoulders and a passing lane make even the climb along this stretch of rte. 26 tolerable for bikers. The best places to fish in the Newry/Bethel area are at the mouths of the smaller rivers, where they empty into the Androscoggin. Non-resident fishing and hunting licenses are available at Mountain View Store, West Bethel; Bob's Corner Store, Locke Mills; town offices in Locke Mills and Bethel also provide fishing licenses.

After crossing over the wide bridge leading into **Bethel,** look for the Ranger Station on your right (past The Gem Shop on the left). This is an important stop for hikers or fishermen — we recommend you get a package of brochures on campsites and National Forest activities, especially if you plan to take the Evans Notch Rd., one of our favorites, south from rte. 2, page 75.

Just past the Ranger Station, a shortcut jogs sharply to the left, passing some industrial buildings and a lumber yard. A third of a mile further, take another left, back onto 26 south to avoid Bethel, if this is not a planned stop for you. However, if you haven't been here before, we highly recommend visiting this pretty, old-fashioned mountain community, see page 61.

If you're hungry, Bethel has plenty of interesting restaurants. Closest to rte. 26 is the SUDBURY INN, 207/824-2174. Straight up Main St. from the highway, this is a charming place where the atmosphere may be country, but the tastes are sophisticated (seafood mousse in puff pastry or lemon walnut chicken).

South of town, there are pretty views of mountains and farms in the valley to your left. This is a good place to begin an Androscoggin River canoe trip, if you can find someone to meet you in Rumford, 22 miles northeast. *The river offers largely a smooth-water trip through open, scenic hills; no obstructions, if you take your canoe out before the dams at Rumford.*

If you decide to drive or bike, rather than canoe, you'll pass REMINGTON HILL BED AND BREAKFAST, 207/824-3513, on the left. *About three and a half miles past Telstar High School, 26 passes through the hamlet of Locke Mills. Look for Howe Hill Rd. on the right, a quarter mile past the post office, then cross the bridge, and continue about a mile along this road to MT. ABRAM SKI AREA. With over a thousand foot vertical drop, but limited snowmaking, Mt. Abram is a bargain, especially when there's a lot of natural snow. Rentals, ski school, Nordic trails. Also restaurant and lounge, entertainment, ski shop and repairs.*

Bullwinkle Country

Locke Mills and **Mt. Abram** make a nice bike trip in warm weather; even non-skiers will get a kick out of this low-key mountain, still owned by the family that originally developed skiing here in the 1950s. Trails are named for Bullwinkle characters, and the clocks in the rustic base lodge are labeled "Pepsi" and "Hires." Mt. Abram seems caught in a time warp — no frills here — just plenty of attention to details, like well-groomed slopes and friendly people.

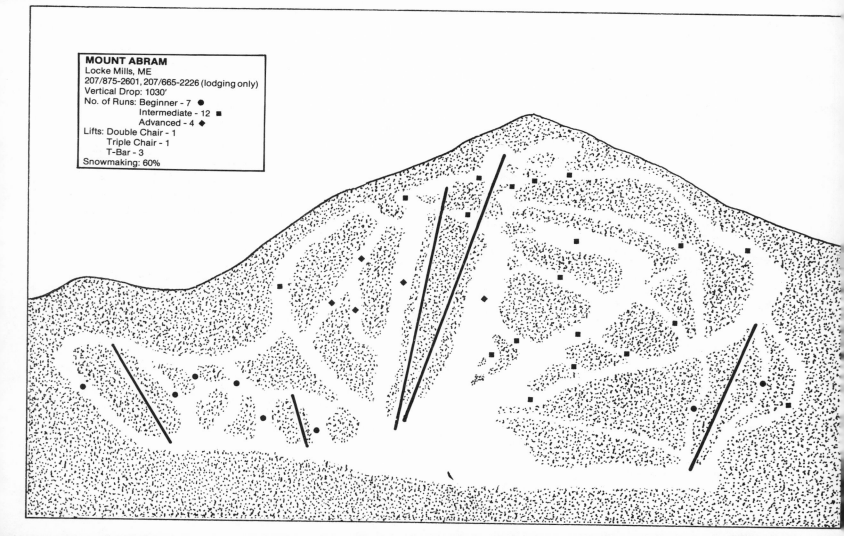

MOUNT ABRAM
Locke Mills, ME
207/875-2601, 207/665-2226 (lodging only)
Vertical Drop: 1030'
No. of Runs: Beginner - 7 ●
Intermediate - 12 ■
Advanced - 4 ◆
Lifts: Double Chair - 1
Triple Chair - 1
T-Bar - 3
Snowmaking: 60%

As rte. 26 leaves town, you'll pass South Pond on your right with bass, lake trout, perch, and pickerel just waiting to be caught. North Pond on the left offers both fishing and picnicking. After four miles of lakes and tree farms, you'll come to the town of **Bryant Pond.** There are several antique shops, a couple of bed and breakfast inns, and the Woodstock Historical Society here, but little else. Christopher Lake, aka Bryant Pond, is a good place to fish for landlocked salmon as well as trout.

> Bryant Pond has the distinction of being the last community in the US to use crank telephones.

West Paris, approximately four miles south, is hardly bigger, but Perham's, another mile on the left, is popular with rock hounds. *Open Monday — Saturday 9–5; Sunday 1–5 pm (daily except Thanksgiving and Christmas). Gift shop, museum of Maine minerals; maps of nearby quarries to visit and dig in. If you didn't already take one of the quarry sidetrips from Bethel, page 69, you might want to do so now.*

A couple of miles south of Perham's, you'll see a picnic area on the right. *Grills, shelters, water, restrooms.* Just below the picnic tables is **Snow Falls,** a 40-foot waterfall that drops to the gorge of the Little Androscoggin, with a bridge across its width for viewing. Less than a mile past the West Paris town line, you'll see a road to your left that promises spectacular mountain views and a village that time seems to have forgotten.

Turn left past the sign for Long Look Farm onto Paris Hill Rd., and continue through the village, returning to rte. 26 in South Paris.

Paris Hill, *National Historic District*

As you climb the hill up to town, look on the right for "Paddiwack Farm," dating back to 1798 but added on to in the 1880s. The impressive, three-storied brick home on the left was built in 1813. When you reach the common, you might want to park and walk around a little. *Walking tour and hiking maps available at the library.*

> "Old Brick" was the home of Charles Deering, who founded International Harvester.

"Sunday evening as Mrs. Stone, the well-known seamstress, was gathering soiled linen for her Monday's labors, two frisky bovines, which perambulate the streets of Paris Hill, locked horns and engaged in mortal conflict. Having learned that the high [ground] was their own special territory, the cattle were not sufficiently thoughtful to select a vacant spot in which to settle their dispute, the result was that one of the creatures was pushed against Mrs. Stone's wagon, overturning it, throwing her out and injuring her severely. . . everybody in Oxford County knows that the streets of Paris Hill are little better than a barnyard."
OXFORD DEMOCRAT, June 1877

The large white frame home just north of the common is Lyonsden, named for the lion's head over the door; the figurehead was from the first vessel Lyonsden's owner, Admiral Henry W. Lyon, commanded. The Greek Revival First Baptist Church was completed in 1823, with a bell from Paul Revere's foundry. Behind the church is perhaps the most photographed site in town, the birthplace of Hannibal Hamlin, Lincoln's first vice president, with the White Mountains behind it. And next to the Hamlin home is the old Oxford County Jail, born-again as Hamlin Memorial Library.

"Northlands," as the Hamlin birthplace was originally called, has long been the home of well-to-do individuals, including a developer of the Florida grapefruit industry, who substantially renovated this home.

Quarried in Oxford, the Maine granite in the library was hauled up Paris Hill in the snow by oxen.

Hikers may want to explore the **Cornwall Nature Preserve.** *Open to the public for photography, hiking, and nature study; overnight camping permitted ONLY with permission (see Conservation Commission members at Paris Hill Town Office on East Main St. in the center of the village).*

Paris Hill's Main St. will lead you down to modern-day **South Paris** and **Norway,** two communities that are often hard to separate. For years both were known for manufacturing: Norway for shoes, South Paris for wooden toys. Although today the factories are gone, these towns offer plenty of food and drink.

When In Paris

There are a number of restaurants in the Paris/Norway area — including the ubiquitous strip of fast-food outlets. For the most value at the least cost, try MARKET SQUARE, 207/743-2844, across from the Cooperative Extension Service on Main St. in South Paris. Home cooking and daily bargains may win out over the franchises, after all.

Undoubtedly, the finest restaurant in the area is MAURICE RESTAURANT FRANCAIS, 113 Main St., 207/743-2532. The decor is low-key with local photography the highlight; the service is superb, as is the cooking. Start with a bloody Mary (the tomato juice base is chef-made). Pate is delicious, though it could be even better if allowed to stand at room temperature before serving. Scampi are large and tender, while fish has been gently poached. It's an effort to save room for dessert — though the sweets are equally tempting.

Although MAURICE is inexpensive by city standards, there are cheaper, more casual places as well. GOLDSTREET'S, 207/743-9783, past Maurice on the strip in Norway, shares the same management, but is less dear — and attractive in its own way.

Rte. 26 will lead you south to Gray, where you can speed home on the Maine Turnpike. For those who would like to see a little of the seacoast en route, **COAST GUIDE: Seabrook, New Hampshire to Freeport, Maine** *may be just what you need. If unavailable at your local bookstore, you can order by sending $10.95 (including postage and handling) to Glove Compartment Books, Box 1602, Portsmouth, NH 03801-1602.*

INDEX

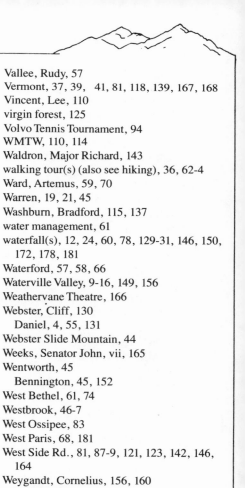